# The Wildest Game

# The Wildest Game

BY PETER RYHINER
as told to DANIEL P. MANNIX

J. B. LIPPINCOTT COMPANY
*Philadelphia & New York*

# Contents

# Illustrations

Neither this book nor the adventures recounted in it could have come about without the help of many friends all over the world. I would like to express my gratitude to them here. Some of them are: Juan Bossard in Argentina, Theo Meier in Bali, J. van Dyck in Belgium, George Koechlin in Brazil, Peter Huggler in Canada, Major Aubry Weinman of the Dehiwela Zoo and Thilo and Mae Hoffman in Ceylon, René and Lotti Zerr in Egypt; P. Balakrishnan, M. P. Cherian, E. P. Gee, A. J. F. d'Mello, Mr. Brittain, S. Gosh, Asish Bose, Francis and Mary More, B. V. Ramanjulu of the Madras Zoological Gardens, Pat Stracey, Frank Thonger and Otto Wenger in India; Max Joss of the Consulate of Switzerland in Tokyo, Fritz and Anni Luethi in Mexico, Peter and Flo Vischer-Martin in Puerto Rico; Alexis and Jacotte von Goldschmidt-Rothschild, Jacky and Maily Maeder ("Shikar and Safaris"), my mother, M. C. Ryhiner-de Sturler, who keeps the records, and Paul and Uschi Seiler ("Tropic") in Switzerland; Kurt and Louise Mueller and Prince Sanidh Rangsit in Thailand; and in the United States August A. Busch, Jr., and Trudy Busch who own "Hairy Josephine," Clyde Gordon of the Staten Island Zoological Gardens, Hugo Mayr of Swissair in New York, John Moyer of the Chicago Museum of Natural History, René and Katherine Perret, Ivan T. ("Chief Guru") and Alma Sanderson, Freeman Shelly of the Philadelphia Zoological Garden and George P. Vierheller of the St. Louis Zoological Garden.

PETER RYHINER

# Introduction

I BELIEVE that I have seen the last of a great wild animal trapping era. I have caught gorillas in the Cameroons, orangutans in Borneo, rhinos in India, jaguars in South America and king cobras in Siam. I have transported 136 elephants, as opposed to Hannibal's forty-five . . . and handled single shipments of wild animals valued at $100,000. Today, such shipments are no longer possible and I doubt that they will ever be again. Currency restrictions, conservation laws, regulations against importing or exporting many species, and increased transportation costs have all taken their toll. In the future, the transportation of rare animals will probably be arranged on an exchange basis by the large zoos, working through their respective governments.

Only fifteen years ago, it was different. Any young man with a knowledge of trapping and handling wild animals could plunge into the jungles of the Amazon, take his chances among the wild tribes in the interior of Africa, or strike up an acquaintance with a rajah in hopes of being able to trap tigers in his state. You needed little capital, only a willingness to take risks and a feeling for wild game. You might die of fever, a native spear, or be mauled by one of your trophies, or you might clear $35,000 on a single shipment as I once did.

Following the last war, there was an enormous boom in the animal business. Zoos had been unable to obtain any new speci-

9

mens and for the first time in nearly ten years the world was open to collectors again. Also, the airplane had come into its own. Animals could be flown in by plane from remote districts where formerly it had required weeks to transport them. Then, too, a collector could take a shipload of animals to New York, London, or Antwerp, find out what new specimens were wanted by the local dealers, and fly to Brazil, Kenya, India or Indonesia . . . arriving at any place on the globe in seventy-two hours or less. Previously, simply getting from one place to another took months by ship. The whole world had suddenly become the collector's compound. I have made three trips in a year from the Far East to the United States, bringing the animals over by ship and flying back to save time.

Animal collecting during this fabulous period was a very different business than in the days of the justly famous Frank Buck. Modern transportation and huge demands made big cargoes routine, as the contrasting lists of animals collected will show.

| Buck | Myself | |
|---|---|---|
| 39 | 136 | Indian elephants |
| 60 | 62 | tigers |
| 28 | 72 | spotted leopards |
| 20 | 23 | black leopards |
| 10 | 3 | clouded leopards |
| 4 | 3 | snow leopards |
| 20 | 32 | hyenas |
| 52 | 25 | orangutans |
| 31 | 135 | gibbons |
| 3,000 | 10,000 | smaller monkeys |
| 20 | 4 | (Asiatic) tapirs |
| 120 | 45 | (Asiatic) antelope and deer |
| 9 | | *Pygmy water buffalo |
| 1 | 4 | gaur (wild cattle) |
| 1 | | *babirusa |
| 2 | | *African Cape buffalo |
| 18 | 50 | African antelope |

\* Cannot be imported today.

| Buck | Myself | |
|---|---|---|
| 2 | 9 | giraffes |
| 40 | 43 | wild sheep and goats |
| 11 | 24 | camels |
| 40 | 75 | kangaroos |
| 2 | 6 | Indian rhinoceros |
| 40 | 62 | Asiatic bears |
| 90 | 125 | pythons |
| 1 | 35 | king cobras |
| 100 | 40,000 | small snakes |
| 5 | 150 | monitor lizards |
| 15 | 300 | crocodiles and caymans |
| 500 | 10,000 | small mammals |
| 100,000 | 2,000 | birds |

Of course, these different records are the products of different eras. Before air travel, it was impractical for collectors to go jumping around all over the world and so collectors confined themselves to certain areas . . . in Buck's case, southeastern Asia. Also, there was formerly no point in collectors' bringing back huge cargoes of wild animals; there was simply no demand for them.

On the other hand, in Buck's time there were few import or export restrictions. In the last few years, I have found it virtually impossible to import any cloven-hoofed animals because of the threat of rinderpest, hoof and mouth disease, anthrax and other ailments. No modern collector can bring in antelope, deer, buffalo or pigs as Buck was able to do. Buck could export all the orangutans that he wished from Indonesia. Today, exporting these great red apes is almost impossible due to conservation laws passed since Buck's time. So I have made this comparison only to give some idea of how matters have changed since World War II.

Because of the airplane, a collector can now easily cover many areas instead of confining himself to only one or two. In addition to the above list, I have also imported:

## South America

42 pumas
36 jaguars
22 South American tapirs
34 rheas (including the rare white rhea)
25,000 smaller birds
12,000 small mammals
6 maned wolves
8 spectacled bears
250 boas and anacondas
500 cameloides (llamas, guanacos, vicuñas and alpacas)

## Africa

5 gorillas
32 chimps
40 zebras
20 ostriches
8 cheetahs
6 rhinos
6 hippos
3 pygmy hippos
6 striped hyenas
20 small cats
12 wild dogs
250 large birds
700 small birds

I have also exported from North and Central America to European and Asian zoos: sea lions, Kodiak bears, ring-tailed cats, raccoons, opposums, armadillos, coati mundis, kinkajous, bobcats, woodchucks, prairie dogs, many reptiles, amphibians and birds.

The question I'm most frequently asked is, "How do you catch wild animals?" Of course there is no one answer, for virtually every species requires a different technique. Some are caught with nets, others in pits, some chased and lassoed from cars, still others taken in box traps or with snares. In this book,

I've tried to explain as many trapping methods as possible. However, I want to make clear that most trapping is not done by the collector but by native hunters. No foreigner, even though he may have spent years in a country, can ever equal the skill of these men. The collector's principal task is to keep the animals alive after capture.

Collecting animals is dangerous work but much of the danger comes from poisonous insects, sunstroke, and tropical diseases. Wild animals will seldom attack a human except under the most extreme provocation. The greatest danger comes from a captured animal that has escaped in a compound or on shipboard.

I have never used a gun (except on one special occasion) and I never carry firearms. I consider the damned things a menace. There is too much danger of injuring a valuable specimen unnecessarily or, in a crisis, shooting one of your own native helpers. Besides, a man working with wild animals is too busy to worry about personal risks.

Generally when setting out to capture an animal, I don't have any qualms over the animal's feelings about the business. It's like a game between us: his brains and strength against my skill. Although I realize that many people feel that capturing wild animals for zoos is inherently cruel, under proper conditions I know of no reason any animal should be unhappy in captivity and I find that most animals adapt themselves to it very easily.

I doubt if anyone would seriously suggest that all zoological parks be abolished. They give pleasure to many people, especially children, and keep alive the popular interest in animals which makes much of conservation work possible. If the parks are to exist, the animals must be captured.

Animals show no indications of resenting captivity once they grow accustomed to it. Escaped animals often return voluntarily to their cages. The popular belief that wild creatures enjoy roaming over wide areas is quite untrue. Most wild animals remain by their own choice in very small areas—invisible "cages" that nothing but the last extremes of hunger or thirst can force them to leave. Even the great cats do not travel except when absolutely necessary. If a plentiful supply of food is at hand, they seldom move more than a few hundred yards a day and then only from a drinking hole to their favorite lying-up spot. Nor do caged animals repine as would humans so confined. Animals are not capable of abstract thinking and so do not suffer from boredom.

There is no question that caged animals are healthier and live longer than wild animals. F. C. Selous, one of the greatest of all African hunters, once remarked that he could tell at a glance the hide of a zoo lion from that of a wild lion. The zoo lion's pelt was much glossier and showed no trace of mange. Wild animals do not lead the ideal existence most people suppose. If they become sick, they simply die, and diseases are much more prevalent among them than is commonly supposed. When they grow old and can no longer fend for themselves, they die a slow, agonizing death unless predators pull them down. As the number of wild animals does not increase under normal conditions and nearly all are very prolific, the mortality rate among them is obviously very high. Gorillas, for example, are one of the least prolific of all animals but a female will probably give birth to twenty young during her lifetime. Of this number, not more than one or two survive—otherwise, the number of gorillas would be constantly increasing, which we know is not the case. In captivity, there is no reason why all the young should not survive.

If animals are unhappy in captivity, they should certainly hate the man who has dragged them from their happy homes to a life behind prison bars. My animals do not hate me. Four tigers I captured in India and sold to the Vero Beach Zoo remembered me two years later. They ran up to the bars, purred, and arched their backs to be scratched. A leopard I sold to the Zurich Zoo knew me after four years. I could go into the cage with him although he would instantly attack a stranger. Some chimps that I sold to the Colombo Zoo in Ceylon remembered me for six years. Whenever I went by their cage, they would go mad with delight. Even if there was a large crowd, they'd instantly pick me out and start dancing around the cage, shouting to me with shrill chirps and cries. Dr. Aubrey Weinman, the director, always let me into their cage and we would have a big celebration. I find it hard to believe that these animals would behave this way if they were really unhappy.

There is also another aspect to the animal collecting question. Many species of animals are fast disappearing . . . not due to collectors but to hunters, the march of civilization and other factors. Several species exist today only because scientists have been able to study them in zoos. The American bison and the Australian koala would be extinct now if some specimens hadn't been kept in captivity and their needs become known to zoologists. There are several species which today are found only in zoos, the European bison, Przewalski's wild horse, the Père David deer, and the Barbary lion, to name only a few. The wild ones have all been killed off to make room for the expanding human population.

When you consider how many animals are shot for sport every year, the very few taken for menageries are negligible. I suffered considerable twinges of conscience about taking six Indian rhino calves, in spite of the government's assurance that the reserve where they roamed was becoming overpopulated, for there are only approximately 350 of these rare animals left. But a few months later, two sporting politicians in Nepal shot twenty-six rhinos in one week simply for fun. My rhinos are doing well in captivity. In the Basel Zoo, a pair that I captured have had a calf, thus starting a new line of these almost extinct creatures. With the rapidly expanding population in West Africa, the wild gorilla is almost surely doomed. But now zoologists have managed to induce gorillas to breed in captivity. In the Columbus Zoo, in Ohio, a little female was born December 23, 1956. Her name is Colo and she is doing well. The perpetuation of the race may well depend on babies like Colo. Lions now breed so easily in captivity that there is almost no demand for wild specimens. The same may someday be true of all the rarer species.

Today, there are only three men, besides myself, who handle large shipments of animals. Of these, two are over seventy. When they retire, I doubt if anyone will take their place. Animal collecting is becoming too difficult. Still, I am glad to have partaken in the great elephant keddahs in the foothills of the Himalayas, the wild pursuits after rhinos across the African veldt, and the capture of rheas with bolos by Argentine cowboys on the pampas. It has been a great period and I am happy to have seen it.

# Chapter 1

# One of the world's rarest animals

SHAIK SUBRATI is the only man I've ever known who could identify a rhino simply by drinking a glass of its urine. He would sniff the full glass as though savoring a fine wine, drain it, smack his lips and then announce with confidence, "Ah, that was Joymothi. She's in very good shape today."

Subrati was the best animal man and jungle craftsman to work for me in my years of collecting wild game. Without him, I'd never have gotten the almost legendary Indian rhinoceros . . . possibly the inspiration for the mythical unicorn. And I shudder to think what would have happened had we failed in that lunatic venture. For suddenly and without warning I'd found myself stuck down one of those blind alleys that seem to booby-trap the animal business. My career seemed finished, my prospects nil, my immediate future grim indeed.

It was in 1950. I was collecting animals in Siam (now Thailand, but I still like to call it Siam) with Mercia, the exquisitely lovely Eurasian girl I'd married a few months before. We had a nice lot of specimens, including six black leopards, four tigers, several dozen gibbons, hundreds of small birds and twenty good-sized king cobras. It was Mercia's first experience at animal trapping and she had brought thirty-four trunks full of fashionable clothes. At first she even insisted on wearing high-heeled shoes which are hardly practical for jungle work, but she was learning and after the first couple of weeks changed to a sarong and sandals. Mercia was particularly good with baby animals and I had great hopes for her.

Our headquarters was a small village named Suratthani in southern Siam which we had selected because it was only twenty miles from a telegraph office. Late one afternoon, a telegram arrived from my old friend Theo Meier. He was in Bangkok, passing through on his way from Europe to Bali, and he wanted me to have a drink with him.

Theo had once taken me in and nursed me back to health when I was dead broke and discouraged. This was the first time in thirteen years that he had left Bali and as I doubted I would be returning to the island I might not see him again for an elephant's age. I left Mercia in charge of the animals and rented a sampan to take me across the river to the railroad station.

I was worried about Mercia. She was very good with leopards and tigers, but I didn't altogether trust her to take proper care of the cobras. Mercia was nervous with snakes. Unfortunately, Subrati was off on a trapping expedition but as I planned on being away only a couple of days, I was sure Mercia could handle matters until I returned.

There were no seats on the train, so I sat on some boxes between two carriages. I arrived in Bangkok somewhat dirty and tired at noon the next day. I was still wearing my jungle clothes, sandals and a stained pair of old khaki drills, having had no time to change. I went at once to the swimming club where Theo had said he'd meet me. Sure enough, there he was, a short, dark man looking almost Oriental after his many years in the Far East. He too was wearing sandals and a brilliant Balinese blouse of his own design.

"Peter, my old friend!" he shouted in a voice that could be heard halfway to the Floating Market. "Come and have a glass of this mekong! It's nearly as good as the tuak we used to drink in Bali."

We embraced and had the mekong. It tasted a little like gin laced with sulfuric acid and the effects were almost immediate. Afterwards, Theo took me to a European bar where you could get real Danish beer and then we went to a native restaurant for namprik—a paste of shrimp and rice, seasoned with limes. We ended back at the swimming club drinking gimlets and eating coriander leaves mixed with fried, hair-fine spaghetti, shrimp and limes.

We had much to talk over; my animal trapping adventures, an exhibition of modernistic art Theo had seen in Paris (he is a skilled painter himself, somewhat in the Gauguin manner), the communist situation in Malaya, a collection of West-Coast-African ivory carvings I had made and was hoping to sell in New York, whether the scrap left over from the war on some of the Pacific islands was reclaimable, and a new religious sect that was springing up in the Celebes started by an old witch doctor who could apparently call butterflies to him by an act of will. At two o'clock in the morning, we still hadn't talked ourselves out but the bar was closing and I remembered that I had no hotel accommodations.

"Think nothing of it," said Theo when I wondered aloud about where I would sleep. "Spend the night with me. I'm at the Palace."

I thought I knew every hotel in Bangkok but this one had escaped me. Theo roared with laughter when I said so.

"It's not a hotel, you ninny. I mean the royal palace. I'm staying with Prince Rangsit."

"I have no decent clothes," I protested.

"Neither have I. The Prince won't mind. You'll like him. Let's have another drink before the bar closes and we'll go. What about some champagne this time? I'm tired of gimlets. Waiter, Veuve Cliquot, '47, and two fresh glasses."

We had to finish the champagne in a taxi en route to the palace as the bar closed before we'd emptied the second bottle.

The palace was a huge, rambling white building, partly European and partly Oriental in architecture. When we got out under a gigantic porte-cochère servants in brilliant blue and white livery prostrated themselves. I like to see well-trained servants. Theo led the way inside.

We went through room after room, walking on Persian carpets so thick we seemed to be ankle deep on clouds. Theo went so fast I didn't have time to see much, but I noticed on the tables some brass Buddha heads that must have been 2,000 years old and are the most valuable of Siamese antiques. They come from remote temples and by Siamese law cannot be exported, although some are smuggled out of the country. Theo took me to our quarters where the servants helped us undress. No amount of liquor ever has any effect on Theo but I needed help. There was a magnificent tiled bathroom, imported from the United States, with yards of shiny chrome faucets but instead of a shower there was a china vase full of water in the bathtub with a dipper beside it so I was able to dip the water over myself Siamese fashion. After the servants had withdrawn, Theo and I lay on our beds naked as neither of us had pajamas and talked until dawn before falling asleep.

When I awakened, it was late afternoon. A slender, dark man, completely naked, was standing by the bed regarding me somewhat curiously. He had obviously come in to use the bath and found me there.

"Savadee—greetings," I said.

From the next bed, Theo roared, "Get up, you fool. That's Prince Rangsit. Don't lie in bed when you're talking to a prince."

I sprang up and the Prince and I shook hands. As we were both nude, I felt somewhat embarrassed but the Prince didn't care. He asked if I'd enjoyed my sleep, invited both of us to dinner to meet his father, the regent, and then disappeared into the bathroom.

Theo told me that the Prince was a great sportsman and an excellent businessman. Instead of lounging in his palace as do many Oriental rulers, he had worked hard building a large trading company and made a fortune. He was a keen shikari (hunter) but the demands of his business limited his hunting trips.

We had dinner that evening in the great dining hall. Each of us had three of the liveried servants standing behind his chair and a little lamp by his plate as the lights in the room were purposely kept dim. The Prince's father was a very old man, dressed in Western clothes. He was also the King's uncle and regent. The King was a young man finishing his education in Europe and was the grandson of King Mongkut, the sovereign of *Anna and the King of Siam.*

The old regent's mind was obviously still clear and sharp, and he could drink and smoke as much as we younger men. I am sorry to say that two weeks after our meal, the old gentleman died. He was certainly gracious to put up with two wandering Europeans in sandals and ragged clothes at his table.

Dinner was finished and we sat back to enjoy our cognac and Havana cigars. The cigars were the best I'd ever smoked, with a rich, potent flavor, but mild. Prince Rangsit explained that he had them made up especially for him in Cuba. The regent was chatting with Theo about the care and breeding of fighting crickets and I felt perfectly happy and relaxed.

The regent reached for his cognac glass and said casually to me, "Oh, by the way, I just signed a bill that will affect you. All shipments of wild animals from Siam are forbidden." Then he continued his talk with Theo as though he had asked me if I was enjoying my cigar.

I sat stunned. Six months' work and all my savings had gone into my animal trapping. I'd spent my last ticals (the Siamese currency) in having the shipping cages made; the animals were to go out in two weeks. The Antwerp Zoo was cabling me $3,000 against the cargo so I could pay the loading charges at the docks. Mercia and I didn't have more than a few Swiss francs between us. We couldn't even pay our passage out of the country.

Prince Rangsit said gently to the old regent, "But, my father, surely this law doesn't apply to Peter as he came here in good faith and has spent much time and money making his collection."

"I know, I know," said the old regent somewhat irritably. "It will be hard on him. But the people will have it so. They know that animals are worth a great deal of money and they resent having them taken out of the country." Then he went back to his conversation with Theo who was looking at me aghast.

As for me, I could neither speak nor move. I had to force myself to think. The extent of the disaster grew worse as I considered it. Now I could not even pay my bills in Suratthani. I had two partners in the venture who would be ruined. And Mercia . . . After months of hard work, enduring jungle fever and insects, handling leopards and the terrible cobras she dreaded so, she would have to be told that it was all for nothing. What would she think of me? Although I was not conscious of making a noise, Theo later told me that I groaned aloud.

Theo managed to interrupt the regent to ask, "Your Excellency, can nothing be done to help my friend?"

The old man blinked at him with watery eyes. "Something done? Do you know how this country stands? In the north are the Chinese reds. In our hills are bandits hired by them. In the cities, fear and suspicion of all Europeans. We balance on a razor's edge over the pit of hell. We must have the people's confidence and support. Do you think I would risk their resentment for the sake of a few leopards and monkeys?"

What he said was true and looking at the sad faces of Prince Rangsit and Theo, I knew it was hopeless.

Theo took me to the train. He said nothing and there was nothing he could say. As the train pulled out, he shouted after me, "Remember, you and Mercia can always come to Bali and live with me."

It was kind of him but there are few wild animals on Bali and I could not make a living there. The next morning, I stumbled off the train at Suratthani in the grip of a depression so terrible it was like madness. I could not face Mercia or my partners with the news. As I crossed the river on the sampan ferry, I wished that it would sink or that a bandit would shoot me from the bank or that anything would happen to spare me the ordeal ahead. Yet while I had these thoughts, I knew that they were childish and I was ashamed of them.

Instead of hiring a car I walked to our compound for now every coin was precious. Mercia met me at the gate. In the graceful sarong that showed her figure to advantage, she looked as though she had just stepped off a South Sea set in a Hollywood studio. But for the first time, my heart did not jump at the sight of her. Instead, I tried to think what I would have naturally said. I called, "How are the animals? Oh yes, and how are you?"

I was never able to fool Mercia for an instant. She said at once, "What has happened? Tell me the worst."

I told her. If there is too much seasoning in a dish or a train is five minutes late, Mercia goes into fits of hysterical temper that are terrifying to watch but in a crisis she is always calm. She stood there with her hands folded in front of her like a child, her delicately carved face expressionless. She was looking towards the jungle trail that led to the west where we had expected to ship the animals, but her eyes did not focus. She said slowly, "Then there is no help for it. We must get the rhinos."

I gave an angry laugh and went by her. Without turning around she said, "The gin is in the box under the bed. We only have one bottle left."

"I don't need gin," I retorted. But later I changed my mind and emptied the bottle. Sometimes liquor helps you to think.

Mercia knew nothing about the animal business. All she possessed was a savage determination that would listen to no reason and admit of no obstacles. Her remark about the rhinos was typical of her fierce single-mindedness.

Three months before, I had received a cable from Dr. Hediger, director of the Basel Zoo in Switzerland, which read simply, "Ship rhinos at once." Puzzled, I had cabled back that I was not in Africa. I got a longer cable in reply. Lothar Behrend, a bizarre old German collector in Argentina with whom I'd once been in partnership, had known I was in the Far East and cabled Dr. Hediger asking if he wanted Indian rhinos. Of course Dr. Hediger did—so did every other zoo director in the world. Behrend had simply taken for granted that I could get them. He might as well have taken for granted that I could get a pair of Abominable Snowmen.

There are only about 350 Indian rhinos left, which makes them one of the world's rarest animals. Approximately 300 of this number live on a reserve in Assam, a province of India north of Bengal and bordering on Tibet. Another fifty or so are in Nepal. No foreigner can get a permit to shoot or capture one and no one but an idiot would even try.

However, after getting Dr. Hediger's second cable, I began to think a bit. A couple of years before, I'd been having drinks with an English tea planter in the bar of the old Spence Hotel in Calcutta. I'd told the man that I was in the animal business and he at once assumed a knowing look.

"I'll wager you'd like to get your hands on an Indian rhino," he said grinning.

I grinned too. "I certainly would."

The tea planter hiccuped and placed his finger alongside his nose. "Tell you what, write Pat Stracey. Got the name? Pat Stracey. That bloke can get you anything. Senior conservation officer of forests at Assam. Just mention my name."

"What is your name?" I asked.

The tea planter winked at me. "That's a secret. 'No names, no pack drill, eh?' Just tell old Pat you know me. Wonderful chap, old Pat." And putting his head on the table, the planter went sound asleep.

I took down Stracey's name and address on a slip of paper torn from an envelope I had in my pocket. Then I forgot about the incident. I didn't think about it again till I got Dr. Hediger's cable. By a miracle, I still had the scrap of paper. I wrote to Pat Stracey.

Naturally, I got no answer. I hadn't expected one. But I'd made the mistake of mentioning the incident to Mercia, together with the information that an Indian rhino was easily worth $10,000. After that, Mercia was determined to get a rhino—several rhinos. She had haunted the post office waiting for Pat Stracey's letter which never came. Personally, I doubted if there even was such a man. The planter was slurring his words and might have said "Tracy" or "Macy" for all I knew.

After drinking the bottle of gin, I fell into a restful sleep and didn't wake up until the next morning. Meanwhile, Mercia had been organizing things, and had done very well. She had been able to sell most of the animals to local merchants who were willing to speculate on getting export permits later. A number were bought by an old Chinaman who, I learned later, sold them to the Peking Zoo, sending them by a cargo ship that had been smuggling arms to the guerillas in the hills.

Apart from the financial loss, it was heartbreaking to lose the ones that had become pets. I remember especially two baby gibbons Mercia had raised on a bottle. They clung to her, moaning and sobbing, and Mercia was in tears too. It was pitiful to see them in the shipping crate, clutching each other like little orphans and crying to Mercia for help. Mercia made the old Chinaman who'd bought them promise to sell them together and he said he would, although whether he was able to keep his word or not we never knew. That's the worst of the animal business, having to sell the ones that love and trust you.

In spite of the money that Mercia had received for the animals, we were in desperate straits. The cash, and it was almost nothing, had to be split three ways between my two partners and us. One of them was an ex-mining engineer who'd given up a good job to go into the animal business. He took the few ticals coming to him and vanished down the river in a sampan. The other man, a Swiss, who'd put his life's savings into this venture, went to Bangkok by train. Years later, I met him in Algiers where he was working as foreman of a brickyard.

Mercia and I added up our share. We had enough to pay our

debts in Suratthani and a little bit over but not enough to start
animal trapping anywhere else. Finally Mercia said quietly, "I'll
have to sell my clothes."

For most women, this wouldn't seem too great a sacrifice but
it meant everything to Mercia. Mercia always took great pride
in always being smartly dressed, especially as a Eurasian in the
presence of the rather dowdy British *mem-sahibs*. To lose her
fine clothes would be the greatest of deprivations to her.

However, there was nothing else to do. Before going to the
merchants to see what they'd offer, we stopped at the post
office to get our mail. To our astonishment, there was a whole
sack of it. The clerk explained indifferently, "There have been
serious floods which held up all the mail for a month."

We sat down on the porch of the post office and tore open
the letters. They were the usual thing. A crazy American millionaire wanted to buy a white elephant for the Pope. An English lord wanted to get a dozen zebras to train for polo, having
heard somewhere that zebras were very quick on turns. There
were a number of cancellations and some new orders, none of
which made any difference to us now.

Then I found a letter from the Indian Forestry Department.
It was postmarked Assam. Over the return address was typed
"Patrick Stracey."

I sat staring at the letter. Far from feeling relief, I hated Pat
Stracey at that moment. I knew what the letter would be: a
polite brush-off. It could be nothing else. Why had he bothered
to write me? Why hadn't he merely ignored my letter?

Mercia snatched the letter out of my hand and ripped it open.
She glanced through it eagerly, her lips parted and her bosom
heaving. Then she screamed, "He's giving you two permits—
to get a pair! That's about 80,000 francs! We're saved!" and
she began to cry quietly.

I read the letter in a daze. Stracey was indeed giving us the
permits—why, he didn't say. There was a hitch to it. The permits cost 20,000 rupees each, roughly about $5,000. Then I'd
have to go to Assam and catch the rhinos myself. But Stracey

promised me the help of the forestry department and the free use of elephants for the job.

Thank heaven we had enough money from the sale of the animals to cable Dr. Hediger. Dr. Hediger was willing to pay 80,000 francs (about $20,000) for the two rhinos but that was C.I.F. (cost, insurance and freight) Basel and no money in advance. Of course, Mercia and I could no more raise the 40,000 rupees for the permits, plus our plane fares to Assam and the expense of getting the rhinos to Basel, than we could rob the vault at Fort Knox. After desperate cables, Dr. Hediger finally sent us 30,000 francs—about $7,000. For that, we could fly to Assam and get at least one rhino.

We left for Bangkok to get the plane. We had disposed of all our animals except one, a huge red-faced monkey the size of a small child and far more powerful than a man. He had been a pet and was tame, in so far as he'd lost his fear of humans. He was the roughest, meanest monkey I've ever seen. He hated Mercia and used to throw his dung at her with an extraordinarily good aim. He saved all his dung and kept it in little piles in case she got within range. He loved durian which is a horribly messy fruit and Mercia used to gather it for him, knowing that durian is one of the greatest delicacies for either man or beast. But it never changed his dislike of her. Mercia hated him, too.

No one would accept this monkey even as a gift so we had to turn him loose. He was always breaking out of his cage anyway and we took for granted he'd run off into the jungle. Instead, out of sheer contrariness, he refused to leave us. Finally Mercia left a pile of durian on the bank of the river and while he was eating it, we and Subrati jumped into a sampan and the boatman shoved off.

When old red-face saw we were leaving him, he went into a perfect spasm of fury, turning somersaults with rage and dancing up and down on the bank. Mercia screamed at him, "Now you can go and gather your own durian! And I hope a python gets you!" We crossed the river with Mercia screaming at the monkey and the monkey screaming back at her.

# Chapter 2

# Capturing
# the "living fossil"

To REACH Assam, the northeasternmost state of India, we had to fly over the foothills of the Himalayas, one of the bumpiest rides I've ever endured. Subrati and I were old travelers and therefore virtually immune to both airsickness and seasickness, but poor Mercia nearly died. By the time we landed at Jorhat, she was so weak that Subrati and I had to carry her off the plane.

We hired an ancient car to drive us to the Kaziranga Wild Life Sanctuary where the rhinos lived. It was a sixty-mile drive over terrible roads and did nothing to improve Mercia's condition. I really became afraid for her but there was nothing we could do except to push on. The country was weirdly beautiful, reminding me somewhat of a lunar landscape. There were great ranges of mountains over which our car panted, knocking and boiling, and then we plunged down into vast plains covered with the high, yellow ekkra grass. A few minutes later, the car would be crawling on a narrow track through a jungle, the road so completely overshadowed with creepers and interlocking branches that we seemed to be in a tunnel. Then would come a magnificent scenic bit along the side of a ridge among the miles of tea gardens, worked by imported coolie laborers with colorful pieces of cloth wrapped around their heads.

We reached Kaziranga and put up in a dak bungalow left over from the British days. These dak bungalows are a godsend to travelers. They are scattered all over the country, never more than a day's journey apart, and were built by the British administrators for their use during inspection tours. Although many are now falling apart we were lucky to find a good one. Poor Mercia collapsed on the rickety old bed and I left Subrati in charge of her while I went to find Pat Stracey.

Instead, Pat found me. He drove in with some of his rangers in a beaten-up English landrover while I was still asking the natives where I could find him. Pat was a Eurasian and looked like a slender, dark-complexioned Englishman. He was a cheerful, lively fellow with a great sense of humor and turned out to be one of the most capable men I've ever encountered. We managed to get a bottle of whisky from a tiny, thatch-roofed store and returned to my bungalow to discuss the rhino situation.

On the veranda we sat down in two dilapidated bamboo chairs while Subrati made our drinks. I was particularly curious to know why the foresty department had granted my request for a permit so easily and I asked him frankly.

He replied, "Your request just happened to come in at a good time. Fifty years ago, there were only about ten rhinos left and it seemed almost certain they'd become extinct, and they had to be rigorously protected. The locals hunted them mercilessly for their horns. As you probably know, the horn is supposed to be a powerful aphrodisiac and sells for 100 rupees an ounce. That's a fortune to people here. However, since we started protecting the rhinos, the herd has built up until now we have between 340 and 360 of them."

"That still doesn't seem like a large herd," I remarked.

"It's about all the sanctuary can stand. It's 164 square miles but we have to fight for every inch of it. The people want the land for rice paddies and crowd in from every side. They drive their cattle in to graze and the cattle carry diseases which infect the rhinos. As they increase in numbers, they're apt to wander off the sanctuary and then there's trouble between them and local farmers. We had a case of it just the other day."

Pat told me that an old male rhino had been driven out of the sanctuary by younger males and the old fellow's mate had followed him, an unusual example of devotion among the big beasts. Outside the sanctuary, the pair discovered plenty of paddy fields filled with succulent rice and proceeded to have a feast. The villagers tried desperately to drive away the two monsters that were ruining their only crop but the rhinos promptly charged and scattered them.

The village hunter was called in, armed with an ancient shotgun loaded with buckshot. He fired at the old bull and wounded him. Until now, the bull's attacks had not been serious; he wanted merely to scare the people off, not to kill. Now he charged in earnest. The hunter tried to run but a rhino can do a good 35 mph and the man hadn't a chance. The bull tossed the man and then trampled him to death.

"When I found the corpse, it was completely skinned," Pat told me over his drink. "The rhino's mate had licked off every inch of skin with her tongue. Why, I don't know unless she was trying to get the salt."

I remembered that 800 years ago Marco Polo had written that the Indian rhino will skin his victims in this curious manner.

"The old bull chased some boys who'd been with the hunter up a tree and held them there for eight hours while his mate was 'skinning' the dead man," Pat went on. "The boys had to sit in the tree and watch it. Must have been a sticky sight for them. Then the bull went to the village and cleared everyone off the streets. A man drove in from another village in a 1914 car and the rhino charged and overturned it. The man hid under the car and the rhino couldn't get at him, although the old chap spent a long time snuffing around and trying to dig the man out with his horn. By this time, the villagers had gotten word to me what was up. I came and shot the bull. Nothing else to do. The female went back to the sanctuary as soon as she saw her mate was dead.

She's taken up with another bull since then and has a nice little calf."

It was because of this incident and several like it that Pat had decided to give me a permit. Besides, as he cheerfully admitted, "For what you're paying, we can run the whole department here for a couple of years."

Pat told me what I found hard to believe, that the Indian rhino seldom uses its horn as a weapon. The horn is softer than that of his African cousin. The Indian rhino's real weapons are his teeth. "They slash with the big incisors and can disembowel an elephant with one blow. But you'll go out on old Akbar, our best *kunki* (pad elephant). Akbar is a bull with big tusks and he's used to handling rhinos."

Later that afternoon, Mr. E. P. Gee drove up to the bunga-low. Mr. Gee is a tea planter; a thin, schoolteacherish man who wears glasses and doesn't drink or smoke. He is a bachelor and has devoted his life to the preservation of the Indian rhino. I believe that he was largely responsible for the creating of the Kaziranga Sanctuary. I'd heard of Mr. Gee and was afraid he'd oppose my taking a pair of young rhinos, but he was enthusiastic over the idea. "Possibly they may be induced to breed in cap-tivity," he said in his precise, English voice after refusing a drink and settling in a chair which Subrati hurriedly produced. "If anything should happen to the herd here, it would be a comfort to know that the race was being perpetuated elsewhere."

The great question was how the young rhinos were to be captured. "In the old days, the mothers were always shot in order to obtain the young," Mr. Gee explained. "I am confident that this expedient will prove completely unnecessary."

"It had better," interrupted Pat decidedly.

"Quite. My suggestion is this. Dig pits. Cover them over with light reeds and earth. The rhinos always follow the same paths through the grass. Or one can find a pile of their dung and dig the pit there. Rhinos always go to the same pile when it becomes necessary for them to evacuate and they back up to the pile, which should render the problem even more simple."

"That's true," agreed Pat. "The poachers used to hide behind the dung heaps and shoot the poor brutes in the arse.
Filthy bastards, those poachers. We've got 'em fairly well
cleared out now, thank heaven."

"The unfortunate rhinos really have had a miserable time of
it," said Gee with a tenderness in his voice men usually only
employ when speaking of a beloved child. "The unhappy creatures actually have no business being alive in this age, you
know. They're one of the oldest types of mammals in the
world today, really living fossils. I hope when the Assamese
discover how highly Europeans prize them and what excellent
publicity they will bring the country, the people may be induced to be more tolerant towards these remarkable creatures."

Although Pat Stracey and Mr. Gee seemed very cordial, I
thought it might be a good idea for them to see Mercia. One
look at Mercia clinches any deal, as far as men are concerned.
I went to get her and found my pretty wife tossing on the
lumpy, dirty bed with a headache and in a very bad mood. "I
thought in Assam we'd be living with a rajah instead of in this
smelly hovel," she snapped at me. "You're always running off
to meet some prince or rajah. Well, I wish you'd find one now.
How could you bring a decent woman to such a filthy old dak
bungalow?"

I told her that Pat Stracey and Mr. Gee were on the veranda
and the success of our trip depended on them. Mercia grumpily
got off the bed and peered through the window.

"My God, a chi-chi and a thin old bespectacled planter in
sweaty clothes," she muttered contemptuously. "I should get
dressed for trash like that!" and she flung herself back on the
bed.

I went back to the veranda and explained that my wife was
still feeling the effects of our plane ride. We resumed our rhino
talks. Fifteen minutes later, Mercia joined us in a ravishing
Japanese silk gown that clung to her figure like wet paper. She
was overjoyed to meet dear Mr. Stracey to whom we owed
everything, fascinated by Mr. Gee's accounts of tea planting,

and deliriously happy over our adorable little bungalow. When the two entranced men left, we could have sailed the *Queen Mary* up the Brahmaputra River to Assam and loaded every rhino in the place on board with their wholehearted assistance. And, most important of all, it was arranged that we need pay only part of the permit fees at that time, so we could afford to trap two rhinos.

The next morning, Mercia and I went out to the elephant lines to inspect the animals we would use and especially Akbar, who was to be our pad (riding) elephant. We found him easily, for Akbar was the biggest elephant there, one of the biggest Indian elephants I've ever seen. He stood 9 feet 3½ inches at the shoulder and had magnificent 5½-foot tusks. His mahout, a slender, brown little man in a loincloth, proudly showed off the big bull.

"Akbar is seventy years old, sahib, and comes from the Garo Hills, where the biggest elephants grow." The Garo Hills are the area celebrated by Kipling in *Toomai of the Elephants*. "Once a wounded tiger attacked him during a big *shikar*. Akbar charged the tiger and knelt on him until the tiger died. He got that scar on his shoulder from the tiger's claws. This scar on his flank comes from a fight with a wild rogue elephant that attacked him when Akbar had four men on his back. Akbar fought the rogue for five minutes and finally drove him off, although he was hampered by the weight of the men. They were afraid to dismount. The scars on his trunk are rhinoceros bites. He has killed three that attacked him."

"Is he perfectly safe with people?" asked Mercia anxiously, for Akbar was watching us suspiciously out of his little eyes and running his trunk towards us in a manner suggestive of a great python moving towards its prey.

The mahout swelled with indignation. "*Mem-sahib*, there is a story told in the bazaars that Akbar has killed twelve men. It is a foul lie. He has only killed two. One was many years ago, a low-caste farmer who tried to keep Akbar from eating his plantains when the elephant was hungry after a long day's fast. The second man he killed only a few days ago. This man was a thieving grass cutter who had stolen some of Akbar's ration of salt. All the mahouts knew of it but the stupid courts desire proof so this man jeered at us and we were helpless. Akbar did nothing, biding his time. Then one afternoon while I was taking him for his daily swim, Akbar saw the grass cutter. He broke away from me and pursued the thief who ran into a hut. Akbar followed him inside and there impaled him on his tusks. When justice had been completed, I called to Akbar and he came like a pet lamb. I mounted on his neck and together we went down to the river to cleanse the blood from his noble tusks."

"Didn't the authorities say anything?" I asked. A man-killing elephant is almost invariably shot.

"They demanded his death, so Stracey Sahib said to them, 'Good. If you kill Akbar, you must first kill me.' But they have decreed that the tips of his beautiful tusks must be cut off. Stracey Sahib is fighting it and with Allah's help, he will prevail. Ah, my beloved, would these cruel men who know nothing of us elephant people mutilate thy beauty? May they roast in hell together with the pariah dogs who were their mothers if such a thing is done." The man threw his arms around the great bull's trunk and Akbar fondled him with the tip, making little crooning noises.

Mercia promptly announced that if necessary she would go to Nehru himself to prevent this crime, thereby completely winning over the mahout. She doubtless meant it too, at least at the moment. We arranged to start out on Akbar at dawn the next day, accompanied by another elephant, named Mohan. Pat Stracey would ride with us and another ranger would be on Mohan. Travelers in the sanctuary always go in pairs in case of accidents. An elephant may be attacked by a rhino and disabled, leaving his riders helpless in the vast, swampy preserve.

We were delayed the next morning because Mercia, in spite of all the luggage she had insisted on bringing to Assam, found that she had forgotten her topi. "If I go without a topi, I'll get

sunburned and people will think I'm a native!" she cried. I told
her to stay in the bungalow but she refused to do that either.
"I want to see anything that's worth 40,000 francs," she
snapped. Finally, she compromised by wrapping her head in a
shawl.

Pat was waiting for us impatiently. The rhinos are only out
during the early morning and late afternoon; during the heat
of the day they lie up in the thick ekkra grass. Akbar knelt so
we could climb to the pad on his back. These pads are big,
straw-filled mattresses with ropes along the sides to serve as
handholds. As an elephant moves with a curious lurching sway,
balancing yourself on the pad is quite an art. The mahout sits
on the elephant's neck and directs him with his knees.

The sanctuary is a semi-swampy area lying along the south
bank of the great Brahmaputra River. To the north, the foothills of the Himalayas rise toward the dead-bue sky, and on a
clear day you can see Mount Everest. The Brahmaputra is a
very erratic river, changing its course so frequently that often
the ghats (wharfs) have to be moved eighteen miles or more as
the river floods and creates a new channel. Most of the sanctuary is covered by the great ekkra grass, higher than a man's
head even when he is on the back of an elephant. Only on
elephants is it possible to penetrate this great area, for a man on
foot would not only become lost in the dense grass, but he
would be unable to cross the cat's cradle of waterways that
cover the sanctuary. Even for an elephant the going is not easy,
and Akbar would frequently stop and test the soggy ground
with one of his great feet before moving carefully forward.

The area was interlaced with a network of rhino trails leading
through the ekkra and we saw plenty of tiger pad marks in
the soft earth of the paths. Once we even saw one of the great
striped cats. He was gliding along a rhino trail and stopped
when he saw us. Akbar stopped also, lifting his trunk and waving the tip slowly back and forth to pick up the scent. The
tiger watched us for a few seconds before pouring himself noiselessly into the ekkra.

"Tigers are another nuisance in the sanctuary," said Pat who was sitting on the pad behind Mercia and me. "Last year they killed four young rhinos. Didn't get a chance to eat them, though. The mother rhino always drives them away even though she can't always save the baby."

Then we saw our first rhino.

He was a big bull, weighing well over 4,000 pounds and lying in a *bheel*, a rhino wallow. It is because rhinos spend a great deal of their time in these bheels that they are nearly always heavily coated with mud. We moved towards him slowly, Akbar carefully parting the ekkra with his trunk as he went to make sure we wouldn't come unexpectedly on another rhino in the thick stuff. We came closer and closer until it seemed to me that we were looking directly down on the big fellow. Then Pat reached out and touched the mahout on the arm and he stopped Akbar.

Rhinos have poor sight and as we were upwind of him, this bull was unconscious of our presence. He lay like a great pig, luxuriating in the wallow. All around him were white herons who generally accompany a rhino, feeding on the insects that he disturbs while plowing through the ekkra. Suddenly the whole flock rose in the air like a cloud of white confetti blown by a sudden breeze. At once, the bull reared up and looked around him, his huge ears (the Indian rhino has much bigger ears than his African relative) twitching about independently of each other, like two sonar listening devices ready to catch the faintest sound.

I was fascinated by the great beast. The Indian rhinos are the largest of the rhinoceros clan and this old bull must have stood some six feet at the shoulder and weighed over two tons. His skin hung in great folds, giving him the effect of wearing armor plate, and he had only one horn, while the African rhino has two. His nose was upraised and he was sniffing loudly, trying to catch our scent.

Mercia was inching around me to get a better look and the bull caught the motion. Without the slightest warning he exploded out of the bheel and stood on the soft ground, the water pouring off him and both ears cocked forward. He had changed suddenly from a peaceful, wallowing pig to a dangerous wild beast . . . an armored tank directed by a tiny, uncertain brain.

Akbar quietly curled his trunk out of harm's way and lowered his head to meet the charge with his tusks. The rhino stood considering us for a few seconds, much as the tiger had done, then gave a grunt and, swinging around with surprising nimbleness, trotted off down a path through the ekkra. In spite of his size he seemed to float over the marshy ground and moved much faster than an elephant could have done.

"They seldom charge now," said Pat with paternal pride. "They know that we won't hurt them. It's these damn poachers that cause all the trouble. If one of them wounds a rhino, of course that makes him vicious and after that he'll charge the first strange object he sees."

I spent the next three weeks going out morning and evening to watch the rhinos, for I needed to know a great deal about the animals to make sure of keeping them alive during the long trip to Europe.

Because of the melodramatic books and motion pictures made of the animal collecting business, most people think that capturing a wild animal is a difficult, dangerous affair, but once captured the animal is simply shoved into a crate and shipped off like a box of oranges. Actually, capturing a wild animal is usually a fairly simple business; the trick lies in keeping him alive after capture. This is a complicated, highly technical affair, and the collector must be as familiar with the animal's mental characteristics as with his physical habits.

For example, virtually all wild animals have what my friend Dr. Hediger calls a "flight distance." That is, a definite distance they will allow an enemy to approach before running or fighting. In theory, a cage for an animal should have a diameter of double the animal's flight distance so when he retreats to the center he always feels safe from a man standing on the outside. If the cage is smaller, the animal becomes so emotionally upset that he will not eat or sleep. Of course, in practice it is rarely possible to construct a cage of this size, certainly not a shipping cage. Therefore, the animal's flight distance must be artificially reduced, generally by taming. When Pat Stracey took over the sanctuary, the flight distance (or in this case, attack distance) of a rhino was as far as he could see or smell a man. I discovered that, due to Pat's care, the attack distance of the rhinos had been reduced to about thirty yards (about the distance we'd been from the old bull). This was of crucial importance to me in planning an enclosure for the young rhinos before I dared to try shipping them.

I made several other interesting observations. The Indian rhino calves always walked in front of their mothers where she could keep an eye on them. In Africa, the white rhino calves behave in the same way, but the black rhino calves go behind the mothers, a curious fact for which I can see no explanation. From my point of view, this was an important point as it made trapping a calf far easier. If the calves had followed the mothers, the adult would have been caught in a pit rather than the calf. Until now, I had been uncertain whether to dig the pits in the trails or by the dung piles but now I determined to use the trail method. I also studied the rhinos' feeding and bathing habits. They bathed constantly—in fact, seemed almost semiaquatic (completely unlike the African rhinos which live in the arid bush country), and their favorite food was young bamboo shoots.

As I knew that Dr. Hediger hoped to get the captured pair to breed, I watched carefully for any signs of rhinos mating so I could give him some tips. At last, I was lucky enough to witness a courtship. It was astonishingly rough, the bull coming up behind the cow, lifting her hind legs clear of the ground with his horn and then pushing her along like a man with a wheelbarrow. This sexual play was apparently necessary, for the cow refused to allow him to mount her until he had repeated this performance several times.

Although Pat Stracey was always helpful and interested, the

mahouts became increasingly restless over these long trips into
the swamp. There was always the chance of meeting a tiger
or being charged by an irritable mother rhino worried about
her calf. The mahouts didn't bother about their own safety
but they were concerned for their precious elephants. I would
have given up my researches at the end of the first few days,
but Mercia urged me on.

"For heaven's sake, Peter, stand up for your convictions,"
she told me when I was discouraged after a day's work with the
sullen mahouts. "Don't let the natives walk all over you. If
these beasts die on our hands, we won't get a franc for them.
Find out all you need to know."

But after three weeks, even Mercia was beginning to get restless. "The next time I go on a trip with you, I'll bring along
some books to read," she grumbled. "I'm sick of riding elephants or sitting in that dak bungalow with no one to talk to.
Besides, I think you simply enjoy watching those bloody rhinos.
You must know all there is to know about the brutes by now."

There was something to what Mercia said. I did get a great
satisfaction from watching the big, lumbering animals and there
were plenty of other animals in the reserve too: wild buffalo,
swamp deer, hog deer, black-necked storks, and adjutant storks.
Every time I went out I saw something new. Still, Dr. Hediger
was beginning to send me irritable cables from Basel, and I
knew Mercia was right.

First, I directed the building of a corral near the bungalow.
The corral covered slightly more than an acre of ground, ample for the flight (or attack) distance of the young calves. It
also included a good grove of bamboo where they could feed
and a stream that they could use for a bheel. The corral was
made of heavy teak stakes firmly planted in the ground, covered
with bamboo stems lashed together to serve as a "bumper" in
case the rhinos charged the corral wall. I didn't want the calves
to hurt themselves against the heavy stakes.

At the entrance to the corral, I had constructed a narrow
"bottleneck" like the chutes used for examining cattle. Before

putting the rhinos in the corral, I wanted to be able to check them for possible wounds or other injuries as a result of the trapping. Also, I wanted them to quiet down for a few hours before turning them loose in the corral. A newly caught, frightened animal will often rush around a large corral so madly that he hurts himself.

When the corral was finished, we set about digging the pits. I had carefully checked the paths used by the mothers with suitable calves and knew exactly where the traps should be placed. I wanted calves about two years old, fully weaned but still running with the mothers. Ten pits were dug, each 6 feet deep and 10 feet long by 5 feet wide. I kept them narrow so the calves could not turn around. A pachyderm caught in a pit large enough so he can thrash about in it will often injure himself in his struggles to escape.

The Assamese covered each pit with a layer of rushes and sprinkled earth on top. They did an expert job, for when they had finished, no one could tell the trap covers from the surrounding ground, including the men themselves. Later, when men had to go out to examine the traps to see if anything had been caught, several fell in by mistake. I had to send out mahouts on elephants to rescue them.

I fully expected to have my two calves in a few days, but nothing happened. Finally I found out what the trouble was. The mahouts were checking the traps, riding close to them on their elephants and then looking down from the advantage of their heights. Rhinos have a keen sense of smell and the odor of an elephant lingers a long time. The rhinos had simply abandoned the polluted paths.

I had fresh pits dug and insisted that the Assamese go on foot to check them. They didn't like this idea at all as they had to follow the rhino paths through the ekkra, and there was always a possibility of meeting a rhino or a tiger. At last, I had to go with them. I admit after a few days I sympathized with the Assamese. You could generally hear a rhino coming; they made quite a lot of noise, for the paths were virtually tunnels through the dense grass and their great bulk scraped against the dry stalks. Then you could dive into the grass and hide until the rhino had gone past. But the tigers moved absolutely noiselessly. We met several of them but luckily always at a distance. We simply stood still until the tiger moved away.

Then one memorable morning as my men and I were plodding along a path towards one of our pits, we heard great snortings and splashings ahead of us. "A rhino, sahib, a rhino!" the men screamed and we all broke into a run.

Instead of a rhino, we found a mother water buffalo and her calf in the pit. The pit was half full of water from seepage, and the two animals were thrashing about, the mother's great horns and staring eyes barely above the surface and the poor little calf nearly drowned. A rhino would have been perfectly all right but the two long-legged cattle were at a disadvantage in the narrow pit. I instantly sent one of the men back to camp with instructions to bring Akbar and plenty of picks and shovels so we could liberate the unfortunates.

One of the natives and I took turns holding the calf's head above water until Akbar arrived. Instantly we set to work digging a ramp down one end of the pit so the captives could climb out while Akbar and his mahout stood watching. The work finished, we leaned panting on our tools, certain the thankful mother would trot away followed by her baby.

The thrashing cow finally got her forefeet on the slope and with a mighty heave freed herself from the mud. The baby followed more slowly. We waited to see them bolt down the narrow path but instead the mother stood looking balefully around. She was only a few yards away and I suddenly realized that I had miscalculated her sense of gratitude.

"Run, sahib, she's going to charge!" yelled the mahout. Even as he spoke, the cow lowered her head and came for me at startling speed in spite of the marshy ground that took her in over her knees at every step.

I flung myself backwards into the grass. All around me were screams and yells as the cow went through the terrified natives, spraying them in all directions. Two of them dove into the pit, several plunged into the ekkra, one man raced towards Akbar with the raging cow after him.

I expected to see Akbar run because even for an elephant a charging buffalo is a terrible sight. Instead, Akbar curled up his trunk out of harm's way and braced himself to meet the charge. As the cow rushed in with lowered head, Akbar took the attack on his tusks. There was a crash that shook the ground under me and both animals recoiled from the shock. The cow backed away, shaking her head, and I thought that she'd had enough but she came in again, this time deliberately going under the bull's tusks to disembowel him.

I saw her disappear under the elephant's body and red blood squirt into the air like a jet from a hose as her horns found their mark. Akbar screamed with pain and fury. He tried to kneel on her but the buffalo was under him, working with first one horn and then the other to reach his vitals. The mahout was screaming insanely and kicking Akbar, apparently trying to force him forward so he could bring his full weight to bear on the buffalo beneath him. The cow drew back again, her black, dripping hide streaked with blood—Akbar's blood. The bull was trumpeting furiously, the natives yelling, and the buffalo bellowing. Then the cow charged for the third time.

Akbar dropped on his knees so she couldn't get under him again and received the charge with both his tusks. Thank heaven the tips hadn't been cut as the government had ordered. I thought the cow would impale herself but buffalos are tough animals. In spite of the fearful punishment she was taking, she kept trying to force home the charge. Akbar half rose and with a tremendous heave flung the cow over backwards. She lay panting for a moment and then staggered to her feet. Slowly, she turned and limped away, the bleating calf trotting behind her.

After this, it was harder than ever to get the men to go to the pits unless they were on elephant back. I was growing desperate. The rains were only a few days away and once they began, trapping would be over for the season, for during those torrential downpours, the pits would be flooded within an hour and become useless. Pat and Mr. Gee were sympathetic but unable to help. Mercia alternated between hysterical fits of fury and hardheaded practicality. She would curse me for delaying the trapping, excoriate the rhinos, and swear at the natives; and then, once her rage had passed, she would go out alone to check the pits. Mercia was absolutely fearless, both with humans and animals.

The rhinos had turned out to be much cleverer than I'd thought. The cows in some way or other sensed the presence of the pits and avoided them. Mercia raged at me, "All this time you've wasted watching these creatures and you don't even know enough to catch a baby!"

I went over and over my notes on the rhinos. Then I had an idea. The rhinos must be mad about salt. That was the only logical reason they would "skin" a dead human with their tongues and there were only a few salt licks in the reserve. I decided to scatter salt over the pit coverings and along the paths leading to the pits. Perhaps the rhinos, in their eagerness to get the salt, would forget caution and be caught.

Subrati and I spent an afternoon spreading the salt. We were out at dawn the next day.

The cover of the first pit was gone; there was nothing but a gaping hole in the ground. We approached it without daring to hope. Inside was a baby rhino.

Subrati and I raced back to camp, yelling with delight.

Mercia burst into tears of relief. Everyone in the camp went mad with excitement. Akbar was still recuperating from his fight with the buffalo, so we started out on another pad elephant, named Jess Pagli which means "the Crazy One." Jess Pagli wasn't fully broken to rhinos but we had no time to think of that. Mohan was hitched to a big transport cage and followed us more slowly. There were five people on Jess Pagli, including Mercia and me. I was carrying a very fine German camera to photograph the transferring of the baby from the pit to the transport cage.

The mahout took us right up to the edge of the pit as there was no longer any need for caution. The baby was a splendid little fellow weighing about a ton. He was splashing around in four feet of water and seemed completely unhurt. While we were admiring him, there was a sudden snort from the ekkra. The mother rhino burst out and came straight for us, her mouth open, her tail straight in the air, scattering mud in all directions as she charged.

Jess Pagli gave a scream of terror and bolted. I was hanging to one of the rope grips of the pad for dear life. The mahout was yelling, Jess Pagli was trumpeting, and through it all came the fierce snorts of the furious rhino. Five people are too much for a single pad even when an elephant is walking slowly and I knew someone would fall. A great, black shape appeared below me and I saw the rhino slash at Jess Pagli's flank with her terrible incisors. The elephant screamed again and now she really began to run but the rhino kept alongside and slashed again. I was still clinging to the camera and was half off the pad. The rhino was just under me.

Jess Pagli reached a broad waterway. Without hesitating, she plunged into it. As she fell away from beneath me, I was left sitting on air. I turned over and dove, with the camera in my hand. My only idea was to swim far enough underwater so the rhino couldn't get me.

I swam until my lungs were bursting and then surfaced. Jess Pagli had finally halted in midstream. There was no sign of the rhino. Mercia was screaming at me, "Don't get that camera wet! It's worth 20,000 francs!"

No one was hurt except poor Jess Pagli who had two bad gashes in her flank. When the mahout had succeeded in quieting her, we returned to camp and got two bulls with tusks. But even the two big bulls refused to face the raging mother rhino and at last we had to fire the grass to drive her away. Then we all worked desperately to put out the fire before it could spread to other parts of the sanctuary.

Mohan had arrived with the transport cage and I told the natives to dig an incline down towards the head of the pit, but to leave a solid wall of earth about a foot thick between the pit and the incline. The cage was pushed down this incline, the doors opened, and the dirt wall dug away. Ropes were thrown around the young rhino and he was hauled into the cage and the door secured behind him. Then Mohan dragged him to the corral.

I was very glad that I'd had the forethought to construct the "bottleneck," for the baby's eyes were full of mud and a mild infection had set in. I washed the eyes with boric acid and treated two small cuts in his legs before turning him loose.

The baby was a male with a little bud of a horn just showing. Everything depended on getting him tame, for an animal as large and powerful as a rhino is extremely hard to handle unless he knows that you don't mean to hurt him. We decoyed him into the bottleneck several times a day, giving him *jagri* (palm sugar) and salt as a reward. Once in the bottleneck, we could scratch his ears and pat him so he soon grew used to us. We had also taken the precaution of smearing the inside of the bottleneck with his dung so the chute would smell homey. Animals are almost completely controlled by odor, and strange surroundings don't disturb them nearly as much as strange scents.

Within a week, the little fellow was so tame that he'd run to us like a big dog to be petted and fondled. Mercia could even ride on his back. He actually got to be a nuisance, following us about and poking us with his stump of a horn to get attention. Mercia named him Gadadahar, after an ancient Assamese king, and when she called "Gadadahar! Gadadahar!" from outside the corral, he would squeak back in reply and butt his head against the stakes trying to reach her. We never heard Gadadahar grunt or snort like the big rhinos. His only noise was the funny little squeak that he had used to call his mother.

We caught three other males before we got a female. "Naturally, because all males are damned stupid," Mercia remarked. We finally got a female two days before the rains broke. She tamed even more quickly than Gadadahar had. We named her Joymothi after an Assamese queen. The two rhinos got along very well together and took their baths lying side by side in the bheel I'd made for them at one end of the corral.

Dr. Hediger had by now sent me enough to pay for capturing permits for both babies and we were ready to start the long trip to Europe. I had hoped to fly them by chartered plane to Calcutta but no plane was available. My next choice was rail but that would mean sending them through East Pakistan, and at that time the railroad lines were closed between India and Pakistan due to the riots. There was only one way left: to float them by flatboat down the Brahmaputra River. This meant a three weeks' trip and exposing our babies to all the dangers of rapids, sudden floods and uncertain native boats, but there was no help for it.

To add to our troubles, the shipping had to be accurately timed. Not every ship that puts into Calcutta is going to Europe or will accept animal freight. Those that do have their regular cargoes and there's often no room for animal cages. I spent several days cabling shipping lines until I found that the Dutch merchant *Alcione* was arriving in Calcutta and would take us and the rhinos. Even then, I did not dare to leave until the last minute. If I arrived at Calcutta ahead of time, the rhinos would be put in the zoo, as wild animals cannot be kept at the docks or even in private compounds because, the authorities argue, if they escaped they would constitute a public menace. There was no telling what infections my babies might pick up if put in a cage that had housed hundreds of other animals, many of them diseased. The *Alcione* would only be in the harbor for eight hours so I had to float the rhinos down the river, arrive during that eight-hour period and load them directly on the ship without delay.

Another unforeseen complication arose. My money was in traveler's checks and no one in Assam would accept them. I went around borrowing five rupees from one man and ten from another until I had enough to fly to Calcutta. There I cashed my checks and returned to Assam with 50,000 rupees in cash. I hated to do it as men have often been murdered for ten rupees in the Orient, but it was unavoidable.

I found Mercia exhausted. The whole responsibility of caring for the rhinos and making preparations for our departure had been left to her. However, she'd done well as she always did. She had gotten a paddle-wheel steamer to tow our flatboat down the river, gotten a lorry to transport the rhino cages to the flat-boat, gotten coolies to help with the loading and unloading, and laid in a supply of food for the rhinos. If everything went right, we had just time to load the rhinos and reach Calcutta before the *Alcione* sailed.

There was no trouble getting the rhinos into the shipping boxes. We had coated the floors with their dung and been feeding the rhinos inside the cages for weeks, so they regarded the cages with affection and were quite content to ride in them. With the rhinos inside, chewing happily on bamboo shoots, we prepared to have cages lifted onto the lorry. I was constantly glancing at my watch for time was of the essence. A delay of even a few hours could mean that we'd miss the *Alcione*.

I had just given the order to have the cages pushed up the tailgate into the lorry when a young forestry official came up to me, looking very natty in his immaculate uniform.

"Your permits have just been revoked," he told me importantly. "The forestry department has decided that no female rhinos are to be allowed to leave the sanctuary. These animals are an important national asset and the female cannot be allowed to leave India."

# Chapter 3

# Rhinos on a raft

HERE IT was again, the same disaster that had struck us in Siam. Perhaps after a long series of protests to the Indian government, I could get the order rescinded but that would do me little good. The *Alcione* would be gone, the Brahmaputra so flooded by the rains that passage on flats would be impossible, and the rhinos probably dead. A foreigner dealing with an Asian official is the most helpless being in the world. There was nothing I could do and the smug ranger knew it. For generations his people had been kicked around by "sahibs" and now was his chance to retaliate.

If I was beaten, Mercia was not. She went into one of her terrifying rages. Even the ranger dropped his haughty air and became nervous. He protested almost apologetically. "I have nothing to do with the order. It has just come through. No females are to be exported. We must keep them here to build up the herds."

"Does the forestry department realize that I've spent five months and 40,000 rupees to get this pair?" I asked.

"That is not my concern. I am only obeying orders." He stamped out to the cages and started to open the door of the female's box.

Mercia threw herself across the door. "You'll have to kill me first!" she screamed.

"Get away from that door," the ranger shouted, struggling with Mercia to release the catch.

He was stronger than she was and managed to tear her hands loose. "Very well, open it! That's a wild rhino and she'll kill me." Mercia did not mention that she had been riding the rhino around the corral the day before. "You'll be held responsible for my death. It'll go on your record that you killed a helpless woman!"

The ranger hesitated. "I'll have the police remove you."

"They can't!" Mercia had both arms and legs locked around the bars in the door. Then she shouted to me. "Don't just stand there, you fool! Call Pat Stracey!"

Luckily, there was a telephone at Gauhati and I was able to find a car to drive me there. Pat might be at any of a dozen places or off somewhere in the sanctuary. I had some qualms about leaving Mercia but from experience I knew that she was quite capable of looking after herself.

I called the sanctuary and a clerk answered. No, Stracey Sahib was not there. No, he was not expected back. No, no one knew where he was. I tried station after station. At last, Pat answered. He had just come in from a tour of inspection and sounded dog-tired.

"All right, all right," he said wearily. "They've mucked things up again. The department is right about having to be extra careful about females, they're our breeding stock. But one more or less won't make any difference and we promised you a pair. Tell that ranger that I want to speak to him."

When I got back to the corral, Mercia was still clinging to the bars like an octopus, surrounded by a ring of cursing policemen and the furious ranger. I gave him Pat's message and he departed sullenly. He returned and gave angry permission for us to remove the rhino.

By now, a large crowd had collected. It was market day and people had drifted into the area from all the outlying towns. When they found that there were two rhinos in the lorry, a whisper of excitement went through the mob.

"He has rhinos!" "Do they have horns?" "Of course, you fool; otherwise, why should he bother with them?" "A piece of those horns would make me a rich man for life!" "Why is this white man stealing our rhinos? We are now a free nation!" "Cut off the horns! The rhinos belong to us! We are no longer slaves to white men."

Mercia said to me quietly, "Get the lorry going at once. This means trouble."

A man pushed his way through the crowd with a long knife in his hand. His eyes were fastened on the rhino cages with a fixed, unblinking stare and saliva ran from his partly opened mouth. I grabbed his wrist. The man ignored me, still pushing on towards the cages. The crowd began to shout and push forward.

I wrestled with the man and the police came to my help, swinging their clubs. The mob was screaming, "Colonialist oppressor! Capitalist exploiter! Cut off the horns! The animals belong to Assam!"

One of the policeman panted, "Let them have the horns! We can't hold them any longer."

The horns were only tiny stumps and if they were gouged out, the baby rhinos might die. One of the policemen went down and was trampled by the screaming crowd. A stone hit another man beside me. He dropped his club and fell back against the lorry, half senseless. The man with the knife was still fighting with insane desperation to reach the cages. He was an old man and probably impotent. Those horns represented his only chance to renew his youthful virility.

The lorry began to move. Mercia had jumped into the driver's seat and started the engine. I pulled myself up on the side as it lurched forward. The car bumped away over the rough road, steadily gathering speed while the mob pursued us, throwing stones and screaming insults until we were out of range.

We went directly to the ghat at Gauhati. The river had altered its course almost half a mile during the last rainy season and a long, rickety causeway on stilts had been built over the mud to the loading ghat. Along this causeway the rhino cages had to be hauled by gangs of sweating coolies. We had no rollers and the heavy cages, weighing well over a ton each, were tugged along an inch at a time to the waiting flat. Mercia walked beside the cages, feeding the babies bamboo shoots to quiet them. I was in constant fear that the mob would follow us to Gauhati but they must have given it up as a bad job. At last the two cages were loaded on the flat and the paddle-wheel steamer began to move down the river, towing the flat astern. We were on our way down a thousand miles of treacherous river to Calcutta.

Mercia said bitterly, "And those were the people who've been after Pat Stracey for the last ten years to have all the rhinos in the sanctuary killed. Now they won't even let us take out two calves!"

We tied up that evening along the bank; the river is too full of sandbanks, shoals and unexpected currents to navigate at night. There were a number of farmers saying their evening prayers on the bank and they called out to ask what we had in the cages. Before we could stop them, the crew proudly shouted back that we had rhinos and instantly there was wild excitement on the shore, some of the farmers hurrying down to the water's edge to view the rare beasts and other racing back to the village to spread the news.

"Now we're in for it," said our captain gloomily. "We'll have every native in the district here before midnight."

He was right. Men and women began pouring in from all directions, some of them, we afterwards learned, from villages fifty miles away. They were a well-mannered, polite lot and the captain rigged a gangplank and let them come aboard the flat to see the rhino. Subrati did a land-office business selling rhino urine which is considered a panacea for all illnesses. Subrati drank a glass of the urine himself every day and had worked out his own method of collecting it. He had a long bamboo, split longitudinally so it formed a trough. When he saw that one of our rhinos was beginning to answer a call of nature, he would hastily hold the bamboo under the animal and drain the urine into a bucket. He sold the urine for two rupees a pint and the demand was far greater than the supply. We opened the front of the cages so the people could at least touch the animals which in itself is thought to bring great good luck.

Then Mercia had an idea. "Look at all that fine, rich grass along the bank," she pointed out. "Wouldn't our rhinos just love that! Let's say that everyone who wants to touch the rhinos has to bring an armful of grass."

It seemed like a good idea and we had the captain announce that an armful of grass was the admission price. There were no objections and soon the bank was covered with stooping figures gathering the grass. Subrati stood by the cages collecting the grass while Mercia and I went to bed. We'd both had a long day and were dead tired.

I was awakened by the sound of running feet, chains rattling, shouts, and the shrill squeaks of the rhinos. Then I heard Subrati yelling for help. I grabbed a half-empty whisky bottle from the table by my bed and ran out. The ship was a madhouse. It was alive with people climbing over the cabin, over the cages, hanging from the anchor cable and crowding the gangplank. I stumbled over the body of one of the crew—dead or stunned I could not tell.

I ran for the flat. As I went I heard the crash of broken glass as the rioters smashed the cabin windows. The rhinos were terrified, screaming like pigs. My first thought was for them. I jumped on the flat and managed to drop the cage doors. The doors slid up and down on grooves and even in the dark I could find the release catches. As the doors thumped into position, I heard Subrati yell again. He was only a few feet from me, on his back and covered with fighting natives.

I drove into the press, laying around me the whisky bottle which broke on the first blow. A broken bottle, held by the neck, is a very deadly weapon at close quarters. The grunts and curses of the natives changed to screams as the jagged glass ripped their faces and hands.

Suddenly the whole flat was brilliantly illuminated. The captain had turned the boat's headlight on it. The light seemed to frighten the natives, for they flung themselves overboard and began swimming ashore. Subrati staggered to his feet, his face streaming blood. He gasped, "Sahib, don't worry. The rhinos are all right."

"What happened?" I panted.

"So many people were coming that the captain tried to raise the gangplank. He was afraid the ship would be swamped. These people had collected their grass and were furious so they attacked the ship. But they meant no harm to the babies."

I heard the dull blows of an axe. The captain was cutting the cable. At once the ship began to move downstream, for the current was strong here. The natives still on the ship hurled themselves over the side in a blind panic. In a moment the water was full of their long, white dhotis and the crowd on the bank waded into the river to help their friends. I could hear the captain bellowing to get up steam in the engines.

I was afraid to leave the rhinos. The crowd began to stone us, quietly and systematically, and again I heard the crash of breaking glass. Subrati and I covered the rhino cages with mats we'd brought to protect the animals from the sun. The stones were jagged pieces of flint and both Subrati and I were hit several times before we'd completely finished the job. Then the full force of the current caught us and we swept downstream and out of range.

I climbed back on the ship. Mercia met me, very pale and shaken. "The rhinos are all right," I assured her.

She looked at me curiously. "How do you feel?"

"I'm not hurt," I said surprised. Then I realized that blood was dripping from a stone cut across my forehead, one eye was beginning to swell closed, and I ached all over.

The captain came aft, swearing. "This is the last time I take rhinos. I knew I never should have agreed to such a crazy idea. Every window on the ship is broken, we've lost the anchor and

I don't know what other damage's been done. None of the crew are dead but that's about all you can say for them."

"It's lucky the people all dove overboard as soon as the ship began to move," I said. "If the crowd had stayed on board they could have easily overpowered us."

The captain grinned. "They thought we were carrying them off to slavery and the rhinos were a lure to get them on board. I heard them shouting to each other that the whole business was a trick. It is said that not so long ago there were slavers on the river and the people still remember them."

Fortunately the ship had a spare anchor and after that we anchored in midstream at night. There was one advantage to the whole business; the rhinos had plenty of fresh grass for the next few days.

For the next three weeks we drifted down the mighty Brahmaputra, one of the greatest rivers in the world. The rhinos stood the trip well and I would have been perfectly happy if it hadn't been for the nagging worry about making connections with the *Alcione*. There was no way of telling how many miles we made each day, and when I questioned the captain, he merely replied, "If it is Allah's will that you reach the ship, you will make it. If it is not, nothing mortal man can do will help you."

Then we came to the great delta at the mouth of the Brahmaputra where the river joins with the even mightier Ganges. This delta covers forty-four square miles of waterways, canals, swamps and streams and reminded me very much of the delta at the mouth of the Amazon. A man was kept constantly in the bow of the paddle wheeler to take soundings with a long pole, and although we grounded several times, the crew was always able to shove us off. The captain told me we were only a day's trip from Calcutta "if Allah wills." It was high time, too. According to my calculations, the *Alcione* would arrive the next morning. We had cut it very fine indeed.

After much pleading and a slight additional payment, the captain agreed to go on at night. It was dull, monotonous work. The crew were tired, the chant of the man taking soundings with the long bamboo poles was like the ticking of a metronome, and the marshy shores stretching away on all sides in the moonlight offered no landmarks, so we did not seem to be moving. I was dozing on the stern when I felt a slight bump. We had gone aground again. I swore and stretched myself. As I did so, I heard the captain shout, "The flat! The cable's broken!"

I bounded to my feet. Caught by the current, the flat with my two precious rhinos was slowly floating past us. On her were Subrati and two members of the crew, all fast asleep. I shouted at them and so did the captain but nothing made any impression. Helpless, we watched them drift away downstream.

The captain snapped, "There're rapids ahead. If the flat hits them, she'll go over."

I jumped into the water with the crew to help shove the boat off but she was firmly stuck on a mud flat. The captain had shaved a bend a little too closely. Even Mercia threw her weight on one of the poles. After two hours of sweating and struggling, the suction under the boat's bottom was finally broken and we were afloat again. We started in pursuit of the flat.

The next half hour was one of the worst of my life. I expected every moment to come upon the flat turned upside down. Finally the boat's headlight picked it up. The flat had run aground on one of the bends, and the three men were frantically waving to us and shouting. We took her in tow again and reached Calcutta shortly after dawn. There was the *Alcione* riding at anchor. We went alongside and the rhino cages were swayed aboard.

The voyage to Europe was uneventful. The news of the rhinos' arrival had been radioed ahead and when the ship docked at Genoa, the pier was black with crowds. Reporters, photographers, newsreel cameramen, radio men, representatives from the zoo, and sight-seers swarmed aboard. Mercia was paralyzed with astonishment. She kept saying over and over, "Have they all come just to see our rhinos? Why, rhinos are only animals. What do these people want?"

Mercia with her stunning exotic beauty made even a greater hit than the rhinos. She was photographed with the babies, photographed with me, photographed sitting on the ship's rail, photographed looking at Europe for the first time, and photographed in virtually every change of clothes she possessed. She was dumfounded by all the attention. Used to being ignored or snubbed by the English, she could not understand why no one cared that she was a Eurasian. She was still in a trance when we loaded the rhinos on a railway luggage car and left for Basel.

An hour or so later, a sharp reaction set in. Mercia seemed to go mad. If anyone looked at her—and because of her striking beauty everyone did—Mercia would go into a wild rage. "They're staring at me because I'm brown!" she wept. Then she feverishly began to unpack the apothecary's supply of lotions, creams and unguents she always carried. "Get out of here!" she screamed at me when I asked what she was doing. I left the compartment and stood unhappily in the passageway smoking a cigar. When Mercia finally appeared, she'd covered her face with a light pancake make-up. When I protested, she yelled, "I won't be taken for an Indian! I won't! They won't let me into a hotel or a restaurant if they know what I am. They may even send me back to Singapore."

New crowds greeted us at Basel. Mercia, after her savage outburst, had suddenly become panicky and helpless. She clung to my arm like a little girl, weeping, "Oh, Peter, what shall I do? How shall I dress? I'll take off the make-up. I know it was foolish. Peter, you must help me. You're all I have."

I sent her to wash her face and went out to greet Dr. Hediger who had arrived at the head of a new battalion of newspaper and cameramen. Flashbulbs were exploding on all sides and I was confronted by a battery of microphones. I couldn't think of a word to say, although Basel is my home and the crowd was full of familiar, smiling faces. I stood stammering and sick with embarrassment.

Someone pushed me aside. It was Mercia, radiantly lovely and smiling. She had changed into an Indian sari and she looked marvelous. She greeted Dr. Hediger and then, being asked to say a few words, spoke for ten minutes, making jokes, describing our adventures, and saying how she'd looked forward to seeing Switzerland which was even more beautiful than she'd imagined. The crowd loved her. Meanwhile, I stood in the background, scraping the side of the platform with my shoe and wondering how the rhinos were.

Dr. Hediger had insisted that the zoo be cleared during the unloading of the rhinos as he was afraid a crowd might bother them. The crates were carefully slid down the tailgate of the truck and the cage doors lifted. The rhinos refused to come out. The elaborately designed pen was foreign to them and they clung to the familiar safety of their old cages.

"I'll get them out," I said. I went into the house that connected with the pen and gave a special whistle that the rhinos had learned to know. All during the long trip, Mercia and I had checked the babies, day and night, at regular three-hour intervals and we always gave that whistle as we came towards the cages. At once there were excited squeaks and my two animals rushed into the pen and began looking for me.

Except that they weren't my babies any longer. I'd sold them. I turned and ran out of the house by another entrance so they wouldn't see me. If they saw me again, they'd expect me to continue feeding and playing with them in this new home. And that couldn't be; I had to make a clean break.

I went to our hotel and found Mercia in our room, prancing with excitement. "We're asked to a big dinner to meet a lot of prominent people," she exclaimed. "Everyone is delighted with me. They don't seem to care what I am. And look at this!" She flourished a sheaf of letters, telegrams and cablegrams over her head.

We tore them open. There were orders from Rome, from Paris, from New York, from Buenos Aires, from Sydney, from Tokyo. Everyone wanted to commission me to get them animals. We were asked to dinners, receptions, conferences, and heaven knows what. Mercia snatched up the letters, ripped them open, dropped them half read, and grabbed for another like a child opening birthday presents.

Finally she said while still poring over the wonderful mail, "Hurry and get dressed. We haven't much time."

"I'm not going," I said heavily.

She stared at me. "Why not?"

"Mercia, I called the babies to get them into the pen. They ran out looking for me and I had to leave them there. We'll never see Gadadahar and Joymothi again," and I began to cry.

Mercia sat staring at me. Then she said slowly, "I think you must be mad. After all, they're only animals."

She couldn't have said anything more cruel. "And you're nothing but a native!" I yelled at her.

Mercia went as white as when she was wearing the pancake make-up. I called room service and told them to send up a bottle of schnapps. Then I sat down on the bed again.

The schnapps arrived and I started drinking. Mercia watched me for a while. Then she got up and started dressing, still not speaking. She put on her evening gown and a stole of snow lynx I'd gotten for her in Calcutta. Then she walked over and stood looking down at me.

"I've waited all my life to go to a big party and be received by Europeans," she said levelly. "This is my chance. I'm not going to give it up for you and those stinking rhinos. Are you coming?"

I couldn't. I couldn't talk to people tonight with the babies locked up in the Basel Zoo, all alone and frightened. I shook my head.

"Then I'm going alone," said Mercia and walked out. I heard her high-heeled shoes tapping off down the corridor. I was glad she was gone. Now I could start drinking seriously.

I drank myself into a stupor and passed out within an hour. But no matter how drunk I became, all night long I got up at the prescribed periods to look for the rhinos and give them their palm sugar and salt. I wandered around the corridors of the hotel whistling for them and it was only when I didn't hear their funny little squeaks that I knew they were gone. Then I'd go back home to my room and drink more schnapps until I could sleep again. I swore over and over that I'd never again make a pet out of an animal but of course I broke my word. I'm still breaking it.

# Chapter 4

# Birth of
# an animal collector

THE RHINOS established me as an internationally known animal collector. I no longer had to beg zoo directors to give me commissions; I had only to pick and choose from the contracts offered me. I'd come a long way from a little boy stumping along the streets of Basel with a couple of turtles under his shirt, hoping someone would give me a franc or two for them so I could buy meat for my pet fox. Yes, a long way . . . nearly fifty thousand miles of travel, jungles, deserts, heat, cold, heartbreaks and a few unexpected successes. I'd lost my first sweetheart because of the animal business, thrown away a promising career, been clawed by a lion, charged by gorillas, nearly lost my leg because of a zebra kick, and alienated my family. But it was worth it—at least I thought so.

I was born in Basel, Switzerland, on January 1, 1920. Nearly every European community has its traditional craft and the traditional craft in Basel was working with animals and plants. Many of the world's great naturalists have come from this little city: the Sarasins who worked for years in Ceylon and the Celebes, Speiser who made a study of New Guinea, Wirz in Borneo, Buehler in Siam, David in Africa and Huber in Brazil. There were many naturalists in Basel and one of the world's best zoos. I grew up in an atmosphere of travel to exotic lands, the scent of animal cages, and the highly technical "shop talk" of animal men, much as a Detroit child grows up listening to talk of automobiles and the jargon of engineers.

My father was a doctor. My mother was born in Singapore, so that in our household the Orient was as common a subject for discussion as the next town. My parents were kind and understanding although implacably bourgeois in their values and ambitions. It was taken for granted that I would enter some reputable profession. Anything else was unthinkable.

Even when I was eight years old, I was determined to be a naturalist and explorer. My parents listened to me with the same good-natured amusement they would have shown if I'd announced that I wanted to be a pirate chief or a knight in armor. But animals were an obsession with me. I filled the house with pets and flunked out of two schools because I was always running off to walk in the woods or lie by a stream watching the fish. At last my parents decided to have a serious talk with me.

"Peter, if you wish to be a naturalist, you must study," my father told me gravely. "You will have to go to a university, take a degree in zoology, and then apply for a position in some museum."

"I don't want to be that kind of a naturalist," I protested. "I want to travel around the world and work with animals."

My parents smiled fondly. "Who will pay your way? You would have to be sent out by some institution to do research and for that you would need a degree."

"I could collect animals and sell them," I said doggedly.

"Our family have always been professional people, not tramps," said Mother decidedly. "Look at your uncles. One is a paleographer, the other an archaeologist. Their future is assured. If you wish to be a zoologist, you must get a degree also."

Two weeks later, I was thrown out of another school for truancy.

My parents did not forbid me to have pets but now they insisted that I would have to pay for their food myself. They thought this would teach me what an expensive luxury animals are. It never occurred to me to give up my pets or even to do better in the new school where they sent me. My only problem was raising money for my animals.

I had a number of Japanese "waltzing" mice (mice which are bred to spin around rapidly in circles somewhat like tumbler pigeons), guinea pigs, salamanders, frogs, toads, a baby crocodile, snakes, lizards, tortoises, and a fennec fox from North Africa that I'd gotten from an animal dealer. The fox was named Fritz and he traveled around inside my shirt with only his nose and bright eyes peering out. When the family cut off my funds, the animals had to pay for themselves and I devoted a good deal of ingenuity to this problem.

I started a breeding program with the mice and developed several distinct strains: pure black, pure white, and black bodies with white heads. Because these strains were a novelty, they commanded higher prices on the market than the ordinary mice. I discovered that dealers would pay me for unusual species of frogs, toads, salamanders and snakes. My biggest moneymaker was the aesculap adder, a very pretty copper-colored snake which isn't a native of Switzerland at all but was originally brought there by the Roman legions. Because these snakes are easily tamed, the Roman ladies used to wear them as ornaments. These are the snakes which appear on the caduceus. Near Basel there were the sites of some old Roman camps and here I found most of my aesculaps. Apparently they had bred and remained in these places for nearly two thousand years.

Even with these projects, I wasn't able to raise enough money to support my private zoo, so I began to stage tortoise races. Each tortoise had a number painted on its back and it was placed around the circumference of a big circle with a pile of lettuce leaves in the center. The first tortoise to reach the lettuce won. These tortoise races were very popular with my contemporaries until their parents protested that I was teaching the children to gamble. There were so many complaints that my parents finally capitulated and gave me enough money to support my private zoo with the understanding that there were to be no more tortoise races.

When I was nineteen, World War II came and I was called into military service. I entered the cavalry and was put in the remount unit. I'd never had anything to do with horses before but by the end of a year I was giving lessons in driving, jumping and simple dressage. I loved anything connected with animals and threw myself into the work with great enthusiasm.

When it became fairly obvious that Switzerland would not be attacked, most of us were relieved from active duty although we still had to put in a month's training from time to time. I was unable to qualify for any profession but my mother (Father had died when I was sixteen) managed to get me a job with J. R. Geigy, the famous Swiss chemical firm. There was only one branch of Geigy's which had anything remotely to do with animals, a new department that was experimenting with an insecticide called DDT. Millions of insects were raised in a huge glass box and then sprayed with this chemical and their death rates calculated.

Watching the dying agonies of a mosquito has never struck me as an enthralling spectacle and even the assurance of the head of the firm that this DDT had a great future failed to inspire me. There were only three of us engaged in this work (it is now Geigy's biggest department) and if I had stayed on, I would have been a wealthy man today. I didn't take much interest in my duties and I had the impression that Geigy's only kept me on for my father's sake. He had been a great friend of the head of the firm.

Between my work at Geigy's and my military service, I didn't have much time for pets and as far as I was concerned, this was a living death. I still had Fritz and he went to the office hidden under my coat. He'd lie curled up on my desk while I was working, watching everything with his alert little eyes, and I was even able to smuggle him into restaurants. I'd hand him bits of food when the waitress wasn't looking and he'd eat them equally surreptitiously. On Sundays, Fritz and

I would go for walks in the woods together, I watching the birds and Fritz concentrating on field mice and rabbits.

In addition to Fritz, I also kept a collection of aquariums and terrariums on a table in my little apartment. They varied from a desert terrarium to a semi-arid to a temperate to a "tropical rain forest" to a swamp and, finally, to the all-water aquariums. Each tank was controlled by thermostats, humidity gauges, fans to provide circulation of air, and lights—ranging from infra-red to ordinary sunlight. I kept a collection of lizards, salamanders, small reptiles and fish, and by altering the "weather conditions" I could study their eating, sleeping and breeding habits. Some of the lizards would only feed in the dark, some only between certain ranges of temperature and others when I pressed a button that caused artificial rain to fall in the terrarium.

I was often away on jobs for Geigy's or on military duty so I needed someone to look after my collection. I'd taken up with a pretty young barmaid who used to feed the animals and check the gauges but she never took any real interest in the work. I had a pair of fan-footed geckos from Africa that I thought would breed if the light were reduced gradually so as to simulate the sunset period when these lizards mate. Once I had to go to Hamburg for the firm and stayed longer than I'd expected. When I got back, I hurried up to the room and asked eagerly, "Did the lizards get a chance to breed while I was gone?" The girl answered angrily, "No, and neither did I."

I was simply living from day to day with nothing to look forward to except massacring more bugs with DDT when my first big break came. Another young Geigy employee returned from a trip to North Africa with a collection of miscellaneous animals he'd bought from native dealers with the hope of selling them in Switzerland for a profit. He had some sand vipers, horned vipers, horned toads, and a few birds. His name was Hans Gagliari and he was married to a pretty, ambitious girl. Hans traveled frequently to Africa for the company and hoped to make some money out of handling animals as a sideline.

Not knowing how to feed or care for his collection, he offered me half the profits if I'd help him with the animals. Naturally, I was half crazy with delight. We disposed of the cargo for such a big profit that we were both dumfounded. It amounted to more than six months' wages at Geigy's. The war had only just ended, and since there had been no shipments of animals since it had begun, the zoos were half empty and desperate for exhibits. Also, many zoos had killed potentially dangerous animals, such as poisonous snakes, for fear that they might escape during air raids. There was an enormous market open to us and prices were sky high.

I wanted to resign from Geigy's immediately and go full time into the animal business but Hans was more cautious. We stayed with Geigy's but started the Zoo Import and Export Company. We had some elegantly engraved stationery made and an imposing price list. Hans luckily was sent back to Algiers on another business trip and this time he returned with a load of more reptiles, several hundred birds, monkeys, Dorcas gazelles and some foxes. The animals were sold before we could unload them from the train and we were deluged with demands for more.

Geigy's didn't send Hans to Africa often enough to meet the demands of our clients, so we had to find some other source of supply. I knew that sailors returning from a cruise often have pets which they're willing to sell so if we could canvass the seaports, we'd probably get a good collection of animals. I turned out to be right. Not only sailors but often ship's stewards will bring back animals to sell and some men make a regular business of it. Fortunately, we had Swiss francs, backed with gold, which were eagerly accepted anywhere. So at the age of twenty, I was launched in the animal business.

After a few weeks, we reduced the business to a system. Every Friday afternoon, Hans and I would sit at our desks with our hats and coats on, impatiently watching the clock until five struck. Before the first stroke had finished vibrating, we'd be out the door and halfway down the stairs. We'd grab a train for Marseilles, Genoa or Antwerp, depending on what news we had of incoming ships. Being unable to afford sleeping compartments we sat up all night and arrived the next morning, tired and dirty. After a quick wash in the public fountain, we'd go down to the docks.

Apart from the animals, I was fascinated by the great ships, the stories of the sailors, the odors of the cargoes and the strange boxes made of teak, mahogany and bamboo stalks in which the animals often traveled. After the dull life in the chemical plant, this was like a fairyland to me. Everything was constantly new and exciting. You never knew what might turn up and sometimes there were fantastic bargains. Once we picked up 600 Algerian tortoises for a song. These are exquisite little fellows with an intricate pattern on their backs which brought us over a 1,000 per cent profit. I remember once getting five African gray parrots—the best talkers of all the parrots—from a sailor for a hundred francs. Later we sold them for 600 francs each. Often you could pick up the reddish hussar monkeys for the price of a bottle of wine. They sold in Switzerland for 300 francs each.

Even more exciting were the rare animals. I remember especially a little lion-headed marmoset, one of the rarest of the marmosets. I called her Mimi and kept her for myself, paying her value into our common banking account. I also kept some frilled lizards and a pair of lovely Brazilian toucans—always, of course, with Hans's consent. The South American animals particularly interested me. Africa was so close that it seemed almost like Europe but South America was foreign, unknown, and mysterious. I longed to go there.

After we had made our purchases, we would hire a horse-drawn cart—usually at the last minute—and make a dash for the railroad station. I well remember those frenzied rushes to catch the last train, the driver shouting, the horses' hooves pounding on the cobblestones, the people leaping out of the way, the policemen shouting and Hans and I perched on top of the load urging the driver to fresh efforts. Most of the baggage-car men knew us and would give us a hand when we reached the station. Some of the animals were too delicate to trust to the luggage car and these we had to smuggle into the passenger car, always a ticklish proposition.

Once we had several tame hussar monkeys and I insisted on taking them into an upper berth with me. A young man and woman had the lower berth and all night long the monkeys kept peering down at them, chattering frantically, and then rushing back to me. The monkeys weren't housebroken and were also nervous from the ride so before long my berth was soaking wet and the berth below me must have been in even a worse state. The young man was furious and kept complaining to the conductor, but we had him well bribed so he refused to do anything. The next morning when the monkeys and I left the train at Basel, the young man stuck his head out from between the curtains. "All I can say is this has been one hell of a wedding night!" he roared at me.

Hans and his wife had a pleasant five-room apartment in a fashionable part of town. We pre-empted three rooms for our animals which his wife thought was a great joke—at least, at first she did. With Hans' apartment as our headquarters, we began shipping animals all over Europe.

Before long, we began to discover some of the ins and outs of the animal business. One of our great rivals at the docks was a Mr. Medici who also met the ships and paid fantastically high prices. We never met Mr. Medici but we soon learned to hate him. Sailor after sailor would tell us, "Mr. Medici was here an hour ago and offered 400 francs for a green monkey." Or, "Mr. Medici is paying 70 francs for chameleons." How Mr. Medici could possibly make a profit at this rate, we couldn't understand. Then to make the matter even more mysterious, we found that often Mr. Medici would return the next day and resell the animals, often for less than half of what he'd paid for them.

After several weeks, we discovered the answer. Mr. Medici was a jewel smuggler. A steward would stuff diamonds down the throat of some animal and sell it to Mr. Medici who would then give the animal a purge. To keep the business from being too obvious, Mr. Medici also had to buy some other animals as a blind.

We also discovered something about customs officials, their care and handling. When we had the 600 Algerian tortoises, we were stopped at the Swiss border by a customs man. He was pleasant enough but decided. "You fellows have been bringing in animals without a permit for some time now," he reminded us. "At first, we let it pass, realizing you were just starting out in this business and didn't know the rules, but we warned you several times and now we're cracking down."

Hans and I were desperate. Getting a permit for an animal took at least a week and we had no place to leave the tortoises. Discouraged, we went to a tavern for a drink. There we ran into a group of our friends and their girls who were having a party. They greeted us with boisterous shouts and we joined them. By two o'clock, everyone was riding very high indeed, except for Hans and me who were still worried about our tortoises. When we explained our trouble, the crowd thought it hilariously funny.

"Come on, let's help Hans and Peter with their tortoises!" a friend shouted. The whole party rushed out to their cars and we managed to hide the tortoises under the back seat of our friend's car. With our friend driving, we headed for the border, the rest of the cars following us, everyone whooping and singing.

We were stopped by another customs official who asked if we had anything to declare. To my horror, our friend shouted cheerfully, "Nothing but 600 tortoises hidden under the rear seat."

The customs man shook his head tolerantly. "You young fellows must have your little joke," he said good-humoredly and waved us on.

During this time, I also made the important discovery that zoo directors are not the high-minded, scientifically impartial demigods that I had always considered them. Directors have their little jealousies and pettinesses like ordinary humans. The Basel Zoo and the Zurich Zoo were rivals. The directors weren't especially friendly with each other and even the employees of the two zoos took part in the rivalry. One afternoon while we were delivering some reptiles to the Zurich Zoo, the director remarked that he badly wanted some llamas. "All the children want to see a llama and we don't have any," he admitted. "I'd pay any price for a pair."

We didn't handle such large animals but we said that we'd keep a lookout for llamas. Later that day, we went to Basel to sell some birds. The director asked if we could possibly take some llamas off his hands. "We have more than we can handle and I'd let them go very cheap."

Hans, who was always a better businessman than myself, pulled a long face. "Unfortunately, all the zoos are in the same position. Overrun with llamas," he said regretfully. "Still, I'll make you a proposition. We'll take a pair of llamas—for a rock-bottom price, you understand—if you'll take a dozen rhesus monkeys at our price."

The director wanted rhesus about as much as he wanted pigeons but monkeys are cheaper to feed than llamas, so the deal was closed. We rushed the llamas to Zurich and made a 700 per cent profit.

That was the beginning of a very profitable business on our part between the two zoos. Both had animals that the other needed and we arranged the interchange—at never less than 300 per cent profit to ourselves. The directors could have saved themselves thousands of francs if they'd only picked up a telephone and talked to each other but the rivalry prevented that, and both men were astonished at our miraculous ability to produce rare animals at the drop of a hat.

At this time, a little tension sprang up between Hans and me. Whenever we managed to get some rare or interesting specimen, I couldn't resist keeping it for myself so I could study the animal. By the time I'd finished studying him, he was a pet and then I couldn't part with him. Although I always paid the animal's value into our fund, this habit of mine annoyed Hans, who was a practical businessman. One day he protested, "See here, Peter, our customers are getting annoyed because you always skim the cream off any shipment we get. After all, this is a business like any other business and there's no place for sentiment."

"It may be a business to you, but it's a hobby with me," I told him. "If you think I'm going to lose this chance to study rare animals, you're crazy. And I'd no more sell any of my pets than you'd sell your wife."

Hans said nothing more but I knew that both he and his wife were irritated with me. I didn't care. My only problem was to find room for my pets in my own tiny apartment. Both Hans and I were making money in what seemed to us fabulous amounts. Hans saved his like the careful chap he was, but I spent mine high, wide and handsome. Every evening I went to a night club with a girl and never bothered to add the check. To handle the overflow of pets and have a "retreat," I bought a little fishing house on the Rhine, really a baby chalet. It was built on stilts over the river and from the porch you could see the Black Forest outlined against the distant peaks and listen to the songs of the boatmen poling their crafts down the current. Across the river was a great cliff, covered with little terraced vineyards, and the scent of the ripening grapes perfumed the air. I arranged a net on a long, swinging arm from the porch and as there was a bend in the river with a strong, in-shore current, I was almost sure of getting a fish or two, often magnificent salmon with firm, pink flesh. There was only one room, with a big double bed, and a tiny kitchen with a charcoal grille where I cooked the salmon. I'd usually rub a fish with salt, pepper, and a little thyme and then sauté it in butter, although sometimes I'd wrap it in bay leaves with a little parsley and garlic. Under the house was my wine cellar, hewn out of the rock, where the wines were always kept cool. After an evening at a night club, my girl and I would generally end up in my little fishing house to sample one of the fresh-caught fish and a bottle of wine.

By now, in addition to my other pets, I had a little tawny owl, a pair of purple-capped lory, a bush baby, a South American kinkajou, some tortoises and a monitor lizard who lived under the bed. All the animals were tame and my main problem was to prevent their fighting among themselves. Everything was running smoothly and the future seemed assured.

Then I had a disastrous love affair. I couldn't imagine a future without the girl in question. I'd never find another girl like her. There seemed no reason to go on living. The future at Geigy's stretched away before me, a treadmill existence without interest and without hope. Even my week-end trips for animals now seemed childish and petty. I'd outgrown the thrill of taking monkeys in an upper berth or smuggling tortoises past a customs inspector.

One evening, an old friend of mine called. It was Jusp, who is now a famous cartoonist. We belonged to a club in which once a month each member gave a dinner which he cooked and served himself. Jusp wanted to know if I was going to the club party that night.

I was tempted to say no. I certainly did not feel like going to a dinner. Then I changed my mind. I had to do something or go mad. I changed into evening clothes and went to the clubhouse. It was a stag dinner with American cocktails beforehand. The cocktails were strong, the wine excellent, and afterwards we had brandy, a special cognac, I recall, about 180 proof. By midnight, most of the members had passed out on the floor and Jusp and I were sitting over our tenth cognac telling each other our troubles.

Jusp glanced contemptuously at the sprawled bodies around us and remarked, "These youngsters don't know how to carry their liquor. They're nothing but animals."

"But unfortunately I can't sell them," I answered moodily.

Jusp had an inspiration. "Why not? Remember those empty packing boxes down in the cellar? Let's put half a dozen of these drunks in the boxes, nail them up, and sell them to your partner as chimpanzees."

The idea struck us both as killingly funny. I primed Jusp as to what to say and he called Hans's apartment while I listened.

A sleepy Hans answered the phone and Jusp said importantly, "Ah, Herr Gagliardi? This is Señor Medici. I have six chimpanzees. All young stock. I wish to sell but I must dispose of them immediately. You . . . ah . . . know my problem perhaps. Because I am leaving Switzerland at once, I can let you have them for 800 francs each."

A young chimp in good condition was easily worth 3,400 francs and I could hear Hans babble with excitement on the other end of the wire. He begged Señor Medici to bring the chimps over immediately.

Jusp and I rolled six of the drunks into crates, got a truck, and loaded them on board. Then we drove to Hans's apartment. We met Hans on the stairs, hopping up and down in his excitement. His wife, in wrapper and slippers, was equally overwrought. By dint of tremendous efforts, we got the crates up the stairs and into the apartment, Hans and his wife hauling while Jusp and I pushed from behind. Hans's wife produced a hatchet and they broke open the crates. Out stumbled the drunks, still in evening clothes, and fighting mad.

At the expression on the Gagliardis' faces, Jusp and I collapsed on the floor in helpless laughter. Hans tried to reason with the drunks which only made matters worse, and a fight started. By the time it was over, most of the furniture in the apartment had been wrecked and the other tenants had called the police.

The next morning Hans told me that our partnership was dissolved. Now that I had sobered up, the whole business didn't seem nearly as funny as it had the night before. I apologized humbly but Hans and his wife were furious and wanted nothing more to do with me. I admit it was a stupid trick and I'd never have done it if I hadn't been drunk and in a state of despair over my broken romance.

But this was not the end of my troubles. When I went back to Geigy's the next morning, the place was a madhouse. A cage of mangabey monkeys that I'd ordered from a French dealer had arrived in Basel and been delivered to Hans's apartment but Hans had refused to accept it. The express man, knowing I worked at Geigy's, had delivered the cage there. The office workers were delighted with the mangabeys and some idiot opened the door. In a matter of seconds, the place was alive with monkeys. Mangabeys are especially agile monkeys and getting them down from the lighting fixtures and filing cabinets was almost impossible. The president of the firm heard the tumult and came out to see what was going on. He'd hardly taken three steps before he was covered with monkeys fleeing from the office force.

The president didn't have much sense of humor and my reputation in the firm hadn't been very good to begin with. The monkeys were the last straw. Rather than be discharged, I resigned.

Everything seemed to be happening to me at once; I'd lost the girl, my partnership with Hans had been dissolved, and now I was fired. I was sick of Switzerland and decided to leave the country. South America had always appealed to me. It had great uncharted wildernesses; no one knew much about the animal life there, and there'd be less competition from other animal collectors than there would be in Africa or Indonesia.

I said good-bye to my unhappy mother and drew what money I had left from the bank. In spite of my extravagances, I had over 50,000 francs (about $12,000). I got a ticket for Buenos Aires and packed my few belongings.

The saddest part of my leave-taking was disposing of my pets. The reptiles and birds could go to the zoo, but finding homes for Fritz and little Mimi, my marmoset, was harder. I finally found friends with whom I knew they would be safe, but even so, parting from Fritz who had been my companion for twelve years was dreadful. Then I took a train for Marseilles, the same train I'd taken so often on my trips with Hans after animals on the waterfront, and embarked for Argentina and my new life. I was twenty-five years old and already felt as though I'd lived a lifetime.

# Chapter 5

# The incredible
# Lothar Behrend

I HAD never imagined a city like Buenos Aires
in 1945. To a European, it was so modern that it seemed to
have arrived yesterday out of a mail-order catalogue. Great
skyscrapers, acres of plate-glass windows, wide boulevards filled
with gigantic cars dripping chrome, and yet from the top of
one of these skyscrapers you could see the jungle stretching
away into the distance, as deep, impenetrable and untouched
as before Columbus came to this new world. Men wearing suits
cut by Bond Street tailors and ladies in the latest Parisian crea-
tions jostled Indians clad in homespun serapes and wearing sandals cut from old automobile tires. The paper would announce
that the authorities were concerned over the increase in traffic
fatalities due to the enormous influx of high-powered cars and
then, in the same issue, that a child in the suburbs had been
killed by a puma the night before. Nothing in my European
background had prepared me for such bewildering contrasts
and I wandered about in a daze.

Although I knew no Spanish, I spoke German and French
fluently and knew a little Italian so I could manage to make
myself understood. I took a room in a small hotel and asked
the clerk where a man would go to buy animals. He suggested
the bird market and gave me the necessary directions. The

Buenos Aires markets stretch for miles and offer everything from shrunken human heads to electric refrigerators, but I finally found the bird section, led there by the twittering, squawks and whistles of thousands of caged birds.

I felt like a child turned loose in a candy store. There were toucans, toucanettes, swans, cardinals, finches, siskins, parrots and macaws. There were mammals too; tiger cats, coatis, agoutis, monkeys with prehensile tails, squirrels and pacas. I wandered about, trying to compute how much a dozen green cardinals or fifty chingolo song finches would bring C.I.F. Antwerp, allowing for shipping charges, insurances, and currency exchange. I tried to bargain with the Indian bird trappers, using a mixture of French and Italian. It was difficult work and I noticed a slender, dark man dressed in immaculate white watching my efforts with amusement.

I was deep in negotiation for a pair of orioles with an Indian who, I strongly suspected, knew no more Spanish than I did, when the stranger strolled over and translated for me in the man's native dialect. They chatted for a while and then the stranger turned and said to me in German, "He wants 250 pesos for the orioles which is about 80 Swiss francs, although I haven't seen the latest currency exchange figures. Of course, he'll come down but why bother with soft-billed birds? They're a nuisance to feed. In fact, why bother with birds at all? The insurance is prohibitive, the damn things keep dying on your hands, and the market is uncertain."

"I'm in the animal business," I explained.

"So was I but I got out of it. You will too if you're not a fool. I collect butterflies now."

"There can't be much money in that."

"Oh, I make a living. I just got back after taking a trunkful of them to Paris. It wasn't a bad trip, I cleared 25,000,000 French francs on the deal. Some specimens I sold for a million francs each to Baron Rothschild. He's very fond of butterflies."

"He must be!" I gasped. "Tell me more about the butterfly business."

"Let's have a drink then." He took me to a little cantina and over a sangrillo (red wine and water, iced) he told me about his curious profession.

My new friend's name was Serge Patoffski. He was a Bulgarian and specialized in collecting rare insects for rich hobbyists. He had a list of half a dozen millionaires who were willing to pay virtually any price for certain species and in addition he supplied many of the retail houses in Europe and America with butterflies, moths, beetles, and spiders, although why anyone would want to buy a spider is a mystery to me. He was a remarkably handsome man, looking like an artist with his black curly hair, big liquid eyes and delicate frame. His hobbies seemed to be women, butterflies and food, in that order. He told me that he had spent nearly all of his 25,000,000 francs in a three months' spree in Paris, going into detailed descriptions of the ladies who had enjoyed his favors and the meals he had eaten which he remembered down to the ingredients of the sauces and the vintages of the wines. Then he switched to the subject of butterflies and in five minutes I was completely drowned in a sea of Lycaenidae, Uraniidae, Areiidae, Lithosiidae, Pieridae, nervures, pupa, larvae, cocoon patterns and heaven knows what else. Serge was an excellent artist and to illustrate his points he would make quick but amazing detailed drawings on the tablecloth. By the time we had finished our drinks, the cloth was covered with sketches of nude women, soufflés, caterpillars and butterflies.

"I'm starting out again in a few days on a new collecting trip," Serge concluded. "We'll fly to Manaus, go up the Amazon by steamer, then up a tributary by boat, then up a backwater by canoe and spend about a month collecting. Then back to Paris again."

It sounded wonderful. No wonder Serge despised the animal business.

"Like to come?" he asked suddenly. "I get lonely on these trips and it's nice to talk to another European. We'll split the profits."

I jumped at the offer. Serge and I spent the next week preparing for the expedition. There was a surprising amount of apparatus that had to be taken along: nets, collecting boxes, special paper in which to wrap the insects so their delicate wings wouldn't be injured, preservatives for certain small insects, and even a case of Carlsberg beer which Serge assured me made the best bait for butterflies. The Carlsberg beer was especially hard to come by and was murderously expensive but Serge insisted that it was vital to the success of the expedition.

After arriving in Manaus, we loaded our supplies on a river steamer and started up the Amazon. Then at a small landing we transferred to rowboats and after another week's travel, finally reached a native village where we took canoes. Serge seemed to know every inch of the district, for he directed our canoemen to a narrow channel completely overgrown by mangroves and invisible ten feet away. Our men paddled up waterways so narrow that the mangrove roots on either side scraped the sides of the dugouts. We went on and on through a maze of channels but Serge never seemed in doubt. At night, we swung our hammocks from the roots and slept as well as we could with the buzzing swarm of insects.

The heat was beyond anything I'd ever imagined. It was like being smothered in a superheated, wet blanket. At night we basted in our own sweat and by day the red-hot sun roasted us alive. The insects were the worst. We moved in clouds of mosquitoes that rose from the roots as we passed. Nearly as maddening was the constant mist of tiny gnats that passed easily through our head-coverings and crawled up our noses, mouths and ears. We drank the channel water and I developed a crippling case of dysentery. Even Serge began to show the effects of the trip. He lost his usual lighthearted manner and became silent and morose.

Until now, I'd admired Serge as a clever chap who'd been able to gull a group of simple-minded millionaires into paying a million francs for a butterfly. Now I considered the Bulgarian an idiot for letting a group of unscrupulous capitalists swindle him. Those butterflies were cheap at a million francs. They were worth a hundred times that. We went on and on day after day, living in a fog of insects, fever and exhaustion. I no longer cared about the butterflies, I only wanted to lie down and die.

Finally we reached solid ground, the dugouts were beached and we crawled up the bank. There was a little forest glade covered with grass as fine as a putting green, a spring of cold water and great trees that protected us from the sun. As soon as we could sling our hammocks, I climbed into mine, but I was too tired to sleep. I lay there restless and feverish while Serge busied himself around the camp. Then he came over to me.

"We're here at last," he announced. "What do you say we each have a bottle of beer to celebrate? I've put it in the spring so it's cold."

There was nothing in the world I wanted as much as a bottle of beer. We both opened a bottle and never had anything tasted nearly as good. After we'd drained them, Serge remarked, "Let's have another bottle. After all, how much beer can a butterfly drink?"

That seemed logical so we opened another bottle. We had another after that and another. I finally fell asleep and for the first time since starting on that devilish expedition, I had a good night's rest.

When I awoke the next morning, I saw Serge examining the empty beer bottles, tilting them so he could see if there were any dregs in the bottoms. I watched him idly and then a horrible suspicion came to me.

"My God, don't tell me we drank all the beer!" I shouted.

"Every drop," Serge admitted. "What shall we do now?"

I hadn't an idea. Serge tried to improvise some other baits from sugar and some plant juices but they weren't very successful. We caught only a few butterflies, and then started back.

When I returned to Buenos Aires, I'd had enough of butterfly collecting to last the rest of my life. Even if we'd gotten the million-franc variety, it still wouldn't have been worth it.

For collectors, the butterflies must be just out of cocoons because even the slightest shower will damage their wings enough to ruin their value. They must be netted only after they have alighted and folded their wings so that the fluffy, feather-like scales will not be damaged, and the body must be pressed at once in a special fashion that kills them instantly. It's a great art and one that I had no wish to acquire. I'd rather have sprayed flies with DDT at Geigy's. That was one trip where we could have used some DDT. Never before or since have I seen so many bugs.

I went to my hotel room and spent three days in bed, drinking enough beer to flounder a camel. It was a stupid disaster but everyone in the animal business is crazy. If they weren't, they wouldn't be in it. When I'd recovered, I asked the desk clerk if he had any more good ideas.

"If you are interested in animals, why don't you see Lothar Behrend?" he asked.

"Lothar Behrend!" I yelled. "Is he in Buenos Aires?"

"Certainly, señor. At this hour, you can always find him at the Munich Beer Hall."

Lothar Behrend was a legend in the animal dealers' world. Suddenly, out of a clear sky, dealers in a dozen great cities would receive a cryptic radiogram, "Arriving at Marseilles [or London or Antwerp] on such-and-such a date on the S.S. So-and-So," Signed, Lothar Behrend. That would be all, but even before the ship docked, a dozen dealers would go out in tugs to meet her: Chapman from London, Chevez from Marseilles, Fockelmann from Hamburg, all with cash in their pockets. On board would be Behrend with fifty or sixty thousand birds and some other animals as well, although he specialized in birds. Often over a hundred thousand dollars would change hands in a few minutes, Chapman taking £10,000 worth, Fockelmann 120,000 marks' worth and so on. Also, Behrend, like Serge, had his "millionaire list" and would bring back special birds at fabulous prices for a few wealthy fanciers.

For me to meet Behrend was like a buck private meeting the

general but I decided to chance it. Perhaps Mr. Behrend would
be in a good mood and drop a few words of advice. I could
only try.

I followed the clerk's directions to the Munich Beer Hall.
It was down a side street and had an entrance like the carved
doorway on a cuckoo clock. The interior was dark and smelled
heavily of beer. On the walls were shelves laden with orna-
mental steins and framed sayings such as "He is not drunk who
from the floor can rise and drink some more." There was a
carved oak bar running down one side of the room and tables
in obscure corners full of refugee Germans.

A waiter directed me to a table at the far end of the long
room. Here was sitting a group of the most remarkable-look-
ing people I'd ever seen. There was a man who could only
have been an ex-Prussian cavalry officer—immaculately dressed,
wearing a monocle and sitting as straight as a pillar in his chair.
There was also a dwarf wearing a pince-nez, an Indian in a
filthy serape, a swarthy man with earrings, an effeminate man
with peroxided curly hair, and a dapper Frenchman with a carefully waxed moustache and the Legion of Honor in his button-
hole.

At the head of the table sat an enormously fat man in his
shirt sleeves drinking from a stein as big as a chamber pot. His
great belly hung in folds over the piece of rope he used for a
belt and sweat ran constantly off his face into the foam of his
beer. He was red as a boiled lobster; indeed, he seemed ready
at any moment to fall down with a stroke. He wore huge steel-
rimmed glasses and had wavy gray hair. Occasionally he
belched so loudly that the steins on the wall rattled, and once
he lifted his ponderous bottom and broke wind with such a report that I thought the little dwarf would be blown off his
chair.

I approached the table and asked for Mr. Behrend. No one
answered. After studying me for a few seconds, the fat man
said, "Why do you want Mr. Behrend, boy?"

"I hope to go into the animal collecting business."

Everyone laughed, the fat man loudest of all. He took another swig of beer and smiled at me beneficently.

"The animal business? Go out and sell neckties or ladies' panty-waists for a living. What do you know about the animal business? Oh yes, you've had a few pets, no doubt. You know that a macaw you can pick up from an Indian for three pesos will bring you $50 in New York, so it seems easy. Therefore you take a boat to South America, land in Buenos Aires without a sou in your pockets, and expect to go into the animal business."

He smiled and buried his face in the stein while the others guffawed.

"I have 40,000 francs," I explained. "I know it isn't much—"

A fountain of beer shot up from the stein as the fat man choked. Everyone stopped laughing and looked at me with new interest. The fat man said unbelievingly, "Not— not in Swiss francs?"

"Yes, Swiss francs."

The fat man leaped to his feet and shoved the dwarf off his chair. "Sit down here, my dear young friend, sit down here! I didn't catch your name? Ah yes, Ryhiner, Peter Ryhiner. Of *course* I've heard of you. I consider this an honor. I am Lothar Behrend. Mein Gott! Forty thousand francs! Waiter, a stein of beer for Señor Ryhiner!"

Immediately I was the center of attention. The rapid conversations flicked around my head like lightning. They were in German, French, Spanish, English and Portuguese, all jumbled up. A man would start a sentence in German, come to a word he didn't know, put in the Spanish equivalent, and then finish the sentence in French. Behrend shoved his great bulk between me and the others and began to question me about my work with animals. As I explained my different techniques, he kept muttering, "*Wunderbar!*" or "*Schön, ach schön!*" At last he brought his fist down on the table with a crash.

"Silence! I have come to a very important decision!"

Everyone kept quiet. Behrend announced, "I have decided to make this young man my partner!"

There were cries of astonishment and everyone pressed forward to congratulate me. I didn't know whether I was awake or asleep, I was so surprised and delighted. Before I was through shaking hands, Behrend leaped up shouting, "Come! We will go at once to a lawyer and draw up the necessary papers. When I, Lothar Behrend, make up my mind, I do not delay!"

He was rushing me out of the beer hall when the waiter quietly interposed himself with the bill. After scowling at him, Behrend began to go through his pockets, becoming more annoyed as he found nothing. "Must have left my wallet at home. Ah, here is a fifty-peso note . . . no, it is only an old laundry bill. Waiter, simply put the bill on my account."

As the waiter made no move to obey, I said, "Please, let me."

"No, no! Impossible! I would not hear of it. Still, merely as a loan . . ."

I paid the check which, judging from its size, must have included everyone's drinks. Then we hurried off to the lawyers.

The partnership papers were drawn up in record time and then we dashed away to the bank, Behrend waving the contract in the air as we ran to dry the ink. At the bank, I drew out 12,000 francs. I was about to have them changed into pesos when Behrend hissed, "No, no! Not here!" He took me to an alley where a rat-faced little man operated a black market exchange. Instead of the legal rate of two pesos for the franc, he gave us seven. Some of the notes were counterfeit and Behrend blasted him with a stream of profanity like a flame-thrower until he changed them. Then Behrend hailed a taxi and told the driver to take us to the docks.

"I have a cargo just come in from Africa," Behrend explained, lighting a long, thin cigar while I sat panting on the seat beside him. "Nothing striking, you understand, just half a dozen servals, some chimps, a few score antelopes, several hundred of the rarer birds and, of course, an assignment of monkeys—green, dianas and other guenons."

Nothing striking! Here was really the fabulous Lothar Behrend of my dreams! I sat rubbing my damp palms together and trying to seem as though I were used to handling such cargoes.

"There has been a little confusion over the shipping charges," Behrend went on. "The captain of the vessel won't allow the animals to be unloaded until he is paid. Can you imagine it, the swine refuses to accept my check!"

"No!" I exclaimed, deeply shocked.

"Incredible, isn't it? That I, Lothar Behrend, who could send a cable to Louis Ruhe in New York and receive fifty thousand dollars within an hour or pick up a phone and have Chapman wire me ten thousand pounds, should be annoyed over a few pesos. The irony of it is amusing. I refuse to become annoyed."

We arrived at the wharf and Behrend hurried off to the ship while I paid the taxi driver. When I reached the gangplank, I found him stopped by three raging gypsies, two men and a woman. All three were screaming like goshawks while Behrend tried to calm them.

"You swindling German pig, where is our monkey?" the woman screeched, clawing at his face. "You took our money, now where is the monkey?"

"My dear lady, I am going on the ship to get him," said Behrend. "There has been a slight delay—"

"Slight delay!" howled the oldest man. "Four weeks!"

"Let me at him! I'll scratch out his eyes and eat them for lunch!" raved the woman.

"You will have the monkey within a few minutes if you only let me go aboard," Behrend pleaded.

"We've been hearing that story for a month now," growled the young man, but they finally let us pass.

The captain met us at the entry port. Never had I seen such a hard-faced, unfriendly-looking individual. His first words were, "Not so much as a piece of dung do you take off this ship until I get my money."

"Captain, it hurts me that you do not trust me," said Behrend with great dignity. "My new partner, Señor Ryhiner, will pay you your shipping charges."

I counted out the money into the captain's hand and then he let us on board. Behrend had not exaggerated the size of the cargo. The ship's decks were covered with cages and there were more below. I wandered around from cage to cage, my eyes popping out. At last I was in the big time. What would Hans say to something like this!

The gypsies had followed us aboard and were loudly demanding their monkey. Behrend said irritably to me, "Give them one of the monas from that cage over there."

I opened the cage gingerly, for monas can give you a nasty bite. There were a couple of dozen monkeys in the cage and I managed to grab one by the back of the neck and haul him out. At the last minute, he twisted around and bit me savagely in the hand. I let go with a yelp of pain. The monkey skittered across the deck and down the gangplank.

"Stop him!" bellowed Behrend but the dockside workers had no intention of grabbing an infuriated mona. They scattered in all directions as the monkey galloped down the dock, his long tail held straight up in the air. He came to the foot of a giant crane and went flying up it like— well, like a monkey.

"No matter," said Behrend crossly. "Get another."

I demanded gloves. While Behrend and I were arguing, a deputation of dockworkers marched onto the ship led by their union representative.

"Captain, there is a ferocious wild animal loose and under the terms of our contract, we demand double pay for working under dangerous conditions," announced the union steward.

The captain ranted and swore but the steward refused to be moved. Finally the captain turned to us and jerked his thumb towards the monkey who was now on top of the eighty-foot crane making faces at the crowd below. "Get that monk down or you don't unload," he said briefly.

Behrend, with his enormous bulk, couldn't possibly climb the crane so I started up it. The crane looked plenty high from the dock but it looked even higher when I was halfway up and made the mistake of glancing down. As long as I had the cross-bars of the crane to use as a ladder, the climb was easy but the crossbars stopped near the top and there was nothing but a single girder. I shinnied up it and managed to grab the mona by the tail. He clung to the girder with both hands and feet, screaming his head off, and I couldn't budge him. I needed one hand to hold onto the girder and the other hand was clutching the tail.

I heard a wild yell of "Hold him, Peter, I am coming!" Looking down I saw Behrend swarming up the crane waving a gunny sack, his face streaming sweat and his great belly heaving convulsively. Together we managed to pry the mona loose and get him in the sack. Then we returned to the dock.

The gypsies were delighted with their new acquisition and the girl impulsively threw her arms around Behrend's neck and kissed him loudly. They wanted to know how to take care of him and instantly Behrend entered into an amazingly detailed discussion of the care, feeding and psychology of monas. I knew enough about monkeys to realize that here was a genius talking. The gross man, still gasping from his climb, outlined vitamin and calory needs, susceptibility to temperature changes under various conditions, diseases, parasites, mental reactions and many other matters, while the gypsies listened respectfully. When they left, we went back on board the ship and prepared to off-load the cargo.

Behrend was everywhere . . . hiring a truck to move the cages to his compound, checking the animals, directing the men at the booms how to swing out the heavy boxes, moving some of the more delicate specimens into a warehouse on the dock so they would be out of the sun while the bigger cages were put on the floor of the truck. I was helping as best I could when one of the seamen told me that Señor Behrend wanted me in the hold.

I descended the ladder and felt my way along the dark between decks. I found Behrend feverishly stuffing black and peach-faced lovebirds into his capacious trousers.

"Hurry!" he snapped at me. "Get some string and tie it around your trouser legs. Then fill your pants with birds."

"But why?" I asked in amazement.

"Because they are parrotine birds, you sheepshead, and it is illegal to bring them into the country. Some may have psittacosis. Be quick!"

Although lovebirds are small they have sharp beaks and I had no wish to have a dozen or so of them packed around my private parts. But there was no arguing with Behrend. We loaded ourselves with lovebirds and then I started for the ladder.

"No, no, you fool, grab a small crate and carry it off the ship. It looks more convincing when you pass the customs inspectors."

I seized a cage containing a pair of bush-tailed porcupines and Behrend followed me with a crateful of pygmy rails. We passed the customs inspectors without difficulty and unloaded our trousers in the warehouses where Behrend had already thoughtfully prepared a cage to hold the lovebirds.

We departed in the truck, sitting on top of the pile of cages while the driver leaned on his horn and dodged between push-carts, donkeys, and leaping pedestrians. Behrend was in a jovial mood now that we had gotten the cargo and pressed me for more tales of my animal studies. I did my best and at last he laid a sponge-like hand on my knee and said sincerely, "Peter, all my life I have been looking for a partner such as you. You have a God-given instinct for our dumb friends. Ach, what a team we will make! As soon as we reach the compound, I will begin to instruct you in your new duties."

I went hot with pride. To be commended by the famous Lothar Behrend was almost more than I could bear. All his crudities, all his shady dealings, all his abuse banished in the delight of his praise.

The truck drove us to the slum section of the city and stopped before a ramshackle house with a tiny back-yard surrounded by a high stone wall. To add height to the wall, a line of old window frames had been run along the top, and the glass painted white to make it opaque. "This is my compound," said Behrend briskly, jumping from the pile of cages. "Give me a hand with these boxes."

"Don't the neighbors complain about your keeping wild animals here?" I asked.

"Certainly, but I have the police well bribed. Oh, they have to stage a raid once in a while. In fact, I'm expecting one any day now, but a few pesos sets everything to rights."

We carried the crates into the minuscule yard. It was already packed with cages, pens and enclosures of every sort and description. Animals tied to stakes were bounding about everywhere; you had to yell to be heard above the chorus of barks, whines, screams and yelps on all sides. But in spite of the confusion the animals were in prime condition, there was no smell, and the feeding and drinking pans shone like newly cleaned silver.

While we were finding places for the new arrivals, a group of zoo directors arrived, all very important men and dressed in amazingly formal clothes, considering the heat. Behrend left me to finish placing the cages while he showed them around. He immediately changed from a sweating, profane, fat man to a gracious, educated host pointing out the rarer mammals and birds, discussing their habits, identifying species and subspecies with the skill of a great scientist, subtly flattering the group and deferring to their opinions although it was obvious that he knew far more than the whole lot put together. The directors were clearly impressed and I saw them whispering together and making notes. We were all set for a big sale and Behrend was rubbing his hands in anticipation and smiling broadly.

There came a wild pounding on the door. I moved to open it but Behrend stopped me. "It's only the police, you idiot!" he hissed. "They'll go away in a few minutes."

But the noise continued. Behrend ignored it although our guests were growing increasingly more nervous. Suddenly there came a crash and through the window frames sailed a dried zebra skin, complete with hoofs and head. It was as hard as a board and it zoomed past one of the director's heads, missing him by inches before smashing into the side of a pen.

"Ah yes, a Grevey's zebra," remarked Behrend blandly. "The narrow, vertical flank stripes are quite distinctive. Now in this next cage we have some fine coscoroba swans which will justify careful examination."

The furious screams from outside the wall were growing louder. A director said nervously, "Really, señor, you had better see what those people wish."

"Certainly, your excellency," replied Behrend politely. Raising his voice, he shouted, "My friends, is anything the matter?"

"Matter!" roared half a dozen voices. "We paid you for a live zebra, you German swine, and you send us a hide!"

"Unfortunately your zebra died in transit, so I decided to send you the skin as a little memento. But if you are not contented, honest Lothar Behrend—whose motto is 'Never leave a dissatisfied customer'—will be glad to make a readjustment. Come and see me tomorrow."

"Assassin! Robber! Filth-eating foreign bastard!" shouted the disappointed zebra buyers.

The zoo directors left hurriedly without making any purchases. Behrend stumped about the yard muttering to himself and cursing the treacherous nature of the Argentinians. Then he turned to me and said mildly, "Peter, the time has come for you to enter upon your new duties."

I trembled with anticipation. What would be my first task? Quiet some savage jungle animal, prepare the formula for some rare bird, or discover why some valuable reptile wouldn't eat?

"Yes, Lothar, what shall I do?" I asked breathlessly.

"Do, you pig-dog? Why, grab a scraper and pail and start cleaning out those cages! That's how all good animal men start," and he stamped into the house.

I grabbed a scraper and pail and started cleaning out the cages. At twenty-six, I had entered into my new partnership with the world's greatest animal collector.

# Chapter 6

# A collector in
# South America

I soon found that Behrend lived according to a rigid schedule. He rose at 4 every morning and went to the market to buy food for the animals. He would allow no one else to perform this vital task and selected the food with the care of a great chef whose reputation depends on his meals. He fed the animals himself and then we cleaned and scrubbed the cages. "Always oversee the cleaning yourself," he often told me. "Nothing gives you so good an insight into the condition of the animals as their droppings."

The cages and enclosures were cleaned by 7. Then Behrend went through his huge stack of cables, all the time keeping up a running commentary that went something like this, "English general in Sussex wants chinchillas. Umm. He'll pay in pounds. Can use them to bribe that local chief in Malaya to get the gibbon ape concession. Change it into francs and use it to buy gazelles in North Africa. Sell them in Italy . . . illegal, but the customs officer is a drug addict and we'll bring him in some morphine at the same time from Tunis. Here's a rajah who's a falconer and wants two harpy eagles. Have to send them by plane—all nonsense sending birds by ship nowadays. We'll get some black panthers from him in exchange. Sell them to a zoo I know where the director doesn't want them but he can make out a bill for the board of trustees saying he paid $7,000 for them and I'll only charge him five. He and I can split the difference. I'll have the money paid to my credit in Madagascar to avoid the income tax and we'll use it to buy giant tortoises smuggled from Prison Island near Zanzibar."

Then he would begin to send out cables. Behrend seldom wrote letters but sent fifty or sixty cables a day to all parts of the world. At 10, he would go to the customs office to arrange for export and import permits. Then at 12, we went out for lunch. He always ate a huge lunch, first sending the chef a quarter gallon of wine to insure special service.

After lunch, we would return to the compound, Behrend peeling off the numerous coats he wore during the cool morning hours as he went. Until 7 we worked with the animals, studying them, feeding them, playing with them, or just looking at them. We then went out for supper, usually to the Munich Beer Hall, and Behrend talked or played cards with his cronies until midnight. We followed exactly the same routine on Sundays except for getting the permits. We used that time for the animals.

The men who sat around the little table at the beer hall were as strange a collection of human flotsam as Behrend himself. The ex-Prussian officer had come to Argentina to train their cavalry but been discharged during the war. Behrend had given him a job sweeping out the compound and he always reported for work looking as though he were about to pass inspection. After clicking his heels together and saluting, he'd grab his broom and make the dust fly. The dwarf was an Englishman who sold special unpickable locks to wealthy Argentinians for safes. He had a ghost as a friend and a seat was always saved at the table for the ghost. Once he told us that the ghost was getting married and we had a wedding celebration. Later, the ghost's wife had a baby and the dwarf assured us with tears in his eyes, that he was to be godfather. There were three or four remittance men who'd married Indian girls, a man who shrank sheepsheads for the tourist shrunken-head trade (a sheepshead, properly shrunk, looks exactly like a human head), two German divers who were trying to find the safe on the sunken *Graf Spee* (later one of these men was killed in an underwater fight with English divers after the same booty), a man who photographed couples on the beach and then blackmailed them with the pictures, and several cosmopolitan individuals who spoke a dozen languages perfectly, represented themselves to immigrants as fellow countrymen, and then swindled the unfortunates out of whatever jewelry or trinkets they'd brought to give them a new start in this strange land.

All these men told amazing tales but none could compete with Behrend. With his pot of beer before him and in his mouth a long cigar which did not interfere with his drinking in the slightest, he'd reel off story after story. He had an amazing memory and I never heard him repeat himself.

Behrend was the black sheep of a wealthy industrial family in Dresden. As a boy, he had bred some rare parrots and made a name for himself in avicultural circles. To discourage his passion for animals, his father gave him a small sum of money and told him to try to make a living out of his collecting. Behrend promptly departed for Abyssinia, stayed there a year, and returned with a cargo of birds. He sold them, repaid his father, and had enough left to set up in business as a collector.

From 1928 to 1939, Behrend was the top collector for European zoos. His shipments were fabulous. He was not only a brilliant animal collector, he was also an expert naturalist. Any strange bird or animal that was considered impossible to keep in captivity was a challenge to Behrend. He would shut himself up for weeks with the creature, often not eating or drinking while he worked with the problem. He discovered the formula for feeding hummingbirds which is now sold commercially for people who wish to attract them to their gardens. He was the first man to keep African sunbirds alive, feeding them a specially adapted baby food from long-necked tubes designed to simulate the nectary of a flower. He was the only man who could keep the rare giant armadillos alive, giving them a prepared food which he wouldn't allow even me to mix. In spite of his abuse and his open dishonesty, I knew that I could learn more from Behrend in a week than from any other collector in a lifetime.

Behrend had married an Argentinian girl and made Buenos Aires his headquarters. When the war came, animal shipments all over the world were stopped. Behrend had never saved a peso and he was bankrupt. For four years he wandered about Patagonia, living as best he could. There was a law that a starving man could kill a sheep as long as he hung the fleece on a fencepost for the owner, for sheep were so common on the great ranges that the meat was considered worthless; and five gallons of wine sold for the equivalent of 25¢. So by doing occasional odd jobs for farmers, he was able to exist.

After the war, Behrend returned to Buenos Aires to find that his wife had gone off with a policeman. He went back into the animal business but his four years of wandering over the pampas had affected his mind and he no longer had the swift, certain touch that had made him famous. He was still a brilliant man and, in my opinion, the world's greatest field naturalist, but his mind was like a clipper ship racing along under full sail with the tiller lines frayed almost through. Always aggressive, he now mistook bullying for firmness. Only his uncanny knowledge of animals was left him, and to share this knowledge I was willing to endure his frequent rages, clean out pens, and ask no questions about the fate of my 40,000 francs.

At least for a time I was willing, but I had no intention of spending the rest of my life as Behrend's cage boy. Behrend sensed this and one day when I was at the brink of revolt, he called me into his office.

"Peter, you have passed your apprenticeship," he told me impressively. "I am now sending you out on your first assignment. I'm kept too busy to do any trapping myself, but I've established trapping stations in different parts of South America. First you will go to Mendoza in the Andes and send back a collection of cougars, horned frogs and giant hares which the Indians have gotten. Next, you go to Asunción in Paraguay and pick up some military macaws, parrots, capuchin monkeys, capy-baras, agoutis and toucans. You can return with this lot by steamer down the Plata. Then go to Gran Chico in Brazil and pick up some hyacinthine macaws. There's always a demand for them."

It seemed a simple enough job and I was glad to get away from Buenos Aires and Behrend for a few days. As it turned out, this was the beginning of the wildest six months of my life during which scenes and events flashed past me as though I were in a runaway express train, charging through an Alice-in-Wonderland world.

I flew to Mendoza to pick up my cargo. The Indian trapper had one young cougar and two very sick-looking marras (giant hares) in cages. That was all.

"Where are the other animals?" I demanded.

"Señor, the jungle is full of them," the Indian assured me.

I spent the next three weeks in Mendoza organizing the trapping. The gauchos were expert trappers but without some kind of stimulus behind them, they'd rather sit in front of their huts, sip maté and watch the girls go by. First we put out a number of box traps baited with sheep for the cougars, the gauchos showing me the trails which the animals followed on their rounds. When it came to the horned frogs, my Spanish wasn't equal to the occasion but I drew some pictures of the animals, coloring them with a box of paints the women used for make-up. The horned frogs are about six inches in diameter, big enough to snatch up a stray mouse, and brilliantly colored, green or vivid orange on a chocolate-brown background. The Indians recognized them at once and the next time it rained took me out at night with torches. We got several dozen of the strange creatures, collecting them with hand nets as they can bite viciously.

Feeding the frogs presented quite a problem. I had all the children in the villages out catching bugs until at last I hit on the idea of putting out meal covered with wet rags. Grubs and beetles collected under the rags and soon we had a permanent supply of frog food at the camp.

Getting the marras was a sport rather than a task. Several villages joined in the hunt, each village contributing a small pack of long-legged, half-starved dogs. We followed the dogs on horseback until they jumped one of the great, three-foot hares from its form and then everyone went at full gallop, the men hallooing to their horses and riding hell-for-leather regardless of holes or unexpected gullies. When the hare had had enough, he would turn at bay and hold off the dogs with savage kicks. One of those kicks delivered with the full force of the hare's long hind leg was no mean blow and the dogs stood respectfully aside until one of the horsemen was able to dash up, throw himself to the ground and toss a blanket over the quarry.

I soon found that the hares could not be kept in cages unless they had a hiding place. They would dash themselves against the wire so desperately that several were killed. I put boxes in the cages and kept the bucks separated as they showed a tendency to fight. After that, I had no more trouble.

We got three cougars in our traps, one a female who gave birth to two kittens the next day. As the mother was too nervous to feed her babies, I raised them on goat's milk, feeding them from a whisky bottle with a piece of cloth stuck in the mouth on which they could suck. The mother's swollen nipples bothered her and at last we had to rope her and rub her with camphorated oil to dry up the milk.

I sent my cargo to Buenos Aires by train and then went on to Asunción. Asunción is the principal city of Paraguay, but its outskirts are nearly overgrown by the jungle. Our agent there was a fat German trader who lived with his five Indian wives in a mud hut. The place was alive with children.

The German only had about half of the animals he had promised to get but considered himself the injured party. "That bastard Behrend told me I'd make a fortune out of this animal business," he complained. "But he's always broke and I have all these accursed animals to feed. He never told me that I'd have to keep them six months before he sent someone to pick them up."

I showed him the money I'd brought and that made an instant change in his attitude. Within an hour we were surrounded by Indian trappers, summoned by shouts, racing children and loud beatings on a tin washpan. The German explained to them what I wanted and then retired to a pile of old clothes which served as a bed, with his youngest wife and a jar of wine.

Asunción was an animal collector's paradise. The jungle around the little town looked like a zoo. Parrots flew through the trees in flocks like rooks at home. Bands of monkeys swung through the branches, worth $50 each F.O.B. New York. On the trails, we saw the tracks of capybaras and agoutis and once we passed a group of coatis, their long striped tails sticking up above the terns like a column of barber poles.

The Indians taught me how to trap these animals and each species required a special technique. For the capybaras, big, guinea-pig-like rodents some three feet long, pits were dug along their trails, the same method I was to use years later to catch the Indian rhinoceros. For the agoutis, snares made of lianas were put in a circle and the Indians sat in the middle, drumming on the ground with two twigs to imitate the stamping of a male in rut. Both females and males came—the female for romance and the males to fight—and were caught by their delicate legs in the snares. The young macaws were taken from their nests by expert climbers and the toucans were caught with bird lime, smeared on the rocks near the streams where they came to drink.

The monkeys were the hardest to catch. First, the Indians spent several days putting food around a tree that stood on the edge of the forest or in a glade. It could not be too far from the other trees or the monkeys wouldn't come to it, nor could it be simply part of the jungle or there would be no way of isolating it when the time came. After a week or so, bands of monkeys would come daily to get the food and the tree would be loaded with them . . . chattering, fighting, and playing tag through the branches. Then one night the surrounding trees would be cut almost all the way through. When the monkeys came to the "food tree," men with machetes would rush out and cut down the neighboring trees while other men carrying nets made of lianas would run forward and make a circle. Some of the monkeys would make a rush for safety, only to be caught by their tails as they tried to climb over the nets. Most would remain in the food tree until that, too, was cut down and there was a wild scramble to catch as many monkeys as possible in the ensuing panic. By preparing the food trees in different parts of the jungle, we got several dozen spider monkeys, capuchins, and howling monkeys, each species in its own section of the jungle.

I learned a great deal from the Indians and I never tried to tell them how to trap. Even when I was fairly experienced they knew far more about the business than I. The only times I interfered were when it was obvious that their methods would injure the animal. Primitive people rarely try to take an animal alive; they're interested only in food. But I did learn a number of basic trappings techniques that were to stand me in very good stead.

I learned more from the Indians than trapping methods. I hadn't forgotten Behrend's injunction to get as many as possible of the magnificent hyacinthine macaws. These noble birds, the largest of all the macaws, are a brilliant blue with yellow around the eyes and beak and with their long tails are nearly five feet high. They are the most intelligent of the parrots and often develop an almost embarrassing devotion to their masters, so much so that there are numerous cases on record of a hyacinthine refusing to eat if his master goes away and simply dying of a broken heart. They are quite rare but I offered the Indians extravagant prices for young birds and soon every man, woman and child in the neighboring villages was out looking for hyacinthines.

They brought me in six young birds, a fair quantity, but I could have used a hundred. Determined to impress Behrend, I went out with two guides and traveled along jungle trails to

villages far in the interior. After I'd told the natives what I
wanted and waited a few days, their trappers would bring in a
few macaws . . . three in one village, four in another, two in a
third. I left the birds behind with careful instructions as to
feeding and pushed on greatly pleased. I now had some thirty
young hyacinthines, scattered throughout eighteen villages,
waiting to be picked up on my return journey.

One of the young birds had an injured toe which I treated
before leaving him behind. In the next village, two nestlings
were brought in and one of them also had an injured toe. Exactly the same toe. A horrible doubt suddenly struck me. I
hastily began to backtrack. It was just as I'd feared: I'd been
buying my own birds over and over again all along the way.
When I got back to Asunción, I only had the original six.

The Indians had seemed so simple and childlike that I'd never
have suspected them of playing such a trick. I discovered then
that simple, childlike people are perfectly capable of extremely
clever, intricate and unscrupulous business methods.

I loaded my cargo on a river steamer and returned to Buenos
Aires. It took two days and a night and was my first experience
in transporting animals. I'd made the mistake of separating the
monkeys only according to species. Now every band of
monkeys has a "head man" who does not allow the young males
to get too close to the females in heat. Crowded together in a
cage, it was impossible for the young males to avoid a female
and this drove the "head man" wild. I had to re-sort the monkeys, putting the "head man" in with females only. Then the
young males fought for supremacy among themselves. This had
to be solved by arranging that two young males of about the
same strength, were never placed in the same cage. If they
were there was a battle to the death. In the wild state, a defeated
male can escape and the victor will not pursue him far but in
a cage he is trapped and the victor will kill him. But I discovered that a powerful young male could be safely kept with
a dozen weaker males; they instantly recognized him as the new
head man and accepted his rule.

The military macaws were the biggest problem. The cages hadn't been made strong enough to withstand their terrible hooked beaks and they were always escaping. Fortunately, they were still too young to fly but recapturing them was quite a job. They could whip off a finger with a single snap and even their claws were surprisingly sharp. I finally developed the knack of grabbing a bird behind the head, popping him into his cage, and then letting go fast. Still, by the time I reached Buenos Aires, my hands looked as though I'd been in a fight with a dozen wildcats.

I'd counted on at least a day or two of rest but when I arrived at the compound with my cargo, I met Behrend at the gate dancing with rage. "You're two weeks over your allotted time!" he bellowed at me. "We've nearly lost the biggest shipment in animal history because of you! You leave at once for the Dominican Republic."

Without even giving me a chance to change my clothes or bathe, he rushed me to a taxi and we started for the airport. On the way, he explained what had happened.

For years, Australia had been a closed market to animal collectors as the government rigorously protected its fauna. However, Sir Edward Hallstroem, a millionaire in Sydney, was an ardent parrot enthusiast and Behrend had promised to send him an almost unknown species of conure parrot from the Andes as well as a large shipment of South American animals in exchange for Australian animals. Sir Edward agreed and Behrend had spent two years before the war trapping in the Andes in search of the parrot. He had nearly died of fever, been chased by Indians, gone mad and wandered through the jungle singing German drinking songs, but had finally gotten the conure. He had sent off the shipment and now, at last, the Australian return shipment was coming.

"Of course, the United States is the prime market today because of the number of its zoos and because the payments are made in dollars," Behrend told me as we were speeding towards the airport. "But it's almost impossible to get animals through their red tape, and some animals, especially parrots, can't be imported at all because of the psittacosis. However, America is trying hard to make friends with Trujillo, the dictator of the Dominican Republic."

"Why?" I demanded.

"Because he keeps out the communists, you fool. As part of the American program to placate Trujillo, animals can be imported from the Dominican Republic to the United States with very little trouble. Being a farsighted man, I went to Trujillo a year ago and talked him into founding the Trujillo National Zoo with a $5 million loan he got from the United States. Now in exchange for some of our Australian animals, he will let us off-load the cargo in the Dominican Republic for a few weeks. That will establish the animals as coming from there and they can go to the United States. The Australian ship is arriving at Cuidad Trujillo in a few days and you must be there to meet it."

I flew directly to Cuidad Trujillo. For $5 million dollars American, I expected to find a big, completely equipped, modern zoo but there was nothing but a rambling dirt wall and a few forlorn animals in crude cages, picked up cheap from a traveling circus which had gone bankrupt. The director was a harassed Belgian who had married an Indian woman.

What had happened to the $5 million dollars, the Belgian didn't know. He supposed most of it had been stolen by the committee of five experts whom Trujillo had set up as the zoo's board of trustees. We still had three days before the ship was due and Behrend reluctantly cabled me a thousand pesos so I could have cages built. President Trujillo gave us an almost unlimited supply of free labor and we got the cages knocked together just in time.

By now I'd grown so cynical that I fully expected the shipment to consist of a few mangy kangaroos and perhaps a wombat or two. Instead, the cargo was a breath-taking wonder. There were kangaroos and wombats but also wallabies, Tasmanian devils, the rare echidnas (the only animal except the platypus that lay eggs and suckles its young), hundreds of parrots, rare birds of all descriptions, and a collection of reptiles that alone would have made the shipment unique. The cargo was easily worth $120,000 but its rarity from a zoological point of view was beyond price.

The animals were in perfect condition, with full instructions for their care and feeding tacked on each cage. The Belgian and I worked for thirty hours without a break moving the animals into their new quarters. As soon as possible, I made a complete list of the cargo and Behrend was able to get entry permits to send most of the collection to the United States.

This task was hardly completed when I got a peremptory cable from Behrend telling me to go at once to Marajo, Brazil, an island in the vast delta region at the mouth of the Amazon. Marajo was the nesting ground of the roseate spoonbill and scarlet ibis. A big order had just come in from Europe for several hundred of both species. My contact on Marajo was a Swiss veterinarian who had imported several hundred Indian water buffalo and was working out a breeding program with them. The buffalo are good work animals and provide both meat and milk so the Swiss hoped to make a fortune with them in South America.

I caught a plane to Belem and then took a ferry to Marajo. I met the Swiss, a short, chunky man, and we rode on horseback to his hacienda, a magnificent estate covering several hundred acres. As we could not start trapping until after dark, the Swiss shouted to the servants to bring whisky and we seated ourselves at the big oak table in the living room. I paced myself carefully because there would soon be work to do, but the Swiss consumed bottle after bottle in a fashion that surpassed anything even Behrend could accomplish. He refused to talk about bird capturing after the first few drinks and would discuss nothing except castrating animals. He claimed to be able to castrate more animals per minute than any other man in the world. He showed me his instruments, went into detailed descriptions, and then got fighting mad because he claimed I didn't show enough interest.

Except for the Indian servants, he lived all alone in the great mansion, but he told me that he had once been married. He assured me that his wife had been a startlingly beautiful girl, the only daughter of a wealthy and important Brazilian family. One evening she had walked into the living room carrying a .32 revolver and without comment had begun firing at her husband. "We never did get along very well," he assured me morosely. The Swiss had fallen backward in his chair but his wife had continued shooting until the gun was empty. Then she had left the room.

The wounded man had managed to crawl to the stable and saddle a horse. He had constructed a sort of rope corset to hold himself to the saddle and ridden to the ferry. At Belem, he had gone to a doctor but was refused aid. He discovered a few days later that his wife had bribed the doctor to murder him. He had managed to borrow some money from friends and flew to B.A. where he recovered. Meanwhile, his wife had gone back to her family. "I'll never find such a beautiful girl again," the Swiss told me sadly. "She looked just like Goya's painting of the Duchess of Alba."

After dark, we went out after the birds. The Swiss had hundreds of caboclos (Indian cowboys) on his estate and several dozen of these were rounded up and told to surround the nesting grounds with a long line of nets ten feet high. Then the birds were stampeded into the nets before they could fly. In addition to the spoonbills and ibis, we also got a few of the rare Jabiru storks, one of the biggest of the storks, standing over five feet high, white with black heads. These storks later sold for $150 each in New York.

On the trip back to B.A. I had a lot of trouble getting the storks to eat. They refused everything I offered them. On the third day, one of them snatched up a piece of rotten meat that had been left near the cage by mistake and swallowed it greedily. That was the solution. These birds are scavengers and will not touch anything but partly decayed meat until they have been in captivity a long while. After that, I had no more trouble with them.

When I arrived in Buenos Aires, I found that Behrend had rented another yard and built a pool there where he was keeping manatees. These big, seal-like creatures supposedly gave rise to the mermaid legend because the female has breasts and rears herself out of the water to suckle her young. Behrend fed them seaweed and fresh fish. They would come to him like dogs but were afraid of anyone else. I would have given a great deal to stay and study them, but Behrend packed me off at once to the Matto Grosso to trap jaguars for a new order.

During the next four months, I seldom slept in the same bed twice or in the same country for more than a few days. I watched Indians in the high Andes catch condors by building circular stockades and baiting the birds in with rotten meat placed in the center. Like big planes, condors are so huge that they require a run before they can take off and the stockades were too small to give them the necessary space. In Brazil, I took part in cayman hunts with caboclos. Caymans are the huge South American crocodiles, reaching a length of eighteen feet, and extremely savage. They lie out on the banks to sun themselves and the caboclos gallop up at full speed, lasso the creatures, and then drag them inland where they can be dispatched with machetes. I wasn't interested in the big fellows but Behrend had orders for thousands of small caymans a foot or so long. These are sent to Florida where they are sold to tourists as "baby alligators," the native American alligator being protected by law. I collected harpy eagles for the rajah-falconer, taking the young birds from the nest. The lowest limb of the nesting tree was over 120 feet from the ground and the trunk was too thick to climb, but the Indians shot a light line attached to an arrow over the limb and then hauled up a heavier rope. I discovered how to get boa constrictors and twenty-foot anacondas into their shipping boxes: put a noose around the snake's neck, lead the rope through a hole in the back of the box, and pull. I collected pacas, coatis, peccaries, kinkajous, ocelots, magay cats, tapirs, and birds and reptiles.

Often I was so weary that I seemed to move in a nightmarish world where nothing was real. I remember arriving at Manaus, far up the Amazon, where I had stopped only briefly many months before with the butterfly collector. Manaus is a ghost town with broad boulevards, majestic mansions and a great opera house lined with imported marble. It had once been the heart of the rubber industry until an Englishman managed to start the trees in Malaya and Borneo. The Brazilian industry found itself unable to compete with the Malayan plantations run by efficient British overseers and collapsed. In Manaus, I met a group of adventurers of a dozen different nationalities who were exchanging salt and tobacco with the Indians for para nuts. These men were also running an animal selling business as a side-line, operating under the names of their Indian wives as it is difficult for individual foreigners to have a business in Brazil. I spent several days here for they were able to get giant armadillos, worth $750, and Behrend had at last confided to me his special formula for keeping these delicate creatures alive. I lost two of the armadillos before I discovered that the food had to be put into their cages at night; they were nocturnal feeders.

Manaus was a weird place. Naked Indians in dugouts tied up to the great wharfs built for ocean liners. Now and then half-crazed men would come down the river in canoes or rafts, prospectors, traders, explorers, and crawl into the empty mansions to die of fever or recover and go out and try again. Later, I came on a pitiful sight. I'd gone down the river to Belem with my cargo and there encountered a little group of young Americans who had spent nearly a year animal collecting in the headwaters of the Amazon. They had an amazing lot of rare birds, reptiles and animals which the Brazilian authorities promptly confiscated as the youngsters had no export permits. The young men were destitute and heartbroken. No wonder, for they had spent all their savings and wrecked their health to make this collection.

After they had gone, the customs officials sold me the entire collection for a few pesos.

These young men had left the United States with high hopes, thinking there was nothing to the animal business except capturing the animals. I have said before, and I will say again: the actual capture of the animals (which after all is generally done by local trappers) is a small matter. Keeping them alive afterwards is much more difficult, and then come the problems of obtaining export permits, shipping licenses, computing currency exchanges and getting cargo space. Even if these boys had succeeded in getting their collection to the United States, they would then have had to get import permits, veterinary certificates and so on. Also, an animal dealer must know the market. You may have the rarest bird in the world, but if Griswold of the Philadelphia Zoo or Marlin Perkins of the Chicago Zoo have no more cage space or are short of money at the time, you cannot sell your bird. Or a board of directors may have decided that the zoo needs some big, spectacular birds and, if you have only finches, you are left out in the cold. Or the zoos may be willing to make you a very good exchange but not to buy. All these considerations are vital and in such matters old Behrend was a past master.

I remember once we had an order for a giant anteater and twenty flamingos from the Rome Zoo. According to Argentinian law, the giant anteaters cannot be exported and our shipments were always carefully watched. As the anteaters are nearly six feet long and stand as high as a small dog, there seemed to be no way to smuggle one out of the country. When I protested to Behrend that it was impossible, he went into one of his wild rages.

"Donkey! Have ten boxes made, all marked 'Flamingos.' Put the anteater in one and put the other boxes around him. The customs men won't look in all."

I followed instructions. While I was crating the birds, Behrend asked me, "Which of the flamingos are especially bad-tempered?"

"I don't know," I confessed.

Behrend literally danced with rage. "Pig's snout! Dog's droppings! Find out, and put those birds in the front of the boxes so they'll bite the customs inspectors when they look inside. Aren't you even capable of thinking of a simple thing like that?" Then he paused in his fury and regarded me with sorrow. Putting his great paw on my shoulder, he said regretfully, "Peter, you are a nice boy but I doubt if you'll ever make a naturalist." He walked away, shaking his head unhappily.

Only occasionally did one of Behrend's tricks fail. Once we had a shipment of skunks destined for Zurich. It was a rush order so they had to be flown, but no airline would accept them. Behrend boxed them up and wrote "Saffron finches. *Very delicate*" on the outside. To disguise the odor, we sprayed the box with perfume. The box actually got as far as Rio de Janeiro before someone happened to kick it, after which the plane had to make a forced landing. The skunks were sent back to us by freighter with a note from the airline company which could have caused them trouble had they sent it through the mails.

Behrend drank as naturally as he breathed and I was always concerned that he might drop dead with a stroke, leaving me with all the responsibility of handling the shipments which were constantly pouring in and out, to and from all parts of the world. Ordinarily, Behrend jealously guarded his secret formulas for keeping rare animals and his methods and contacts for exporting and importing. Only when absolutely necessary, as in the case of the giant armadillos, would he divulge any of his secrets. I often expostulated with him, pointing out that if he were taken sick I would have to care for the animals and must know something about the business connections of the firm. No matter how tactfully I made the suggestion, Behrend would go into a blind rage. "Ah, now you have revealed yourself in your true light! You want me to die so you can take over my business! Perhaps you are even planning to kill me, you murderer!" For the next few hours he would regard me suspiciously, whirling around if I came up behind him and refusing to take any food or wine, claiming that I might be poisoning him. Then the mood would pass and he would be the personification of benevolence, giving me information about animals that money could not buy and pulling out a great map of the world he kept and showing, with the aid of tiny planes and ships, how the cargos were moved and in what great cities and remote villages his multitudinous contacts lay.

I discovered that Behrend had had a number of other "partners" but none of them could endure him for more than a few weeks. I stuck on because I knew that nowhere else could I learn as much about animals and the animal business as from this half-mad old man. Often, when the liquor was heavy on him, Behrend would talk endlessly of the golden days of the past when he would come into Antwerp or Brussels with a cargo of birds of paradise, toucans, rare cranes from Africa and unknown species from the Himalayas to be met by the leading dealers of Europe, their pockets bulging with cash. "Ach, then there was no worry about export permits, currency, stupid customs men and irresponsible governments. Those days will come again, Peter, they must come again!" And the great, fat man's tears would fall into the froth of his beer.

I put up with a great deal from Behrend in exchange for the precious bits of information he let drop from time to time but there is an end to everyone's endurance. Mine came after a business that still makes me sick to think about.

I was in Patagonia catching rheas, the little South American ostrichs, with some gauchos. The gauchos caught the birds by riding them down on horseback and entangling them with bolos, three balls connected by strings which, when properly thrown, wrap themselves around the legs of an animal. Money meant nothing to the gauchos and they went rhea hunting mainly for sport so I was there several days before I could get enough birds. Then I got a message from Behrend saying I was to go south at once to Tierra del Fuego to pick up a cargo of penguins. As the penguins were delicate, he was flying down some refrigerator tanks in which the birds could be put for the trip to Buenos Aires.

I sent my rheas by plane to Behrend and flew to Ushuaia. There I met a French doctor who was my contact for the birds. He had gone to Tierra del Fuego with an expedition to study the Indians but the expedition went bankrupt and the members didn't even have enough money to return to France. One by one they had managed, somehow or other, to get away. Only the doctor was left. He was desperate, not having seen or heard from his wife and children for nearly two years. His one chance to raise money was through the penguins.

Catching the birds was pitifully easy. They were trusting little things and would toddle up to you, put their flipper in your hand, and let you lead them away. I paid off the doctor and flew back with twenty-five penguins to Buenos Aires. Behrend already had an air-conditioning unit installed for them and the birds did very well on a diet of fish. The purpose of the air-conditioning unit was not so much to keep the birds cool but to filter the air. The Magellan penguins are extremely susceptible to an air-borne virus infection that attacks their throats and lungs. If put in the open in a warmer climate, they die within a few days. While the penguins were luxuriating in their air-conditioned room, Behrend and I lay in bathtubs full of water panting from the heat and drinking gallons of beer.

The penguins had been ordered by an American dealer, and after making sure that the birds were all right, Behrend flew them to him in air-conditioned units, together with careful instructions not to expose the birds to the open air.

A few days later, we heard that the dealer had sold the birds as part of an advertising scheme to various frozen-food concerns for a window display. Naturally, the poor little penguins all died. When Behrend learned of this, he telephoned the dealer and treated him to a blast of profanity that must have corroded the wires, although unfortunately the dealer couldn't understand Behrend's German oaths.

Although this tragedy wasn't Behrend's fault, it disillusioned me with the whole business. I felt—and still do—that Behrend should have discovered why the dealer wanted so many penguins. In my opinion, the Magellan penguins should be protected by law, for almost none of them survive in captivity unless kept under constant air conditioning.

I brooded over the matter for several days. I couldn't forget the sight of those good little creatures paddling along by my side to the crates, happy as children being taken to a picnic. If I could have gotten hold of that dealer, I think I would have killed him, although I suspected that the fault was also mine for getting the birds in the first place. I decided to get away from Behrend. This was not the animal business as I had dreamed of it. I had no time to study the animals, keep pets, or even eat or sleep. Instead, I was in a maelstrom of currency rates, shady tricks, permits, bribes, and under the thumb of an old man whom I now suspected to be more than half insane.

Having made up my mind, I approached Behrend. He was sitting behind his desk with his huge chart spread out before him. "Lothar," I said firmly. "I have come to tell you—"

He glanced up. "You are leaving for the West Coast of Africa in two hours. I have your passport, money, and health certificates all ready. We're starting the trapping and importing of gorillas on a large scale. It's the biggest animal deal in history, Peter, and the entire affair will be under you."

# Chapter 7

# Africa and gorillas

I'D THOUGHT nothing Behrend did could surprise me, but I stood goggling at him, gargling my words. He went on as calmly as though he'd asked me to hand him the matches. "I've had a man over there for nearly a year, Fernandez, an old-time gaucho. Wonderful fellow, Fernandez, except that he hasn't been able to get any gorillas. But he's cheap and keeps a very accurate expense account. Listen to this: 'One peso for lunch, half a peso for wine.'" Suddenly Behrend turned the color of a ripe eggplant and roared, "What's this? Five pesos for a brothel? Why, when I was there you could get into any brothel on the West Coast for three pesos. They're cheating the poor fellow. However," he continued more calmly, "judging from the expense account he's only spent sixty pesos on brothels in twelve months. Not bad."

"Where am I to go?" I asked. At the thought of being able to collect gorillas, all thought of breaking with Behrend had vanished.

"To Río Muni." I shook my head and expected another blast, for Behrend seemed to know every obscure country, town and river in the world and expected me to do the same. But he said mildly, "I'm not surprised you haven't heard of it. Even the Spanish consul didn't know of it, although it's a Spanish possession. 'It must be French,' he kept telling me. Río Muni is less than a hundred miles square and south of the French Cameroons.

110

You will meet Fernandez there. Follow his advice in all matters, he's the best type of man for this work—very dumb."

"Then why send me?" I asked bitterly. "Because I'm even dumber?"

For the first time since I'd known him, Behrend seemed embarrassed. "Well, a big New York dealer sent Fernandez a cable, with a 200-word reply prepaid, offering him $2,000 for a gorilla. The swindling Yankee! Those gorillas are worth $7,000. Fernandez cabled back, 'No speak English,' over and over for the 200 words."

"How much are we paying Fernandez?"

"That's the trouble, only 180 pesos a month. So he might be tempted to sell us out. These Argentinians are treacherous. I want you to straighten things out and also arrange for a relay service from Río Muni to Recife, Pernambuco, Brazil to handle the gorillas."

Behrend spread out his huge chart to show me the situation. If you look at a map, you will see that the West Coast of Africa makes a great hump with Dakar at the end of the "elbow." Río Muni is just below this hump. South America makes a corresponding hump with Recife, Pernambuco, at the end of its "elbow." From Dakar to Recife is only about 2,000 miles, and virtually all planes flying the southern route pass between these two points.

"We don't know how the gorillas will stand flying so you are to establish checking stations under reliable men at Douala in the French Cameroons, and Dakar. If the gorillas are all right, they'll then go from Dakar to Recife where I'll have another man stationed. Then after a few days' rest they can be flown on to New York."

"Why not fly them direct to New York from Dakar?" I said, pointing to the chart.

Behrend turned the magenta shade that preceded an outburst. "Because, you *liederliches Kamel*, they would have to go through London and as even an idiot like you should know that an ape cannot pass through England without special permits, even if the animal doesn't leave the plane."

"How do you capture a gorilla?" I asked.

Behrend nearly exploded. "Don't bother me about silly details, *schwachkoepfiger Nichtsnutz!* The important matter is the currency exchange. There may not even be gorillas in Río Muni. That would explain why Fernandez hasn't gotten any, but that's unimportant. There're some in the French Cameroons. Now don't ask me why we don't trap there! Gentle, indulgent, and soft-hearted though I am, I can grow irritable over too many *bloedsinniger* questions! Naturally the reason is that we have pesos but don't have francs, and to convert would cost us money. If necessary, get the gorillas in the Cameroons, smuggle them into Río Muni, and ship from there."

Like all of Behrend's schemes, it sounded not only fantastic but dishonest. Still, the temptation to see gorillas in their native habitat was too much for me. Within two hours, I was on a plane en route to Dakar.

I had never been in Africa before and would have happily spent several weeks in Dakar if possible. I saw Moors coming from the desert with their camel trains, tall Housas in their blue robes and white caps, the gigantic baobab trees, great herds of long-horned cattle and I wandered fascinated through the strange bazaars. But I was in a hurry to get on to Río Muni. After some trouble, I found a Frenchman named Cousu, a small trader married to a native girl, who agreed to check the gorillas before sending them on to Recife. Cousu seemed like a reliable man and had some simple medical knowledge.

From Dakar, I went on to Douala where I established another "checking station" and then went to Río Muni. Río Muni is such an isolated spot that I could not go there directly. I first had to go by ship to the island of Fernando Po and then take a trading schooner to Bata, Río Muni.

In Bata, I met Fernandez, a dark, squat man with a low forehead and a harassed manner. He was desperate for news of his sweetheart in Argentina whom he hadn't seen for two years.

Behrend had sent him out with the assurance he would only be
in Africa for two months. "I am beginning to think Señor Behrend is not wholly reliable, señor," he told me seriously. I knew
nothing about his sweetheart but even so he was delighted to
talk to someone from Argentina.

His face fell as soon as I mentioned the gorillas. "It is a terrible business, señor," he said sadly. "To get the babies, both
the parents must be killed. Once I followed a gorilla family
with my hunters for several days, hoping for a chance to grab a
little female. Finally the chance came and I rushed for the baby.
She screamed and the mother burst from the bushes, snatched up
the baby, and stood looking me in the face. And such a look!
I could have wept. Then my hunters gave their war cry and
moved in with their spears. The mother screamed for help and
we heard the male coming. Blessed God, señor, what a creature!
Six feet high and as heavy as four men. The natives flung their
spears but he came on with the spears sticking from him like
pins in a pincushion. I managed to shoot him and he fell dead at
my feet. Then we pursued the mother. She, too, died under my
gun and we carried off the baby, screaming for her parents.
She died a few days later, I think of shock."

This was horrible. "Is there no other way?" I asked.

"None, señor. They will not leave the young, they die defending them. Only rarely is it possible to steal a baby. I have
one little male that was captured in this way. The native hunters tracked the family for weeks and then stole the baby while
the mother was away feeding. The male charged and they killed
him but the female followed them for days, screaming for her
baby who screamed back to her. One man told me, 'She would
come almost within spear range and stand there, moaning and
holding out her arms for the baby while the little thing wept
and held out his hands to her.'"

"Fernandez, this I cannot do," I told him. I was nearly in
tears myself.

"I understand, señor. I am going to give up the gorilla business and go into some profession that does not try the feelings so much."

Fernandez had three baby gorillas: two males and a female. As none of the three were weaned, he had hired native women as wet nurses and the gorillas were living in the women's huts. He took me to see them. The filth of the huts was indescribable, and both the women and their children were covered with lice, rotten with yaws and obviously suffering from half a dozen different diseases.

"Couldn't you get better women than this?" I demanded.

"All the native women are like this, señor, and these women are very good to the baby gorillas. They treat them just like their own children."

That was exactly what I was afraid of. Their own children had great pot-bellies from malnutrition and had wide black rings around their eyes which at first I thought were some sort of tattooing but which turned out to be rings of flies feeding on the discharge from the infected corneas.

"The baby gorillas nurse readily enough," Fernandez assured me, pointing to a little male sucking happily at the black breast of his foster mother. "But within a few days, they sicken and die. I do not know why."

I knew why. Gorillas are very delicate and these huts were riddled with disease. I examined the little male. He screamed and fought when I took him from his foster mother and Fernandez remarked knowingly, "That's just how they behave when you take them from their real mothers." It took me a long time to quiet him but finally he snuggled down in my arms trustingly and began to play with my fingers. He was covered with lice, one eye was already badly infected from the flies, and he had infant diarrhea. I knew he could only survive a few more days.

The next baby was in equally bad shape but there was some hope for the third, a little female. I took the native foster mother out of her polluted hut, gave her a good bath, disinfected her thoroughly, and took her into the house which Fernandez and I were sharing. I dosed the baby with sulfa, deloused her, and had the satisfaction of watching her slowly recover. She was a solemn little thing and showed no inclination to play as do baby chimps. I got her a rag doll which I carefully disinfected and she'd play with it for hours, holding it to her bosom as her foster mother did her. She refused to sleep unless it was in bed with her and always looked for it the first thing on awakening. I named her Mponge. For a long time she refused to leave the house, obviously believing that she was in a world full of enemies, and I was very proud when at last she consented to walk across the compound holding tight to my hand. Although never friendly, she gradually lost her fear of humans and would gravely hold court, sitting on her foster mother's knee, when the natives came to see her.

Although I was determined not to do any gorilla catching, I did want to see a gorilla family. Fernandez took me out with his native hunter who had located a family group a few miles from Bata.

The Río Muni jungle was very different from the South American jungles to which I was accustomed. There was almost no undergrowth, for the great trees form a dense overhead mat of branches and shut out nearly all light, so you are walking in a region of perpetual twilight even though the scorching tropical sun is blazing in the sky. The ground is covered with a carpet of dead leaves so thick you seem to be walking on a deep-pile rug. Occasionally we came to clearings where a great tree had fallen or where there had been a native village and these areas were thick with bushes and huge ferns, all trying desperately to reach the light before the saplings which were growing up among them could spread out and cut off the precious sunshine.

Our hunter took us to a village whose inhabitants claimed that a gorilla family had been raiding their fields for the last few weeks and doing enormous damage. We camped on the outskirts of the village while our hunter went off with some of the village trackers to look for spoor (tracks). They returned the next day to say that the gorillas were not far away so we set out at once.

By 5 o'clock they still hadn't located the family and I was ready to return to camp. Then we began to come on fresh dung and bushes that had been stripped of their leaves by the beasts. I took some of the leaves so I could learn something of the great apes' dietary requirements; apparently any young, juicy leaves were good enough for them. Several times our trappers stopped and pointed to freshly broken weeds, the juice still slowly oozing from them. Our hunter who spoke some Spanish told me in a low voice, "We must go very slowly now. If we come on a female unexpectedly and she screams, the male is sure to charge."

I nodded to show that I understood. Fernandez had a gun, an old Springfield, badly rusted, and the natives had spears but I didn't trust these weapons to stop the charge of a furious male gorilla. Also, I had not the slightest desire to kill a male protecting his family.

We went on, moving step by step through a big plantation of ferns higher than our heads. It seemed to me that even if the gorillas were crawling on their hands and knees we would never catch up with them, but I later learned that a gorilla family moves very slowly, stopping constantly to feed. Finally our tracker motioned us to stop and wriggled ahead on his belly through the ferns. We could still see the soles of his bare feet when he stopped. Then he writhed back to us and motioned me to follow him.

I crept after him. Peering through the ferns at a little forest glade, I could see the gorillas, curiously suggestive of a human family on a picnic.

The old male was sitting with his back against a tree, benignly watching the antics of the two babies. He was a huge old "silverback" and although I wouldn't care to guess at his dimensions, gorillas do reach six feet six inches in height and can weigh as much as 600 pounds. His arms were astonishingly long—a big male can have an eight-foot reach. He didn't look ferocious, rather peaceful in fact, but I would have hated to try to grab one of those babies.

There were three females, much smaller than the old male; about the size of adult chimpanzees. There were also two or three youngsters, perhaps three or four years old, but they were off in the ferns and only occasionally appeared. Once they started to fight and the old male looked up and gave a short, angry bark that quieted them immediately.

The babies were playing "king of the castle" on a dead log. To their huge delight one of the mothers joined in the game. They danced and wrestled on the log, the little fellows teaming up to push the mother off. Little Mponge, so solemn now, must once have romped like this and I determined to get her a young chimp as a playmate.

One of the females was sitting by herself and at first I thought she must be sick but then I saw that she had a tiny baby at her breast. While I watched, she held out the baby and examined him for fleas or lice. Then she cleaned him carefully and put him back on her breast. The whole family looked very contented and I wouldn't have disturbed them for anything.

The natives behind us were growing increasingly restless. They had taken for granted that we intended to shoot the gorillas, which was the only reason that they'd taken us to the spot. The family was ruining the crops which meant life or death to them. Besides, gorilla meat is considered a great delicacy.

The old male heard a noise and bounded to his feet. He stood staring at us, although I don't believe he could see anything, and then gave a short bark. Instantly the rest of the family vanished. I don't mean that they disappeared into the jungle, I mean they simply dematerialized. One moment there had been eight of them in plain sight. The next moment, the glade was empty except for the male. How such large animals can move so swiftly and silently, I can't imagine.

The male stood staring in our direction, watching from under his beetling eyebrows for any movement. Then he turned slowly and swung off, touching the ground with his knuckles.

In this position, he looked like a big, black bear. In another moment, he too was gone.

We tried to follow them but now the family was alarmed and moved swiftly. We heard a distant booming and our hunter said it was the old male beating on his chest. "That means he knows we are following and he is warning us to keep away," he said. I decided to accept the warning.

The natives were furious that we hadn't shot the animals and the pleasant smiles with which we'd been greeted turned to sullen frowns. We returned to Bata and I sat down with Fernandez to make plans for the future.

I determined to send Behrend a consignment of drills, mandrills and chimps. The natives kill these creatures regularly for food and often catch youngsters which you can buy cheap. Drills are a big, baboon-like monkey and mandrills, with their brilliantly colored muzzles striped all the colors of the rainbow and gaudy behinds, are always a prime attraction. Of course, none of them can compare with the gorilla but I refused to collect gorillas. Apart from sentimental considerations, I was convinced that the babies were too delicate to make the business profitable. Only a few young gorillas had survived in captivity and those were hand-raised by women who devoted more time to them than the average human baby receives. Even under those conditions, the casualty rates were appalling. Eight baby gorillas died before Toto ("Gargantua's wife") was successfully reared by Mrs. A. Hoyt.

I got a little male chimp as a companion for Mponge. At first, she was afraid of him and would cling to me while watching his antics, like a carefully reared little girl regarding with shocked fascination the pranks of a boy. The chimp, whose name was Jack, was really a handful. All chimps are. He was all over the place, cried like a spoiled child if left alone, and was a natural clown. He loved applause and would caper around wearing a saucepan for a hat or draped in a shawl as long as anyone would laugh at him.

He was very gentle with Mponge and finally won our demure

young lady over. It was very sweet to watch them go off hand in hand to play. Curiously, Mponge hated being laughed at and would go into terrible rages followed by the sulks if we so much as smiled at her. Although I was greatly attached to Mponge, generally I don't like baby gorillas as much as I do chimps, for the obvious reason that gorillas are so much like human being that they can scarcely be considered animals at all, and I tend to prefer animals to humans.

The Spanish authorities in Río Muni were greatly amused at my reluctance to go gorilla hunting. As one man pointed out to me, "You must realize that gorillas are dangerous wild animals and do a great deal of harm to the native plantations. If they would live off in the jungle no one would care, but they like the ripening crops and when a gorilla family moves into a cultivated district, the natives suffer. A gorilla eats as he moves and will pull down a stalk of corn, take a bite or two, go on to the next stalk, destroy that and so on."

"Can't they be frightened away?" I asked.

The man shrugged. "How do you frighten a gorilla? Last week we had a case of a woman who shouted at a gorilla destroying her crop. The gorilla charged her and tore off her left breast. She survived but her family will starve. Their crop was ruined by the beast and recently there was a man who disturbed a gorilla while cutting bamboo. The animal grabbed him by the neck and scrotum. The scrotum came off so the ape wrung his neck. We found the head a few meters from the body. Now no one will go into the bamboo thickets and they must be cleared because we need more room for cultivation."

"What do you intend to do?"

"We must shoot the gorillas; there is no other solution. After we have killed a few, the rest may go back into the jungles and not return. If not, they must all be killed. People are more important than apes. I have postponed the drive mainly because of you. For the money you will pay for export licenses, we can do something to improve the condition of the people here but if you refuse to capture the young gorillas, then I must go ahead. Already there has been heavy pressure brought to bear on me both from the natives and from Madrid."

This put the matter in a new light. After all, I was in the animal business and Behrend had spent years and thousands of pesos arranging for this gorilla business. Also, I had thought of a way to capture the babies without killing the parents: use tear gas. I was sure that the parents would be thrown in a panic by the gas and we could pick up the babies. It was logical to suppose that the adults, after such an experience, would go back to the jungles where they would be safe.

I organized the first hunt carefully. Our hunter had located a band of twelve gorillas near a village and we could count on the cooperation of the community in the drive. The main problem was to keep the resentful natives from killing the entire family in the excitement. I resolved to have a boma (corral made of thorn bush) built in a half-moon shape about a quarter of a mile long and into this boma I planned to drive the gorillas. The boma would have to be fifteen feet high and very thick to make reasonably sure that the family would turn at bay there. Then I planned to use the tear gas. I counted on the panic-stricken adults, being able to escape over the boma but I doubted if the young could follow. That would be the moment for men with nets to rush in.

Our hunter reported that there were three young gorillas of a suitable age with this family—an important consideration, for I did not want to get newborn babies nor yet half-grown adults. With our nets and camping equipment we drove to the village and interviewed the head man. I needed at least a hundred beaters and there were only about thirty able-bodied men in the community, but the head man assured me that when the time came, he could get beaters from two neighboring villages. So I went out with our hunter to locate the family and study the lay of the land.

It was most certainly not the type of terrain I would have chosen for a gorilla hunt. The jungle was cut up by hills, deep ravines and streams. There were great open stretches where the natives had once cleared fields that were now an almost impenetrable mass of undergrowth. The natives will clear a patch of jungle, plant their crops there until the soil is exhausted, and then move on to another location, and it will be fifty years or more before the trees come back. But this was where the gorillas were and there was no help for it.

I wanted to make sure our hunter was really on the track of the family. Often natives sent out to track down some animal will go a few yards into the jungle, take a nap, and then return with detailed accounts of their exploits. I was reassured when I saw some of the curious nests the family had built in the trees for sleeping quarters. I was amused to notice that the inside of the male's nest was bare but the females had carefully lined theirs with soft grass. Then I returned to the village and gave directions for building the boma.

People were brought from the neighboring villages and with the men wielding brush hooks and the women carrying loads, the huge structure was completed within a few hours. Then the drive began.

My beaters spread out in a line over a mile long and began to move forward, beating on drums, blowing on conch shells, waving rattles and shouting. Fernandez took one end of the line and I the other. The net men stayed behind me. I had a knapsack full of gas grenades but no gun. I have never seen the animal yet I consider dangerous enough to justify the trouble of carrying a heavy, unwieldy length of metal through underbrush. Besides, I like to have both hands free in an emergency.

We moved as fast as possible because it was important to stampede the family into the boma, but keeping the line unbroken was a difficult job. Groups of men were delayed by the ravines, patches of underbrush, and the hills. Two natives went ahead of me, cutting our way with brush hooks so the men carrying the heavy nets could follow. We kept in touch with the other groups as well as we could by the sound of their rattles and cries. As we came closer to the boma, the groups closed up until we were a long line of men, walking almost within arm's length of each other.

The gorillas were just ahead. We came on patches of watery dung dropped by the frightened apes. Then we saw where the male had torn down branches in his rage. We were almost to the boma now. Even above the shouts and roar of the drums, I could hear the deep, choking coughs of fury from the old male. The natives around me set their shields and lifted their spears, ready for the charge they knew must soon come.

We burst from the ferns and there ahead of us were the gorillas, running back and forth, trying to find some way over the boma. Unlike other apes, gorillas are not arboreal animals and except for sleeping spend most of their time on the ground. I'd counted on this fact in building the boma. At sight of us, the old male gave his terrible coughing roar and charged at incredible speed, going on all fours at a pace I wouldn't have believed possible.

I flung one of the gas grenades. It exploded in front of the charging male. A cloud of white smoke went up and I was caught in it as well as the gorilla. I flung myself to one side, choking and weeping, having no idea where the male might be. I'd forgotten to provide myself with a gas mask and for a few seconds I was completely blinded.

I crawled away and then stood up, wiping my eyes. There was wild disorder on the boma. All I could see was the natives with their spears and all I could hear was their whoops. I threw another grenade, as much to hold back the natives as to frighten the gorillas, for I didn't want the animals killed. As the smoke went up, I caught a glimpse of either a young male or a female scrambling over the boma. Where the old male was, I had no idea.

Fernandez was yelling and the men with the nets ran to him. I followed, choking and gasping. Fernandez had a young gorilla and the baby had bitten him badly in the left hand. The men threw their nets and we managed to tie the little fellow up. In the excitement, I forgot all about the big male. Later, I learned that he had fled after the first grenade.

We got two of the three babies, the third one escaping with its mother. The male that had bitten Fernandez was weaned but the other, a smaller male, was still nursing. After treating Fernandez' hand and giving him a tetanus injection, we raced back to Bata. I had already arranged with three native women to nurse any babies we might get and these women had been carefully sterilized and kept in quarantine under what was virtually armed guard. I selected the healthiest and most intelligent of the women to nurse the baby male. The other male I took into my own room. He was frantic with fear and rage and I sat up all night with him, trying to calm the terrified youngster. Just before dawn, he dropped off to sleep and I dozed too, sitting in a chair by his crib. I did not dare to put him in a cage.

Mponge immediately adopted the baby, to the considerable apprehension of the baby's foster mother and myself, but Mponge was very careful with him. She carried him around and wouldn't even let her friend Jack come near her priceless possession. When the baby cried for food, poor Mponge was frantic. She wouldn't let us take the baby but sat cuddling and crooning over him, trying to quiet the squawling infant. After infinite tact and patience, we finally got the baby away long enough for him to nurse. From then on when the baby started to cry, Mponge would carry him to the foster mother and stand gravely by until he was fed and given back to her.

The bigger male we named Bobo (he is now in the St. Louis Zoo, stands five feet six inches and weighs over 520 pounds). I gave him a bottle formula designed for babies to supplement the regular diet of Pablum, cod liver oil, wheat germ and raw egg that Behrend had recommended. The original formula did not agree with him very well but by altering the ingredients I finally worked out a suitable combination. I tried it out on Mponge and the other little male and both did well on it, although most of their food continued to come from the wet nurses.

We were still getting in a steady flow of drills, mandrills and chimps as well as some other animals so I was kept in camp while Fernandez conducted other drives for gorillas, using the tear gas grenades. He brought in three more babies, all caught without killing the parents. As soon as the natives discovered that we would rid them of a menace as well as pay them the equivalent of $15 in trade goods for the babies, we had no trouble finding volunteer gorilla hunters and Fernandez was gone for weeks at a time.

I made sure that each baby gorilla had a chimp as a playmate as well as a foster mother—even the ones who were weaned were assigned a native woman as a nurse. Gorillas need continual attention and affection more than any other animal, although chimps also require a great deal of love. The gorillas were far more solemn than the chimps, and I think more intelligent. If one was hurt, the others would instantly rush to his help. It was amusing to see the little males trying to beat their chests in imitation of their fathers and if one managed to produce any noise, he was obviously very proud of himself. I found it impossible to teach them any tricks, while the chimps enjoyed learning them. The gorillas didn't like to perform and even as babies were far too dignified for such antics.

The chimps were not only a lot of fun but a lot of trouble. Once Jacky went around and opened all the cages, letting several thousand pesos' worth of animals loose. There was no use punishing him; after all, it was his privilege as a chimp. Nor could he very well be tied up, he grieved so. The only solution was to put locks on the cages.

When I was sure that the babies were used to captivity and feeding well, I prepared for the first shipment. I'd decided to send over one gorilla as a sort of "trial balloon" and selected Mponge. Everyone was alerted: Behrend, our agents in Douala, Dakar, Recife and New York, and reservations were made on the airlines. Mponge would be flown by Air France from Douala to Dakar and then by Pan-American to Recife. When everything was ready, we embarked on our great experiment.

For this first trip I drove Mponge by car to Douala, a trip of two and a half days over jungle trails and across treacherous fords in rivers swollen by sudden rains. I put her on the plane for Dakar myself. She was listed as a passenger and traveled first class. The stewardess promised to look after her and give Mponge her bottle at regular intervals.

I waited at the nearest telegraph station so I could receive reports as Mponge reached the various points along her 9,000-mile trip. Evening came and still no word. The plane should have arrived at Dakar at 2015. The suspense was terrible but I could do nothing but wait.

Fernandez arrived in an ancient car with Mponge's foster mother. I told them that so far no word had come through. We sat in silence, Fernandez and I by the telegraph operator, the woman in one corner, the whites of her eyes shining in the semi-darkness.

The key began to click. The message was from Cousu, our agent at Dakar. The plane was coming into the field.

We waited in an agony of uncertainty. Then the key clicked again. Cousu was wiring, "Mponge not well. Won't eat and is crying. Suggest hold."

I cabled Behrend in Buenos Aires. The reply came back, "O.K. to hold. Will cancel flight reservation until hear from you."

The time crawled by. I saw the foster mother's lips move. She was praying. Fernandez and I said nothing. An hour passed. Two hours. Three hours. I wondered if Behrend could get another reservation on a westward-bound plane. There were no more flights on Pan-American for twenty-four hours.

The key danced. Cousu wired. "Mponge much better. Has taken her bottle and seems all right. Suggest ship."

I cabled Behrend. The answer came "Have reservation on SAS, Flight 225, leaving Dakar at 0200."

I told Cousu to ship Mponge on. I knew there was nothing organically wrong with the gorilla and suspected her trouble might be airsickness, and I'd gotten in touch with the Dakar airport and learned that the Air France plane had hit some bumpy weather off Liberia and several of the passengers had been ill. But the big transatlantic planes fly so high that they are usually free of atmospheric disturbances, so the next leg of the journey looked safe.

At 0230, Cousu wired that Mponge was on her way. We now had a ten-hour vigil until she reached Recife. Never had ten hours passed so slowly. Again the plane was overdue. Finally I could stand the strain no longer and sent a Telex through the airport at Dakar to the airport at Recife.

I was put through to the girl at the information desk. "Have you heard from Flight 225?" I asked.

"Flight 225 has been delayed an hour and a half," the girl informed me. "They had to put down at Bahia."

This might mean that Mponge had been off-loaded because of some customs regulation. "Do you know if my gorilla is on board?" I demanded.

"The passenger list is just coming in to us, sir. Will you wait a moment?"

I sat sweating, holding the silent receiver. Then the girl reported in her calm, professional voice, "The gorilla is on board and doing well. The pilot radioed that she took her 8-o'clock bottle and has now gone to sleep."

I rushed back to the house in wild excitement. Our hunters, trackers, the foster mothers and all their families were crowded about waiting for the news. When I told them that Mponge was all right, everyone went mad with joy. The drums were beaten frantically and Fernandez and I opened a bottle of whisky and took our first drink in twenty-four hours.

Mponge was kept in Recife for a week to recover from the flight and then sent on to New York. Most American zoos will not deal with a collector directly but insist that animals go through a recognized American dealer. Mponge was sent to Heinz Ruhe, one the biggest animal dealers in the States, and met at the airport by an ambulance with an electric blanket and a veterinarian. The gorilla was rushed to Ruhe's store in the

Bowery and kept under observation. She seemed to have stood the trip well and to be thriving.

I sent two other gorillas to Recife, following this same method. Each time there was the long wait, the uncertainty, the sudden change of plans at the last moment, the chance of something going wrong. But we were slowly getting the business reduced to a system. Each time there were fewer slip-ups and by checking weather conditions ahead of time, we were able almost to guarantee the babies a comfortable flight, the whole complicated system being directed from Behrend's little desk in Buenos Aires.

Fernandez had brought in several more gorillas and we also had a number of chimps, mostly from Siena Leone, Liberia, and Nigeria. These are the white-faced chimps, worth far more money than the more common black-faced chimps of the Cameroons. I kept the babies on a rigid diet which, I'll admit, they didn't particularly like but was good for them. In the old days, collectors had allowed baby apes to eat anything they wanted so the babies filled up on fruit and developed colic and dysentery. My babies had to eat their Pablum, meat and wheat-germ mix first, getting only a little fruit for dessert. I made sure that the littlest ones were doing well on a formula before shipping them off and were sufficiently "broken in" to people so they wouldn't miss their foster mothers too much.

Then came a cable from Behrend. Mponge was very sick and not expected to live.

What could have happened? Every precaution had been taken. If Mponge died, there was something basically wrong with our whole system. The entire project would have to be abandoned. Mponge might simply be suffering from homesickness, to which animals are subject even more than humans. In that case, the sight of a familiar face might help her. In any case, I had to see what was happening. I took a plane from Douala and arrived at New York's International Airport twelve hours later.

I had a Swiss passport and the immigration inspector asked

my business in the United States. "I've come to see a sick go-rilla," I told him. The man nodded, "Oh yes, I've been reading about her in the papers. You must be the West African trapper who got her." He put my papers through in record time and I took a taxi to Ruhe's.

Mponge was clearly very sick. She sat with her head in her hands and hardly knew me. Ruhe had gotten her a day nurse and a night nurse. Dr. Leonard Goss from the Bronx Zoo was in attendance, administering glucose injections. He had no idea what the trouble was, and of course Mponge couldn't help by telling him how she felt.

That evening, a specialist in tropical diseases and a pediatrician were called in but they were unable to offer any suggestions. Mponge was sinking fast and at ten o'clock she was put in an oxygen tent. The doctors were trying everything in their power and I sat outside her room, prepared for the worst.

Shortly after midnight, she passed away.

An autopsy was held immediately. Mponge had died of the flux, a liver complaint caused by parasites carried by almost microscopic snails. If these snails come in contact with humans or apes, the parasites enter the host's blood stream through the pores and find their way to the liver. Many American soldiers died of the flux in the South Pacific during the last war.

Mponge had undoubtedly picked it up in the filthy native hut where she'd been living before I reached Africa. Nearly all the natives have the disease just as they all have malaria but they have developed a partial immunity to it. The gorillas have not.

Fortunately, none of my other babies had been in the native huts so they should be all right. But Dr. Goss told me that my precautions had not gone nearly far enough. I would have to take urine tests, stool tests, blood tests and saliva tests of all the babies and also of all the foster mothers, as the babies might be contaminated by their milk. In fact, the two other young go-rillas now at Recife could not be allowed in the United States until these tests had been made.

Mercia and I.

An elephant camp in India. The animals in the foreground are carrying grass for their suppers.

Mercia and I with mahout on Akbar, trailing rhinos through the ekkra grass in the Assam sanctuary. Note Akbar's "caste mark."

Rhino trapping in Assam. *Above left:* Natives disguise the pit trap with rushes. *Above right:* Our first catch, dangerous and unwanted— a water buffalo! *Below left:* A few moments after this picture of our first captive rhino was taken, the baby's mother burst from the ekkra to scatter the proud captors in terrified flight. *Below right:* The mother rhino vanquished, natives prepare to haul the baby from pit to truck.

At the Philadelphia Zoo renewing acquaintance with two rhinos I'd captured in Assam.

H. Bertolf

Here, at the Basel Zoo, is the offspring of that first pair of Indian rhinos I brought back from Assam.

Elephant training in India. *Above:* Two kunkis (tame elephants) help control a newly caught baby. *Below:* Captured wild elephants test the footing in the trench which forms part of the keddah stockade. In the background are two kunkis left with the wild animals to help quiet them.

This two-year-old cheetah was once the pet of a Kenya game warden. These amazingly swift animals are easily tamed and in India are used to hunt antelope.

*Photos by H. Bertolf*

*Above left:* Malayan sun bears. *Above right:* A lesser panda. *Below left:*
Exercising a tiger on shipboard. *Below right:* A bear cub explores the ship.

The two gorillas were scheduled to leave Recife, Brazil, within forty-eight hours. I obtained a complete list from Dr. Goss of the necessary tests, plus a detailed description of the physical check-up the foster mothers would need, and then flew to Recife.

Behrend flew north from B.A. to meet me at Recife. "Peter, nothing must interfere with these gorilla shipments," he told me in an awed voice. "People are mad about the animals. Only a few days ago, we sent one of the young males to Rio, hoping to interest the zoo there. The gorilla was taken outside for some newspaper pictures. A crowd formed and a man started asking him questions. He had come from São Paolo to Rio to buy a Cadillac, had saved for years to get the money. Instead of the Cadillac, he bought the gorilla. When he took the ape home, his wife left him but after some thought, he decided to keep the gorilla anyway. He had been diseased and was not able to have any children."

"What's he going to do with it?" I asked, astonished.

"Heaven knows. He's named it after his dead brother who was a famous athlete and is building his whole life around it. He is a scrawny little fellow and the gorilla seems to mean something to him."

The remaining male was certified as healthy and I called Fernandez in Río Muni to explain the tests to him. He was frantic. "Señor Ryhiner, I can't do all that! We will have to have a doctor here."

"I'll have a doctor sent from Dakar," I promised him.

"But what will I do until he arrives? I have several more baby gorillas and they are all nursing. How can I test these women? They nearly all have venereal diseases. Can the babies be infected by their milk?"

"I'll fly back on the next plane," I promised him.

I caught a plane and hurried back. At Dakar, I got a doctor and went on to Bata. The doctor set up a clinic and we were able to select strong healthy women as foster mothers. In spite of this, I made a point of getting the babies on a bottled formula as quickly as possible, as I couldn't keep the women away from their husbands and they might become infected at any time.

I now had a large collection of animals, including the gorillas, and I was constantly busy. It cost us $2,500 to deliver a gorilla to New York where we sold him for $6,000 to Ruhe or some other dealer who then resold him to a zoo for $7,500. The capturing had been so well organized that we were sure of obtaining a small but steady supply of young gorillas without having to kill the parents. This was a "crop" that could be harvested yearly without damaging the gorilla population. If a gorilla family was reported raiding a plantation and we could not get around to it at once, we'd recompense the villagers for the damage done so they wouldn't kill the animals. The whole business was working out very well and we had begun sending gorillas to Europe as well as the United States. We had great hopes that some of our babies would breed in the next few years and thus start a "gorilla line" independent of the wild stock.

Then a wealthy American arrived in West Africa. As he stepped off the plane, he made the dramatic announcement that he would pay the natives $1,000 for a baby gorilla.

The purchasing power of $1,000 in West Africa was roughly equivalent to that of $1,000,000 in the United States; it was fantastic wealth. Within hours, whole villages were deserted, everyone having gone gorilla hunting. The wholesale massacres that followed were appalling. Hand-to-hand fights took place between gorillas defending their young and desperate natives. Usually in such struggles the whole gorilla family was killed as well as several of the spearmen. Steel traps were set out which broke the animals' legs. Even if a baby gorilla was captured, he seldom survived more than a few days because the natives had no idea of how to feed and care for him. This meant that another gorilla family had to be attacked and then another.

The American got his baby gorilla and returned home in a fanfare of publicity. The other babies who had been captured were then offered to us—at $1,000 each. We could not possibly pay such a price nor would we if we could, it would have meant more purposeless destruction. Besides, the babies brought in were either dead or dying. Fernandez and I tried to argue with the natives but it was no use. The price of a gorilla had now been definitely set for them at $1,000 and they would let the babies die on their hands rather than accept a cent less.

In a few weeks, Fernandez and I stood in the ruins of a business we had been laboriously building up for more than a year. Fernandez returned to Argentina. I collected what monkeys and other animals we had and sent them to Behrend after cabling him what had happened.

I was preparing to fly back when I got a cable from Behrend. An enormous shipment of East African animals, valued at more than $100,000, had been collected for us at the port of Mombasa. I was to fly to Mombasa and return with the shipment to Rio de Janeiro. The animals were already in transport cages at the docks, so my job was to be a simple one. I took a plane for Mombasa, looking forward to the long return voyage to Rio as a rest for my jangled nerves.

# Chapter 8

# Kenya and big game

I ARRIVED in Mombasa and looked around for my cargo. There wasn't a sign of it and no one knew anything about a shipment of animals. I had the name of the animal trapper so I went on to his address in Nairobi and there hired a car so I could drive out to the trapper's ranch, a day's trip. I arrived late that evening, tired, dirty and in an extremely bad mood.

Standing on the front porch of a rather dilapidated house was a little hard-faced man wearing a stained bush jacket and torn pants. I asked if he was the trapper and he nodded without bothering to speak.

"Where are the animals?" I asked after identifying myself.

"Out in the bush. Where did you expect to find them, all in boxes waiting for you?" he inquired sarcastically.

"That's exactly where I expected to find them," I assured him. "That's where you said they'd be in your cable to Behrend, wasn't it?"

"Oh, that!" he laughed. "I didn't expect him to send someone so soon. I'm not going to have a lot of animals eating their heads off here until I know there's someone to take them off my hands. Besides, I haven't enough pens to hold all the muck Behrend wants."

He did have a few pens and a few animals. Being freshly caught, they were in fair shape but they wouldn't remain so long; the pens were filthy and much too small.

"You'll have to build better pens than this," I told him.

"The hell I will. These animals have to pay for themselves. When I get the money for them, I'll build pens, not before."

I discovered that this man was a Boer who'd come to East Africa without a penny and worked his way up from poverty to a position of comparative comfort. Before the war there'd been an extremely capable animal collector in East Africa, a German named Schultz. He was accused of being pro-Nazi and was thrown out of the country in 1940. This Boer had bought Schultz's furniture at an auction and in a desk drawer he had found Schultz's account books. On paper, the profits in the animal business seem fantastically high so he'd decided to do some animal collecting as a sideline.

My first impulse was to cancel the contract and find another trapper. However, canceling a contract in a foreign country is a long, expensive business with plenty of legal complications. Also, I discovered that although this Boer knew nothing about the animal business, he had hired two very capable men to do the trapping for him. One of these men was the famous Willie de Beer, who'd worked for Schultz and was well known in animal circles. Willie was a giant, tremendously strong and tough as a rhinoceros-hide whip. There was a legend that once while Willie was moving a leopard from the box trap to a transport cage, the leopard had gotten loose and clawed him badly in the left shoulder. Willie knocked the animal out with one blow of his fist, tossed the cat into the transfer cage, and unconcernedly drove back to the farm.

The other trapper was a younger man but also very capable. With these two men, I was confident that the animals could be collected. From Nairobi, I sent a cable to Behrend saying that I'd be in East Africa at least four months and then settled down to the job at hand.

After an interchange of cables, Behrend grudgingly sent an advance against the animals (using some of my 40,000 francs), sufficient to put up new pens. He didn't send enough to put up the kinds of pens I wanted to have built, but at least we had something to hold the animals after they were captured.

Behrend's order included such animals as elephants, giraffes, leopards and rhinoceroses as well as the ordinary antelopes, gazelles, birds and monkeys. I had no conception how you went about catching an antelope or gazelle, let alone an elephant or a rhino. Fortunately, Willie de Beer and his assistant knew exactly how to do it. I went along to watch.

We started out in a car with a little seat strapped to the right-hand front fender. Willie sat in this seat with a long pole that had a noose at the end. His assistant drove the car as though it were an airplane across the semi-open bush country. I'd been worried about what would happen if we met a herd of elephants or buffalo. After the first few miles, I'd have welcomed a herd of elephants as a relief; they'd have made the driver slow down.

Two lorries followed us full of transport cages and "boys," as the native men are called in East Africa. The lorries would stop on a hill and watch to see if we caught anything. If we didn't, the drivers would go to the next hill and stop again.

The plains were covered with game. Never had I imagined such vast numbers of animals. We drove at top speed past tens of thousands of zebras, topi, reedbuck, waterbuck, impalas, hartebeest, wildebeest (called "gnu" in America), Thomson's gazelles, Grant gazelles, duiker, oribi and flocks of ostriches. Willie de Beer told me that in the old days the Boers used to shoot these animals by the thousands merely to get grease for their wagons. It was hard to believe that these zebras, common as sparrows, were worth $500 F.O.B. New York or that the giraffes—and we passed many herds of sixty or more—would bring $5,000 each.

That day Willie was after zebras. His assistant drove at top speed through the center of a herd, cutting it in half. He then spun the wheel and cut one section into half again, keeping up this technique until he had a small group of about twenty zebras isolated from the main body. We drove alongside the galloping animals, Willie miraculously maintaining his seat on the fender.

"There's three good ones in that lot," Willie shouted to me. We wanted only young animals and I could see the three half-grown foals he meant.

"Go ahead," I shouted.

We continued to parallel the group. Zebras will always eventually turn and run in front of a car moving beside them. The small herd suddenly swerved and crossed a few yards ahead of us. Instantly, Willie's assistant jammed his foot down on the pedal and the car leaped forward. Willie expertly noosed one of the young zebras and we stopped with a scream of brakes, the cloud of red dust that had been following the car swirling around us. Willie's assistant had leaped out almost before the car stopped moving and deftly slapped a muzzle on the foal to keep him from biting. To my surprise, the zebra did not resist. He seemed to be in a daze.

A pole with a red cloth on the end was quickly driven into the ground and the zebra tied to it. Instantly we were off again, following the rest of the herd to get the other two foals.

"The boys will pick up that one we caught," Willie told me as we sped away in pursuit of the other two foals, the car careening on two wheels as we followed their turns. Looking back, I could see the lorries moving down the hill with the boys casting off the ropes that held one of the transport cages.

The next zebra was caught a few minutes later, and then the third. Both of them stood as quietly as tame horses while the muzzles were put on and they were tied up. Willie told me that when zebras are first caught, they go into a state of trance from shock but this condition only lasts for a minute or so. Then they put up a terrible resistance, biting and kicking so savagely that it is almost impossible to handle them. Speed is vital and the two men worked together like clockwork. After I got the hang of the business, I was able to help them and we caught a dozen zebras in two hours.

On the way back, we had an accident. The two lorries loaded with crates were traveling side by side across the veldt ahead of our car. Suddenly for no apparent reason, the right-hand lorry made a left turn and the left-hand lorry made a right turn. There was a stunning crash and both lorries turned over, the boys riding on top of the crates flinging themselves clear. Neither men nor animals were hurt and the lorries were finally pulled back on their tires by our car with the boys pushing and as fine an exhibition of profanity from Willie de Beer as I have ever heard.

Following this roping system, in the next three months we got fourteen zebras, three eland, two waterbucks, four wildebeest, eight ostriches, five young giraffes and a number of gazelles. We also captured three young rhinos. In capturing the rhinos, a slightly different system was used. We went out with two cars, one covered with old tires to act as bumpers. When a cow rhino with a calf was spotted, the protected car would engage the mother while the other went after the baby. Even with the protection of the tires, the driver had to exercise considerable skill for the infuriated mother could easily upset the car if she hit it broadside. The driver had to avoid the mother's rushes and at the same time lure her away from the baby. Fortunately, a rhino is a stubborn animal and the mother in her determination to destroy the car would forget about her baby. However, catching the baby had to be done fast. Once his neck was in the noose, a dozen boys would leap out of the car to hold him while the lorry raced up. A transport cage was hurriedly unloaded, the baby pushed inside, and the cage hoisted back in the truck before the mother realized what was happening.

One evening when we were coming back after a rhino hunt, we saw a circle of cars stopped near a thick piece of bush. Willie de Beer drove over to see what was up. A sportsman had wounded a buffalo. His white hunter, together with a native gunbearer, had gone into the cover to finish off the animal. The gunbearer had been walking behind the hunter and both men were intent on the spoor when the buffalo suddenly charged them from behind. The gunbearer had been killed instantly, the buffalo first goring and then trampling on him. When we came up, the hunter was sitting outside the cover smoking a cigarette and looking pale and shaken.

"I should have shot that damned buff before he could get into cover," he told Willie. "But my bloody client had made me swear to let him do all the shooting. 'I'm not interested in a trophy if *you*'ve shot it,' he told me. He hit the bull and then missed on his second shot. Of course, I couldn't let him go after a wounded buff—against government regulations as you know. I had to go in. Now this has happened I'll probably lose my license and I deserve it."

There wasn't much left of the gunbearer, just a bloody mass well stamped into the ground. Willie de Beer shook his head as we drove away. "Thank God I'm not a white hunter and have to put up with fools like that," he said.

Our most exciting hunt was for elephants. For this job, Willie took six cars. A German family living near the Mozambique border had been complaining that elephant herds were ruining their crops and offered to give us every assistance possible.

"That's good elephant-catching territory," Willie told me as we drove away at the head of our cavalcade. "The ground's level and there are plenty of big herds. I don't anticipate any difficulty."

Elephants will stampede when pursued by cars, especially if guns are fired into the air and there is a great deal of shouting and horn blowing. The herd is chased by cars until the babies drop back. Then one lorry stops to collect them while the other cars continue to chase the herd, still honking horns, shouting, and firing into the air to keep the mothers from turning back.

The German's ranch house was built on the slope of a hill. Sitting on his porch with our sundowners in our hands, we could see over miles of country. There were seven lakes on the property and one river. He had a tiled swimming pool near the house and he told us that nearly every morning there were the pug marks of lions around it; the lions evidently regarding the pool as a new sort of waterhole. Through a pair of field-glasses, I could see herds of game scattered over the distant hills. Around the house were enormous fig and baobab trees, the finest I'd ever seen. If I could live anywhere in the world I wished, my first choice would be Bali; my second that ranch house.

Shortly before dusk when the setting sun turned the hills golden as though a gigantic yellow spotlight had been thrown on them, we saw the elephants. At that distance they looked like gray sheep. Through the glasses I could see their enormous ears and catch an occasional gleam of ivory as the bulls slowly turned their heads while feeding. Every now and then a trunk would go up, writhing about like a boa constrictor, as some member of the herd searched the wind for unusual scents.

"There are plenty of babies," said Willie who was studying the herd through his own glasses. "We won't have any trouble getting you a few."

Willie was too optimistic. We spent the next ten days following the herd without success. Either the animals were in dense cover where the cars couldn't go or the groups we found didn't have any suitable young. At last we had to admit that we were beaten.

On the last morning, while the boys were loading our tents into the lorries, an incredible thing happened. A baby elephant came running into camp, crying loudly, and went from one to another of us, his tiny trunk curled up and his mouth open to be fed.

"His mother must have been shot by a poacher," Willie de Beer said. "The natives fire into a herd with poisoned arrows. The herd runs off and some of the wounded elephants die. The poachers watch for the circling vultures to show them the kills. They shoot cows and bulls both. The cow ivory isn't as heavy as the bull but it's worth more pound for pound; finer texture and grain."

Although the baby was so tame, he refused to go into a lorry and he was surprisingly strong. Finally, Willie had the boys dig a hole with a slanting side so the truck could be backed into it until the tailgate was level with the ground. Then we could lead the baby in without trouble.

We drove back along a twisting jungle trail and suddenly came on a whole herd of elephants, the very animals we'd been after for ten days.

The baby was squealing in the lorry—from hunger, not fright —and at the sound, the whole herd charged us. Even Willie de Beer who is absolutely fearless jumped out of the car and ran. I was right behind him. The herd surged around our cavalcade trying to find the baby. I saw one car go over and prayed that there was no one inside. Willie still had his gun and so had the other white men with us. They started firing over the herd and the elephants slowly withdrew, screaming and striking at the cars with their tusks and foreheads as they passed.

We managed to right the overturned car and continued on our way to the German's ranch. Luckily, the German had some goats and I gave the baby goat's milk, pouring it into him through a split bamboo pole. The little fellow was so eager that most of the milk splashed over him and me but finally he got a square meal. The goat's milk didn't agree with him too well but after a few days I worked out a formula of condensed milk and water mixed with corn gruel that did the trick.

We returned with our lone capture to the Boer's ranch. Most of the animals that Behrend wanted had now been collected. The little rhinos had grown very tame. The adults are such sullen, cantankerous beasts that I was astonished when the babies took to following me about like pet pigs, nuzzling for food and holding out their heads to be scratched, but Willie told me that even adult rhinos often tame very easily. "But I wouldn't encourage them," he warned me. "They can become overly protective. A chap named Stanton near Voi had a couple of pet rhinos that would attack anyone who seemed to be threatening their master. Once a friend slapped Stanton on the shoulder and the rhinos damned near killed the fellow before Stanton could drag them off."

Knowing that the rhinos would go to a zoo anyhow, I continued to play with them. The little male especially, became a great pet. He had a funny little squeak, a ridiculous noise for such a big animal, and he used it to express all sorts of emotions, eagerness, irritation, alarm and as a "please-come-and-play-with-me" call.

The tamest of all the animals were four hyena pups we had bought from natives during the first few days of trapping and which were now nearly full grown. They were doglike, playful, and loved to be hosed off when the time came for their daily bath. We made no attempt to keep them penned up; you couldn't have driven them away. I have never understood why people dislike hyenas so intensely. They are simply big dogs and like all dogs will eat carrion when they find it. My hyenas were not skulking or treacherous but some of the best pets I've ever had. I've raised many young hyenas since then, both African and Asiatic, and they were all wonderful pets.

Willie de Beer showed me a number of useful tricks for keeping the various animals. The giraffes, for example, had to be fed from boxes on the ends of poles. "In the wild state, they usually feed from the tops of thorn trees and having to keep bending their necks down to eat puts too much strain on them," he explained. He also suggested leaving the transport cages in the corrals for several days before shipping. "Put food inside and let the animals go in and out so they'll become accustomed to the cages," he advised. "Then they won't resent them when shipping time comes."

Taking care of so many animals occupied all my time so I was unable to make many hunting trips. The zebras had to be wormed regularly. They were all heavily infested with tape- and roundworms which they are able to throw off in a wild state, but in the narrow confines of a pen they were continually reinfecting themselves from their own droppings. I also suspect that in a wild state they may eat certain herbs that discourage the worms even if they don't kill the parasites.

I did take time off to visit Carr Huntley, the famous animal collector in Rumuruti. Carr was a big, broad-shouldered, hearty man who had a pet lioness that rode around in the car with him.

He carried his head slightly cocked to one side as the result of a blow from a charging rhino. His back was covered with scars where a lioness had clawed him. I asked him how it had happened. Carr told me that he had found some lion cubs and was collecting them when the mother unexpectedly returned. His boys, including his gunbearer, had promptly scampered up trees and Carr had been knocked down by the charging lioness. While she was standing over him considering where to take the next bite, Carr's gunbearer managed to climb down from the tree and shoot her.

Carr had a pair of tame white rhinos for which he was asking 17,000 pounds. Although white rhinos are rare, such a price was way out of line. I don't think Carr seriously wanted to sell them anyhow; he made too much money renting them out to motion picture companies. Virtually every picture made in Kenya over the last few years shows Carr's rhinos charging the embattled hero. They'll run to anyone who holds out a carrot for them. Then a quick shot can be inserted of the hero firing his gun and afterwards a picture of a dead rhino taken somewhere in the bush. Those two rhinos have been "killed" by Clark Gable, Victor Mature, Stewart Granger and I don't know how many others.

Later, I saw Carr in Nairobi, his hand heavily bandaged. A few days before his pet lioness had bitten off part of a finger. "She was in heat and a bit irritable," Carr explained apologetically. "I didn't mind her biting off my finger particularly but then damned if she didn't eat it."

I had arrived in East Africa in November. By June we had a nice collection of animals. In addition to the ones mentioned before, we had 4 cheetahs, 4 leopards, 4 oryx, 4 Grants, 4 wildebeests, and 30 smaller antelopes and gazelles. We also had several dozen monkeys of various kinds, scores of reptiles, varying from spitting cobras to pythons, and hundreds of birds. Most of the birds were caught in great nets stretched across ravines. These nets, made in Japan, are called "mist nets" and are made in three layers so a flying bird will become entangled between the different thicknesses. The nets are so light that they are almost impossible to see, even from a few feet away. The Boer had found several of them among Schultz's possessions. The monkeys we captured by using the same system I'd learned in South America: baiting them into a food tree and then cutting down the surrounding trees so they were isolated. The snakes were brought in by the natives who could track a snake through the wavy lines they left in soft earth or sand. The track usually led to a hole and after that it was simply a matter of digging. The leopards were caught in box traps baited with a goat. The cheetahs were run down in cars. Bush babies, little monkey-like animals that live in trees, were caught simply by putting out bait of sweet wine mixed with fruit and then collecting them next morning as they lay around dead drunk.

Many of the smaller animals I'd already handled in Switzerland. How long ago that seemed now! It was strange to see them running around wild instead of arriving in Marseilles or Genoa, neatly packaged in crates. I was beginning to appreciate now all the work and time that had gone into getting them to Europe.

We had almost every African animal except lions and buffalo. Wild lions generally have such poor manes that they are worthless for exhibition purposes and lions now breed so readily in captivity that there is no demand for wild stock. Buffalos carry hoof-and-mouth disease which infects domestic cattle and so usually cannot be imported to any country under any conditions.

Finally the time came to put the animals in their transport cages and ship them by rail to Mombasa. The native carpenters working on the cages were very slow and the Boer was impatient to get the animals off his hands. After the cages were finished, I wanted to feed the animals in them for a few days as Willie had suggested but the Boer refused. We had a violent argument and at last the Boer suggested a compromise.

"According to my original contract with Behrend, I had to take the responsibility of loading all the animals on the ship together with their food," he pointed out. "That would mean I'd lose two or three days in Mombasa. If you'll agree to waive that part of the contract, I'll give you the extra time you want here."

I agreed. It seemed a small point and I could imagine what would happen if my kicking, struggling animals were hauled by brute force into strange boxes, nailed up, and left there to thrash themselves to death. I was still young and inexperienced at the time and knew nothing about contracts. I was only concerned with my precious animals.

I allowed the animals a week to become accustomed to the crates and then we started loading. All went smoothly except for the zebras. The men were tired, hot and trying to hurry the business so several zebras got loose. In ten seconds there was no one in the compound; the teeth and hooves of an infuriated zebra stallion are no joke. We were all hanging from trees, the tops of sheds, and the fence. Then the animals started to fight among themselves. Willie de Beer and I jumped into the compound to separate them. One zebra jumped on top of a transport box and from hence to the lorry. I went after him and in the scuffle the zebra kicked me on the right leg. I nearly fainted from the pain while Willie managed to drag the animal into the transport cage.

I went on helping but my leg began to swell and soon it was so painful I could hardly hobble around. But at last the animals were loaded and we drove to the nearest station on the Uganda-Mombasa Line. This is the railroad, by the way, where construction work was held up for three weeks back in '98 because man-eating lions kept killing the workmen.

When the cages were loaded onto flatcars, I said good-bye to Willie and his assistant who had done such a magnificent job over the last four months. I had several African boys with me and it was only a six-hour trip to Mombasa so everything seemed simple from now on. But we hadn't counted on four low bridges. The giraffes' necks stuck up so high that they couldn't go under the bridges so each time the train had to be stopped while the boys and I pulled the animals' necks down and held them in position while the train went through.

By the time we reached Mombasa, my leg was swollen to twice its natural size and I felt weak and feverish. Then I discovered that the ship, a Dutch freighter named *Straat Malacca*, had been delayed for several days.

I rented a yard where the cages could be put in the shade and made sure that the animals had plenty of water for it was stiflingly hot in Mombasa after the cool of the highlands. By now, I could only walk with the aid of a cane and my leg had blown up like a blimp. I couldn't sleep that night and in the morning I sent for a doctor.

After a quick examination, he told me, "You have gangrene. This leg will have to come off."

"I'd rather die," I told him. It would mean the end of all my ambitions to be a collector.

"That's what they all say when they first hear of an amputation," said the doctor briskly. "But you'll get used to the idea soon. The new artificial limbs made since the war are marvelous."

I begged him to wait for twelve hours and see if the swelling wouldn't go down. After warning me that I was risking my life, he consented. He dosed me with sulpha and injected me with enough penicillin to cure a corpse. That was another night I most certainly didn't sleep. I spent the whole night with my leg in a bath of soda, trying to tell myself that it looked and felt a little better. My boys came in at regular intervals to report about the animals and ask for advice. They were a good lot and I was lucky to have them.

The next morning, the doctor took another look at my leg and told me that there was a bare chance it could be saved. I blubbered like a baby at the news. He told me to stay off it until the ship sailed but the next day my boys reported that several of the animals were down with heat prostration. I managed to get some crutches and hobbled to the yard. Two of the cheetahs were sick and the baby elephant was down on his side.

I had them throw coconut matting over the cages and keep them doused with water, day and night. The sick animals slowly recovered, but as a result of my exertions I was delirious with fever for the next twenty-four hours.

The *Straat Malacca* finally arrived and her captain told me that the animals must be loaded immediately as he could waste no time in Mombasa. I was still running a high temperature and kept blacking out at intervals, but I supervised the loading as well as I could, hobbling about on crutches.

The food which the planter had provided for the animals was now swung aboard but I had no time to examine it. A distracted shipping agent was going over the bills of lading and the impatient captain was virtually shoving him off the ship.

"These will have to be signed and sealed by the custom house," he told the captain.

"We can't wait!" roared the captain. "Mail them to this man at Capetown, that's our next point of call."

"Send them air mail!" I shouted to the shipping agent as he went over the side. "I'll need them to get the cargo into Brazil."

The shipping agent nodded and waved. We had already weighed anchor and the ship was moving out of the bay.

I passed out shortly afterwards. Two of the seamen carried me down to my cabin and afterwards very kindly offered to take care of the animals as in my condition I was in no shape to do it myself. I lay on my bunk with my leg soaking in hot Epsom salts and told them what to do. The only animal who absolutely needed my help was the little male rhino who'd gotten rubbed against the side of a crate during loading. He wouldn't let anyone else handle him so I had to rub the sores with ointment. The rest of the animals seemed to be standing the voyage very well, even when we had some heavy seas. The giraffes looked funny balancing with their long necks as the ship rose and plunged.

The fourth day out, I'd gotten up at dawn to check the animals when I noticed something strange about one of the giraffes. The rising sun was hitting him full in the face and his whole

head seemed to have turned chalk-white. I limped over to examine him more closely. By God, there was almost no flesh left
on his face! The white bones were showing plainly, covered
with tatters of skin. I yelled like a madman and some of the
seamen ran up. Together, we got the poor beast's head down.
We were looking at a skull. The flesh must have rotted off
under the skin and the tortured animal had rubbed the skin free
during the night.

We checked the others. One was also very bad—his lips almost
gone and his cheeks half rotted away. The others had the beginning of the same ailment but not in such an advanced form. I
could not understand what obscure disease had struck them.
I knew they were all right when we loaded in Mombasa. The
captain radioed Capetown to have some of the best vets meet
the ship but I was afraid that it would then be too late.

I did what I could for the poor animals and the crew helped
me as best they could. While we were sponging out their
mouths, I found some thick bits of wiry grass lodged in their
lips. Then I pulled out some great thorns. I had carefully
specified, and had it guaranteed in my contract with the Boer,
that only the finest hay be given the giraffes, for I knew that
their mouths were very delicate. In a wild state the giraffes
will graze from the tops of thorn bushes but their long tongues
lick in between the thorns and bring out only the tenderest
leaves. If their fodder is coarse, or is good-and-bad mixed together, the animals cannot separate it.

One of the sailors climbed up to the feeding boxes and
brought me down some of the "hay" which the Boer had provided. It was nothing but thorn bush. The Boer had saved himself a few pounds by having his boys cut thorn bush instead of
providing the hay we'd agreed upon.

I knew now why he'd been so eager to have the contract
changed. Under the new contract I had no time to check the
food when I arrived in Mombasa.

With the help of some of the good-natured seamen, I went
through the stuff, sorting out what little good material there

was in it. The cook also contributed some lettuce, bread, potatoes, and anything else he could find, so I was able to keep the animals alive. Some of the ostriches also were sick. They are very nervous birds and at every port the booms swinging cargo over their heads drove them frantic. I had to hold up one bird's neck constantly with a forked pole so he could breathe. I tried to put his neck in a sling but it kept rolling out. As the bird could not eat or drink, I poured water down his throat. My leg had begun to swell again and I was haunted by the prospect of an amputation.

After two days of this, we arrived in Capetown. Five vets came on board with the pilot. By now, one giraffe was down and another could hardly stand, although the ostrich seemed a little better. The vets looked them over and reported, "We know about cats and dogs but not about giraffes and ostriches." They then charged me seventy pounds for this important information and left the ship.

At least, we could get good, clover hay in Capetown. I purchased several tons and flung the thorn bush over the side. But in spite of everything I could do, both the sick giraffes died that night. I was barely able to save the others.

Now a new problem arose. The dead animals rotted rapidly in the hot sun and had to be disposed of immediately. I wanted to throw them overboard but the port authorities refused. They would have to be taken out to sea and dumped. I had to hire a tug for this unpleasant task and the tug captain charged me 200 pounds. I watched my poor giraffes going out to sea on the deck of that tug and thought how pretty and happy they'd looked four months before, galloping behind their mothers across the open plains.

Now that they had decent food, the other animals recovered rapidly. The day came to sail and I was positive that I could bring the rest of my cargo safely to Rio. Then I received word from the Brazilian consul that he could not approve the cargo until he received the bills of lading from Mombasa. We were to sail at 4 that afternoon, and the papers still hadn't arrived.

The captain spoke to me not unsympathetically but decidedly. "I cannot delay sailing," he said bluntly. "You must off-load your animals. There is nothing else for it."

I had no place to put the animals on shore and it might take months to find another cargo vessel bound for Rio and able to hold my huge shipment. It would mean complete ruin. I pleaded, tried to bribe the captain and did everything I could to prevent the off-loading. The captain simply called to some stevedores and told them to go ahead. When I tried to interfere, he threatened to call the police.

Three hours before sailing, a clerk from the office of the Brazilian consul raced down to the dock waving the bills of lading. They had just arrived. The Mombasa shipping agent had sent them as he promised but by surface mail, not air mail. They had arrived nearly too late.

The ship weighed anchor and put out to sea. I was finally on my way to Rio with my only slightly reduced $100,000 shipment.

# Chapter 9

# Jaguar loose at sea

BEHREND HAD taken care to notify the Rio press that the biggest shipment of African animals in history was arriving so when the *Straat Malacca* steamed into the harbor, we were met by tugs blowing their whistles, shouting crowds on the docks, and public officials in full regalia.

This was the first time giraffes had ever been seen in Brazil and the crowds could not have been more astonished if I'd had a cargo of dinosaurs. The giraffes were so completely tame that I could lead them like domestic horses. So a parade was staged and we started down the main street, the giraffes going first, followed by the other animals in their cages. When it was discovered that the giraffes' necks were too long to pass under the overhead wires, the excited crowd tore the wires down. It was the greatest triumph of my life and made up for all the months of hardship and disappointments that I'd endured.

A group of wealthy men had purchased a pair of the giraffes for the Rio Zoo, a beautiful place and one of the best equipped zoos in the world but possessing no unusual animals. The director was horrified when we charged them 400 contos (about $14,000) for a pair but such crowds came to the zoo as a result that the donors felt they had bought wisely. Thus encouraged, the director bought two of our rhinos. I am happy to say that the rhinos later bred, the second time in history that rhinos have ever bred in captivity, the first breeding taking place at the

149

Brookfield Zoo near Chicago. This success made the Rio Zoo justly famous in international animal circles.

My leg refused to heal and there was a great mass of raw, pulpy flesh from the ankle to the knee. A doctor who examined it gave me some ointment and told me to keep the leg bandaged at all times, but as I was able to walk on it without much trouble I didn't follow his advice too carefully. The leg felt much better and I was sure it would heal within a few days.

Behrend was furious over the death of the two giraffes and held me responsible. "You're a fool and that Boer is a thief," he summed it up. "Anyhow, you should have checked the food before letting it come on board. I don't care whether you were sick or not." I felt he was right for I was still depressed over the loss of my two poor giraffes.

"However, there is a bright side to the matter," Behrend added after some thought. "Although I paid that *verwahrloster lump* for the animals, I did it in pesos through the Argentinian government. The pesos were later changed to English pounds. The English needed the pesos to buy Argentinian beef. The whole payment hasn't gone through. Now that we have the animals, I'll stop payment on the last draft. I can use the death of the two giraffes as an excuse."

I had returned to South America determined to get a complete account of our financial position from Behrend. It seemed to me that we should make a profit of some $40,000 on the African shipment and I wanted to get my share as a reward for all I'd been through. After savage protests, Behrend finally allowed me to look at his books. I couldn't make head or tail out of them. Some of the animals were to be exchanged for others, which in turn were to be exchanged for still others, and the profit on the final deal depended on currency fluctuations, under-the-table arrangements, and what zoo directors in various parts of the world might be willing ultimately to pay. As soon as Behrend had any money, he instantly "invested" it in experimenting with some new bird or animal or started some fantastic scheme like the gorilla project. When the profits (if there were any) came in, they were so scattered in different parts of the world that it was impossible to keep track of them.

After considerable thought, I decided to remain with Behrend a few more months. I was certainly getting experience which would have been impossible to get elsewhere, and I wasn't yet ready to start out on my own. And also, I was only just beginning to understand the currency exchanges which dominate the animal business.

Our remaining rhino, the tame male, had been sold to the Mendoza Zoo and as penance for my sins in Kenya I agreed to ride in the baggage car with the rhino to Mendoza, an overnight trip. I was feeling low; my leg had started hurting again. It was my birthday, and I felt very far from Switzerland and my friends. For consolation I took a gallon jug of wine into the boxcar with me and the rhino. At the last minute, Behrend gave me another for a birthday present. As the train pulled out, some friends rushed up to the platform and presented me with a third jug. After a few drinks, I felt better. The rhino was squeaking to be let out and as he was perfectly tame, I opened the cage. He sniffed at the jug and as a joke, I offered him a drink. To my surprise, he loved it and squeaked for more. Between us, we finished the jug and I opened another.

"Little friend," I said as I gave him the first drink from the new jug. "We are both far from home and our families."

"Squeak!" said the rhino dolefully. We both had another drink.

"Yet things are not as bad as they seem. I might have fallen off an alp in Switzerland or you might have been eaten by a lion."

"Squeak!" agreed the rhino more hopefully.

"You will have a nice home and not run the risk of being killed by a native poacher for your horn or shot by a rich playboy as a trophy. And who knows, someday I may be a famous animal collector!"

"Squeak!" said the rhino happily.

"At all events, let us have another drink."

"Squeak! Squeak! *Squeak!*" agreed the rhino.

The rest of the trip is vague in my mind. I remember singing drinking songs with my arm around the rhino's neck while he squeaked bravely away, taking what might be called the tenor parts while I carried the bass. A few hours before dawn, we opened the third jug and finished that too. I'd never felt better in my life and I'm sure neither had the rhino.

I was trying to teach him the opening steps of a gavotte when the door of the car was suddenly thrown back, letting in a flood of light. We had arrived at Mendoza. Standing on the platform were the town officials, all in formal dress, and behind them the excited populace, cheering madly. They had even brought the town band which struck up a spirited *paso doble*.

"Señor Ryhiner, everyone has come to see this savage rhinoceros from the heart of Africa," shouted the mayor. "We have heard of these creatures, more ferocious than ten Miura fighting bulls. Where is the monster?"

"Little friend, your public waits," I announced, and the rhino and I staggered out into the sunlight. I was still singing while the rhino squeaked bravely away.

The citizens of Mendoza were very nice about the whole affair. A dinner was given for me, the mayor's only stipulation being that I wear his raincoat as during the trip the seat of my trousers had been torn off in some mysterious manner. It was scorching hot and I nearly died in the coat but there was no help for it.

I was awakened early the next morning by a pounding on my bedroom door. I felt as though someone had run a red-hot poker through my temples and my mouth seemed to be full of zoo-cage sweepings. I managed to open the door and there was a group of frantic keepers from the Mendoza Zoo.

"Senhor, something is wrong with the rhino!" the head keeper wailed. "He does nothing but lie on the floor of his magnificent new enclosure, moaning at intervals and drinking great quantities of water."

I was an old hand at this business. I mixed up a concoction

of brandy, tea, the white of an egg and Worcestershire sauce. I drank half of it myself and told the keeper to give the rest to the rhino, explaining it was a mystic concoction taught to me by an old Kibuyu witch doctor on the slopes of Mt. Kenya. An hour later, the relieved keeper told me that the rhino had recovered sufficiently to eat some lettuce and carrots although he still groaned at intervals and went into a fury if anyone slammed a door.

The trip to Mendoza had made my leg much worse. By the time I returned to Buenos Aires, I was in constant pain, day and night. The leg still refused to heal and I could only sleep in snatches.

One morning I was sitting with the leg propped up on a footstool and had managed to doze off for an hour or so. When I awoke, I noticed a curious phenomenon. My leg was covered with little scales about the size of a fingernail, all reared up at right angles to the flesh. I stared at this spectacle and then reached out to touch them. Instantly all the scales snapped down and my leg was as smooth as before.

I sat and waited. Slowly, one after another of the scales lifted themselves upright again. Carefully, I bent over to examine them. Under each scale was a maggot-like worm. When I touched one of the scales, the maggot promptly slammed his trap door into place. I ran my hand along my leg and in a flash my skin was as smooth as it had been before.

I sent for the doctor. When he arrived, the maggots had lifted their doors again and were enjoying the fresh air and light. The doctor took one look and nodded.

"You didn't get those in Africa but over here," he told me. "They're the larvae of a fly that lays her eggs in raw flesh. I told you to keep that leg carefully bandaged. Were you out in the jungles?"

I told him about the trip to Mendoza. Anything might have settled on me in the boxcar that night.

"That's when you got them. Now I'll show you what must be done."

The doctor produced a long, thin pair of forceps and very deftly began plucking out the maggots. He got seven or eight before the rest took alarm and pulled down their doors.

"Get someone to sit beside you and pull them out," he explained. "It's a long job but you'll win in the end."

I hired a Negro boy but he was so rough that I could only stand the pain a few hours at a time. I could still walk on the leg and often went to the Munich Beer Hall where my affliction was a standing joke. The dwarf turned up one evening with a fishing pole and invited the whole group to go fishing with him. "We don't need any bait. Peter will bring the worms," he explained.

Behrend had a shipment of South American animals destined for the European market and he wanted me to go over with them. As I couldn't do any collecting with my leg in such bad shape, I accepted the job. I also hoped that in Europe I might be able to find a doctor who could speed up the process of healing my leg.

The shipment consisted of 8 jaguars, 12 cougars, 3 tapirs, 8 llamas, 6 guanocos, 2 alpacas, 12 capybaras, 200 nutrias, 16 agoutis, 6 rheas, 100 flamingos, 160 macaws, 200 parrots and 300 monkeys. The cargo was valued at $50,000. The nutrias were the worst to handle. They are big, muskrat-like animals with powerful chisel teeth and they chewed their way out of their cages the first day. Then they staged fights up and down the decks. They were terrible animals to catch for they could whirl and bite in a flash, and their big teeth gouged out hunks of flesh. We had already lined their cages with sheet iron but then they chewed through the wire. They screamed all night and when they weren't chewing their way out they were fighting. Several were killed in these combats. I hated them, but there was a big demand for nutrias in Europe. Magazines were full of ads: "Make a fortune raising nutrias in your spare time! Valuable fur! Clean, lovable little pets!" The price of these overgrown rats had jumped from $4 to $150 and Behrend wanted to be in on the bonanza.

We were to sail from Recife, Brazil, and there I found that a ship carrying another of Behrend's animal cargos destined for Europe had gone on a reef in the harbor. None of the cargo, including the animals, could be off-loaded because of the insurance laws covering "general average." This means that before a cargo can be off-loaded, its total value has to be determined so each shipper can take an equal share in possible loss. The man who was traveling with the animals had to go out to the wreck twice a day to feed the poor creatures and had been doing this for three weeks. Finally the general average was computed and I had the animals transferred to my ship. This cargo included three lions (bred in captivity in South American zoos) and a large number of soft-billed birds.

Feeding the soft-bills was more trouble than taking care of all the other animals combined, even those damned nutrias. Behrend had his own soft-bill formula and it contained fifteen different ingredients, such as minced hard-boiled egg, minced lettuce, ant eggs, fruit and ground ox heart. Half the ox heart was served raw and half cooked and then ground. The formula had to be mixed three times a day. I couldn't make up a large quantity at one time because the mixture tended to sour and the steward refused to keep opening the refrigerator locker. I knew where he kept the keys and one day I stole them and sneaked into the locker, carefully closing the door behind me. While I was inside, somebody saw the unlocked door and fastened the hasp. I couldn't get out and the temperature was below freezing. Luckily there was a vegetable locker which was just a little warmer and I sat in there. When I didn't turn up for lunch, the ship was searched and I was dragged out, half frozen.

The fourth day out, I was taking a shower after finishing my chores when one of the crew burst into my cabin door. "A jaguar's loose!" he shouted.

I thought it was a joke, but more seamen came running in and one look at their faces was enough for me. With a towel wrapped around my middle, I raced for the deck. Sure enough, there in the yellow light of the setting sun was a big jaguar stretched out on the afterdeck, licking his paws and obviously enjoying himself.

A jaguar weighs 400 pounds and is as big as a full-grown African lioness. Except for a tiger, they are the most dangerous of the cat family, quick, aggressive, and powerful. This jaguar had been in a cage with a sliding door and the catches that held the door in place had not been securely fastened. The big cat had simply pushed up the door with his paw and walked out.

I wasn't unduly alarmed. The jaguar seemed quiet enough and I knew that most caged animals return to their cages if left alone. They regard the cages as a haven of safety. If no disturbance was made, it was only a matter of time before the cat returned to his cage.

The captain appeared beside me. He was dancing and gesticulating like a madman. "That animal's a menace to my ship!" he screamed. "He'll kill somebody! Shoot him!"

"There's no need for that and besides I haven't a gun," I told him.

"Well, I'm going to shoot him!" bellowed the captain. Turning to a seaman he shouted, "Get a gun!"

"There isn't one on the ship," answered the seaman.

Below the afterdeck where the jaguar was lying was a cabin called the afterhouse and through the windows we could see two men getting ready for dinner; one in his shorts, shaving himself and the other dressing. Before I could stop him, the captain yelled. "Run for your lives! There's a man-eating tiger just over your heads."

Both men bolted out of the cabin, one covered with lather and the other with flying shirt tails. At the sight, the jaguar sprang up and began nervously pacing back and forth.

"He's going to attack!" bawled the captain. "Sound the general alarm! Tell the passengers to barricade themselves in their cabins!"

Within seconds the ship was a madhouse. Men were dashing about armed with fire axes, crowbars and anything else they could find. A Brazilian actress, who was one of the passengers, rushed out and demanded that she be photographed with the jaguar for publicity purposes. A German woman kept sticking her head out of a porthole and screaming hysterically, "Help, he's got me!" causing a fresh panic each time. Two nuns were so fascinated by the cat that they walked up to within a few yards of him and stood staring. "Isn't he lovely, sister?" I heard one say to her companion who answered, "Sweet! And seems so happy to be at liberty!" Finally I had to lead them back to their cabin, respectfully but firmly.

The jaguar was growing increasingly restless with all this turmoil around him. He jumped down from the afterhouse and began pacing the deck. Here he was among the other cages. The monkeys clung to each other, shaking with terror, and the parrots and macaws set up an unearthly squawking. The jaguar batted at them irritably with one paw before passing on. Then he came to a cage full of wood ducks. Here he paused.

The ducks were worth $50 each and there were 300 of them. I shouted and threw everything I could lay my hands on but the jaguar refused to be distracted. With a quick blow, he ripped loose the wire front and sprang into the cage. There were frantic squawks, clouds of feathers, and ducks erupted from the cage. Some flew into the sea, others into the rigging; others skitted across the decks. The jaguar rushed through them, knocking down ducks with quick left-and-right blows. Then he started gorging himself.

This was growing serious. I asked some of the seamen to help me and we tried to drive him back into his cage by shouting and beating on pans. The cat refused to leave his collection of ducks for a long time but finally trotted off carrying a particularly fat drake in his mouth. Instead of going into his cage, he went into the ducks' cage and finished his meal there. There was no way of getting him out and the bird crate was too flimsy to hold him even if we could have nailed boards across the front. Still, even though he had now fed, he needed water. I put a pan of water in his cage, lifted the sliding door, and ran a string from its catch to the bridge. Then I settled down to wait.

The jaguar had gone to sleep in the ducks' crate. The ship was still full of terrified ducks and the sight of these valuable birds finally got too much for me. I gave a seaman the string and told him to drop the door if the cat went inside. Then I started rounding up what was left of the ducks. I got most of them and by juggling the other animals around, emptied a cage. After putting the ducks inside, I went back to the bridge. The first thing I saw was the seaman, fast asleep. The second was the jaguar in the cage, lapping up the water.

As fast as I could without scaring the cat, I tiptoed across the bridge. I was still a few feet from the string when the jaguar started backing out. I gave one bound and jerked the string. Down came the door—on the jaguar's back. He gave an angry snarl and jumped clear, outside the cage. The door slammed into place and the jaguar stood regarding it thoughtfully. Then he sprang back to his position on the afterhouse and lay down. I knew that he'd never go near that cage again.

There was nothing to do now except wait until morning. I sat up all night on the bridge, thinking of another animal collector who had a black leopard that escaped on shipboard. The cat killed one sailor and badly mauled a second before he was recaptured. This big male jaguar was potentially far more dangerous than any leopard. There had to be some way of capturing him. By morning I had a plan.

There was a small room connecting to the afterdeck where the crew kept old rags and some tools. When it was daylight, I opened the door of this room while the jaguar watched me suspiciously. Then, imitating lion tamers I'd seen, I got a chair and by shouting and waving the chair, I finally managed to drive him into the room. I slammed the door shut, feeling very proud of myself.

A few minutes later, the ship's engineer came up and I told him that the jaguar was finally secured.

"In that room?" roared the engineer. "You can't keep him there! I have to get in there to oil the machinery."

The captain came up and joined in the argument. There was no help for it, the door must be opened again.

"I've changed course to head for the Canary Islands," the captain told me. "The radio operator has alerted the port authorities and they'll meet the ship in the harbor with guns. Damn if I ever take a cargo of animals again."

I let the jaguar out and he promptly sprang back to his usual place and sat licking his paws and enjoying the sunshine. Meanwhile, the ship was being deluged with radiograms from all over the world. The AP and UP offered $1,000 for the exclusive story but the captain angrily refused. The chief engineer took a picture of the jaguar sniffing around the cages but the captain said he'd fire him if the man ever tried to sell it. The passengers had quieted down now and the jaguar was a big attraction; he served to break up an otherwise tiresome voyage.

That night the jaguar broke into a cage containing some king vultures, worth $100 each. He killed three and the others flew into the rigging. I got them down later. That brought the total damage he'd done to $12,000. He was worth about $3,000.

The ship was racing at full speed for Las Palmas in the Canary Islands. We arrived early the next morning. The wharfs were black with people, everyone having turned out to meet us. The captain was raging and tried to keep the reporters and photographers from coming aboard but of course that was hopeless. A smart police launch came alongside, and a small army of policemen with Tommy guns and in immaculate white uniforms covered with gold braid boarded us. With them was a man who we were told was the "best shot in the Canary Islands." He, too, was in faultless white duck and carried a handsome sporting rifle.

I hated to see the jaguar shot. But he was vicious and there was no help for it. With the "best shot in the Canary Islands" leading, we approached the afterdeck.

The noise had disturbed the jaguar. We met him coming around the side of a cabin. He stopped and looked at the crowd in astonishment. At that moment, he didn't look like a savage jungle killer but like a frightened and very puzzled animal, wanting desperately to get back to the safety of his cage.

"Shoot, shoot!" screamed the captain. The best shot in the Canary Islands raised his rifle, took careful aim, and squeezed the trigger. Nothing happened. He'd forgotten to cock the gun.

Then everyone shot. At the first blast from the submachine guns, the jaguar gave a convulsive leap into the air and then ran. The police chased him, pouring burst after burst into the frenzied animal. At last, the jaguar sank down and died, riddled with bullets.

Everyone wanted to have his picture taken with the dead jaguar, grinning broadly at the camera and holding a Tommy gun. I felt a little sick. I blamed myself for the whole business, as well I should have. If I'd known what I know now about the big cats, I could have driven the jaguar back into his cage. With the help of a chair and a long pole, it could have been done, even with my bad leg. I've never forgiven myself for this disaster. It was the worst blot on my whole career.

Counting the loss of the jaguar and the damage he had done, our profit on the voyage was already cut by $15,000. But worse was to come. When we arrived in Antwerp, I found that Behrend had sent by air express a large crate containing a single, particularly tough ocelot. Why Behrend had gone to such expense to send a single cat I could not imagine but I included the animal with my other freight.

When the customs men came to inspect the cargo, I showed them around. When we came to the ocelot's cage, we found the whole floor of the cage covered with parakeet feathers and the bloated ocelot sitting in the middle of them, idly toying with a feather like one of the old-time motion picture vamps playing with a flower.

"What does this mean?" demanded the surprised customs man.

I knew well what it meant. Because of psittacosis, parakeets could not be imported into Europe so Behrend had hidden the birds under the floor of the cage, sure that with such a savage animal the customs men wouldn't investigate too closely. As long as the cage was in transit, the cat had been too nervous to do much investigating, but when the cage had been landed, he'd scented the birds and ripped up the floor.

Three thousand dollars' worth of parakeets gone down that ocelot! Fortunately, my presence of mind did not desert me. "Oh, that's a very rare species of ocelot," I said carelessly. "We feed him nothing but parakeets."

The customs man shook his head wonderingly. "The problems you animal dealers have!" he said and passed on. I followed him with a sinking heart. Problems! He didn't know the half of it.

But more was yet to follow. I next discovered that the bottom had dropped out of the nutria market. Fanciers had found that the animals, used to a South American climate, didn't come into pelt at the right time of year so the whole craze had collapsed as suddenly as it had risen. I couldn't give the damn things away. Meanwhile my leg had become so painful that I couldn't walk on it. I was running a high fever and had spells of delirium. Still, the animals had to be cared for and sent off to their various destinations.

My old friend, Van den Bergh of the Antwerp Zoo, agreed to take the animals off my hands temporarily. He put all the nutrias in one big cage where they staged such glorious fights that for the next two weeks they were the zoo's biggest attraction. Meanwhile, I got a room in a hotel and tried to arrange for the shipping of the animals to the different zoos that had ordered them.

I was sitting in my room with my leg up, half out of my head with fever and anxiety, when there was a knock on the door and my brother walked in. He entered with a broad smile at seeing me again but after one look at my face, he instantly became serious.

"What has happened to you, Peter?" he asked anxiously.

Then he saw my leg with all the little scales reared up as my maggots took a deep breath. He gave a startled exclamation and reached out to touch them. Instantly all the scales dropped down into place. My brother leaped back as though he had been burnt.

"God in heaven, what does this mean?" he shouted.

His expression was so funny that I went off into shouts of laughter. My brother stood regarding me a few seconds and then sent for some brandy. After he had given me a stiff swig, he sat down beside me.

"Come now, Peter, tell me what this is all about," he said gravely.

I told him everything. He listened without comment. When I had finished, he said quietly, "There's is a train to Basel in two hours. You are going home with me and we'll get Gilgian to look at that leg." Gilgian was another of my brothers, and a doctor.

"I can't!" I wept. "I have the animals to attend to."

My brother left the room. He returned in a few hours. He had gotten rid of the animals, sending some off to their destinations and persuading Van den Bergh to hold the others for the time being. Then, half carrying me, he got me into a taxi and onto the train for Basel.

He had telegraphed ahead so an ambulance was waiting at the station. I went directly to a hospital. Gilgian was summoned and he listened while I explained about the maggots and how they had to be picked out a few at a time so as not to alarm the others.

"I think I know of a better system than that," Gilgian said briskly when I had finished. He got a can of ether and carefully sprayed my leg. The anesthetic paralyzed the maggots so they could not close their trap doors and Gilgian got them all out in a few minutes. Then he disinfected the holes and gave me a sleeping potion. I slept for the next forty-eight hours. Three days later, my leg was completely well and has never troubled me again, although on my leg from knee to ankle is a great reddish area like a gigantic birthmark.

While I was convalescing in my mother's home, I received a long cable from Behrend. Instead of the savage outburst I expected after the fiasco of the last voyage, he was full of a new scheme. Since 1918, Russia had been closed as an animal market and virtually no Russian animals had appeared in zoos. By some incredible series of negotiations, Behrend had arranged for an exchange of animals with the Moscow Zoo: the animals Van den Bergh was keeping for us in the Antwerp Zoo against snow-leopards, Bactrian camels, bears and Mongolian geese. I was to deliver my animals in Prague, all except those devilish nutrias, which not even the Russians wanted, and pick up the Russian animals in the same city.

It was these miraculous deals which Behrend could still pull out of a hat that kept me with him. No one else in the animal business could perform such tricks and all my resentment to-wards the old swindler disappeared in admiration. I cabled Behrend that I would leave at once and in spite of my family's protest, took a train to Antwerp to collect my animals.

I arrived in Prague without trouble and the Russian animals were there as promised. A few days were needed to complete the transfer and I stayed in a small hotel, doing a little sight-seeing and a little drinking. One evening an elderly couple came to my room. The woman spoke a little German and she explained their problem.

Several years before, their son had escaped from Czecho-slovakia and was now living in France. He had managed to have a letter smuggled through to his parents, saying that he could meet them near the Czech border and take them to Paris. But they must let him know where and when they would make the attempt. They had no way of getting a letter out. Would I take the letter and mail it when I was outside of Czechoslovakia?

I told them that of course I would, stuck the letter in my in-side pocket, and after listening to their hysterical thanks, forgot about the matter. The next day, I dropped in on the Swiss consul. During our conversation, I happened to mention the letter. He instantly looked grave.

"How do you know that these people weren't *agents pro-vocateurs?*" he asked. "Such agents are often used by the Soviet.

When you reach the border with your animals, you may be arrested. I'd burn that letter immediately."

I was tempted, but the couple didn't seem like *agents provocateurs* and I decided to take the chance. I left Prague with the Russian animals and we traveled to the border by rail, the letter still in my inside coat pocket. At the border, the customs men cleared my cargo through without trouble. I'd forgotten about the letter and was about to re-enter the train when two iron-faced men in plain clothes came up and showed me their identification cards. They were members of the secret police.

"We are arresting you as a foreign spy," one of the men told me curtly.

If ever I cursed myself as a fool, it was then. There was no use bluffing; the letter was in my pocket and I was caught. I put my hand inside my coat to hand it to them and my fingers encountered a pack of pictures of nude women I always carried with me. Behrend had warned me long before never to be without a good set.

"If you have trouble with customs, always hand them a set of dirty pictures," he advised. "It gives them something to seize and keeps them occupied for hours while you get the animals across."

I turned over my collection to the two men. They accepted them with considerable astonishment and began to leaf through the pictures. The policemen burst into shouts of delighted laughter. They called over the customs men who were equally fascinated. The train had begun to move and I quietly stepped aboard as it pulled out of the station. The last I saw of the dread secret police and the customs officials, they were all clustered around my pictures, giggling like schoolgirls and nudging each other in the ribs.

Later, I found that suddenly accusing a foreigner of being a spy is a favorite gambit of the secret police. The man is often frightened into revealing something incriminating. It would certainly have worked with me for I was on the point of handing them the letter when I happened to touch the pictures. I don't believe now that the letter was a trick, or that the old couple were anything but what they appeared to be. I mailed the letter a few days later from Switzerland.

We made a good, although not startling, profit on the Russian animals, the Moscow Zoo having driven a pretty shrewd bargain, but as a prestige affair it was most important. Zoo directors realized that the fabulous Lothar Behrend still had his old magician's touch and the publicity we received was worth far more than the actual cash. Papers all over the world ran the story and a few weeks later Behrend cabled me again. The Maharajah of Mysore wanted to exchange some tigers against some European swans and purebred Alsatians and bulldogs. In addition, I was to pick up a cargo of Indian animals which an agent of Behrend's had been collecting. Behrend also hoped that I could unload the nutrias on some unsuspecting Orientals. "Tell those *kindlicher* Indians what sweet, lovable little animals nutrias are," he urged me. "Explain how they'll make a fortune out of the hides. Tell them anything, but get rid of those *verfluchter* nutrias before they ruin us." I promised to do my best. A week later, I sailed for India.

# Chapter 10

# India and tigers

I HAD an assistant on this voyage to India, a German count. He had never even had a pet frog. I'd run an ad in the Antwerp newspaper and this man answered it, wearing an elegant double-breasted suit and Homburg hat. Mainly as a joke, I sent him to the railroad station to fetch some Bactrian camels I'd ordered. Still in his faultless getup, he led them back through the streets of Antwerp. I still didn't like the man but one evening I found him playing the mouth organ to a sick tapir. The tapir loved the sound and recovered, partly, I seriously believe, to the soothing effects of the music. So I decided to take him.

We arrived in Mysore without trouble and here, at last, I was able to dispose of those nutrias. The Indians were fascinated by the creatures and I told them a long story about what charming pets they made and how valuable their pelts were. I also sold for a good profit some other animals I'd brought over. Altogether, the trip was most successful.

Mysore is a beautiful city. The count and I stayed at the Mysore Hotel, a magnificent building resembling an old palace, but with few modern conveniences. There is a long terrace where we had our drinks in the evening and we could look up a long, straight street shaded by giant banyan trees to the distant hills where the rajah had his summer palace. Near the hotel is a park with lovely water gardens—the water flowing

over marble steps—which keeps the air cool and fresh even on
hot days. The park and the rajah's palace were designed by a
German architect. He did a splendid job, for it looks very
Indian.

I first went to see Behrend's Indian agent who was supposedly
making the big collection of rare mammals, birds, and reptile
that I was to take back to B.A. I had some trouble locating him.
He spent his nights throwing big parties with Behrend's money
in Bangalore, which is famous for its night life, and was unconscious during the day. He had done nothing about getting
any animals and was quite frank about the whole affair. "Of
course I'm living like a rajah and doing nothing to earn it," he
told me cheerfully. "If that fool in Argentina is willing to keep
sending me money, why not?" I had to admit that this was
logical reasoning. One of the most mysterious sides of Behrend's character was his willingness to send large sums to unknown people while he grudged me every peso. I cabled him
what was happening but his only answer was to tell me to mind
my own business. He had often pulled off great coups by trusting to unknowns: in Prague, he had trusted completely to the
honesty of the Moscow Zoo director, and he was positive that
he could tell from a man's letters if the man was sincere. I said
nothing more but arranged by cable with the European zoos
(who hadn't as yet paid for the South American and Russian
shipments) to send the money to me instead of to Behrend. As
I was Behrend's partner, I was legally entitled to receive the
money, although in the past, all payments had been made direct to him. Besides I'd still gotten no return on the 40,000
Swiss francs I'd invested in the concern. I also kept the money
that I'd made on the sale of the nutrias and the other animals.
This gave me a working capital.

I delivered my swans and dogs to the palace. The rajah was
a fine-looking old gentleman and an expert on animals. He had
one of the largest private zoos in the world. Later, I strolled
about the palace grounds. There were three different stables,
one for horses, one for elephants, and one for dromedaries. The

horse stable had 250 box stalls and each horse had five grooms. All the grooms were in uniform. In the tackrooms were saddles inlayed with gold and silver. I've never seen anything like it— before or since.

The tigers hadn't yet been caught but I was prepared for that; for once, Behrend had warned me in his cable. The rajah told me that I could stay at the hotel or go out with his trappers and naturally I chose the latter alternative. Before we started out, I visited the Mysore animal market which is very fine indeed. An old man in a dirty turban and a ragged dhoti began following me about, pointing out some of the rarer birds and animals to my intense irritation until I discovered that he really knew what he was talking about.

"Would you like to work for me?" I asked him. Fortunately he knew English, which is one of my languages.

"That was my hope, sahib," answered the man respectfully.

This was Subrati and that was the beginning of a curious relationship which I think is unknown in other parts of the world. Subrati was my servant but he was also my father, my friend, my instructor and, in some respects, my child. A bond developed between us that has continued ever since.

With Subrati's help, I purchased a number of small birds and animals. I sent these to Behrend under the care of the count. Now that I had Subrati, I didn't need the count, for which I was thankful. He was conscientious and a good worker, but always extremely stiff and formal. I was convinced that he'd never really understand the animal business. Later, as the result of a cable from Behrend, I found out how wrong I was.

The rajah sent out two trappers after the tigers with a retinue of apprentices, servants, assistants and trackers. Subrati and I tagged along with them. Both of the trappers were experts, their profession having been handed down from father to son for many generations. I'd have no more thought of interfering with them than I would have told the captain of a ship what course to set.

Tigers are trapped for many reasons: sometimes merely to

get rid of a dangerous nuisance, sometimes to provide "bagged" animals for a big tiger shoot, sometimes (in the old days) for arena fights when they were pitted against buffalo, packs of dogs, or elephants. Today, they are trapped mainly to sell or exchange for other animals.

The trappers maintained a network of communications with outlying villages and knew what tigers were in the vicinity and where they were to be found. Unlike lions who live in small bands, tigers are solitary animals but each tiger has a fairly well-defined "beat," generally following the same trails and drinking from the same pools. Lions are polygamous and a male tiger seems to have no regular mate. When he scents a female in heat, he will leave his beat to breed her and then return, taking no further interest in her or the cubs. They are about the same size as lions, both animals weighing about 500 pounds, although the tiger is slightly longer, a big male reaching ten feet counting the tail. There is no question which is the better fighter. A tiger will always beat a lion unless the tiger is sick or much smaller.

We were going after a special tiger. An old goatherd living near a small village had noticed that a tiger passed his flock every evening at the same time. The tiger never bothered the goats or the man and after several months, a sort of friendship grew up between them. The tiger began to pass closer and closer to the shepherd and, lonely and bored, the man encouraged the animal. Finally, one evening the tiger, apparently in a playful mood, came right up to the herder. It jumped on the man, knocked him down, and began to carry him about in his mouth like a cat with a mouse. He finally set the man down and went on his way, but the goatherd was mad with fear and badly clawed. He refused to graze his herd until the tiger was gone and the villagers were equally terrified. The rajah had decided to kill two birds with one stone and sent his trappers to get this tiger for me.

The trappers had no trouble learning the tiger's "beat" from the villagers and they set about digging a pit, but a pit of a very special nature. It was fifteen feet square and twenty-four feet deep. At one end of the pit was a tree and a buffalo calf was tied to this tree for bait. A buffalo is always used as the domestic cow is regarded as sacred. Then the pit was surrounded by a stockade five feet high, except in the section near the tree, which was made fifteen feet high. The trap works like this: a tiger, hearing the bleating of the calf, approaches the pit. He can hear and smell the calf so he jumps over the stockade. Down he plunges into the pit and is caught.

I waited ten days for the tiger, staying in a dak bungalow near the village. The time passed pleasantly enough as there was so much new to see. I went out with some of the assistant trappers and they showed me the bird and animal life. I saw leopards, bears, hyenas, wild dogs, sambur, thar (wild goat), spotted deer, barking deer, wild pigs, jungle cats, leopard cats, porcupines and jackals. Flocks of parrots flew through the trees, brilliant kingfishers darted over the streams, and the gray jungle fowl (the ancestor of our domestic chickens) strutted through the jungles. I cursed myself as a fool for not bringing along a guide to the birds. Many were completely unknown to me and although the Indians knew them all, they did not know the European names.

The pit was checked daily and one morning I was turned out of bed with the news that the tiger had been caught. I pulled on my clothes and followed one of the assistant trappers to the pit. A huge crowd had gathered from the village to see the "man-eater" as he was called and the rajah's servants had a hard time keeping the people back. When I fought my way through the press, I saw that stout poles had been laid across the stockade to form a cover over the pit. A hole had been left in the center and, walking over the cover, I looked down at the tiger.

He was the maddest tiger I'd ever seen. I couldn't judge his size for he was crouched at the bottom of the pit, looking up and snarling. While I watched, he suddenly made a bound towards me. He came shooting up like a rocket and in spite of myself I fell over backwards. Later, we found his claw marks within a foot of the top of the pit. I'd wondered why the trappers had insisted on digging such a deep pit but now I knew. A tiger can easily jump over twenty feet, straight up.

The trappers told me that the tiger would have to be left in the pit for several days to quiet down and learn to eat in captivity before moving him to a transport cage. How they were going to get that raging demon into a transport cage, I couldn't imagine, but I left everything in their hands. Water was lowered into the pit through the hole in the "lid" and then, after twenty-four hours, a dead goat dropped in. After the tiger had eaten three goats on three successive nights, the trappers announced that the time had come to transfer him to the transport cage. I looked forward to this operation with considerable interest.

The trappers went about the job in a very businesslike manner. First, a hole was cut in the side of the stockade just big enough to fit the door of a transport cage. The cage was dragged into place and lashed securely to the stockade, the greatest care being taken to make sure that the cage fitted exactly in place. Then the sliding door was raised and a man stationed beside it. I noticed that in the back of the transport cage a small hole about a foot square had been cut—for no reason that I could see, but I didn't ask questions. Animal men don't like to be bothered with questions at a time like this.

The next problem was to get the tiger up on a level with the stockade. Scores of men began bringing baskets of earth which they dumped into the pit through the hole in the "lid." As the pit filled up, the tiger rose higher and higher. Soon he was leaping against the lid with a series of crashes that shook the whole structure, although it looked solid enough to hold a bull elephant. Finally the pit was filled level with the bottom of the stockade and we could hear the tiger raging around inside but he made no attempt to enter the cage.

This didn't seem to bother the trappers in the slightest. One of them called over a little ginger-colored dog no bigger than a fox and pointed to the hole in the center of the lid. The dog jumped on the lid, trotted over to the hole, and crouched down, watching the tiger below him. Suddenly he dropped through the hole.

Scratch one dog, I thought to myself. All hell burst out inside. The dog was barking and the tiger hissing and snarling. Then I heard the tiger charging. He must have gone like a flash of striped lightning but an instant later the little dog came flying out the hole in the back of the transport cage. There was a crash as the tiger charged in after him and the whole cage shook. Instantly the man stationed by the cage slammed the door shut and we had him. I wouldn't have had that dog's job for all the wealth in Mysore.

A team of bullocks dragged the transport cage to my bungalow and the trappers departed to get the next tiger. I didn't go with them. Now that the tiger had been caught, Subrati's and my work was just beginning.

I was mortally afraid that the tiger would break one of his long canine teeth for he grabbed the bars in his jaws and worried them with all his strength. He also flung himself against the bars with such a terrible desperation that it seemed impossible that any animal could stand the shock of such blows without crippling himself. He didn't eat for two weeks and I was frantic, even though the trappers had warned me that a captive tiger would often fast for amazing periods and it didn't seem to do him any harm. I was glad that he'd been well fed in the pit before making the transfer. Those trappers certainly knew their business.

The trappers returned in three weeks with another tiger, the female the rajah had promised. I now had a pair but Behrend had cabled me to get as many tigers as possible. Tigers, unlike lions, do not breed readily in captivity so there is always a demand for them from zoos and circuses. They bring about $3,500, the small Sumatran tigers being somewhat less valuable and the great Siberians, who often weigh more than 600 pounds, bringing as much as $10,000 a pair.

The trappers, having fulfilled their part of the bargain, left me, to my real regret. Never have I seen men for whom I had more respect. I was now on my own. I established a compound at the village as my headquarters and settled down to the job of trapping tigers. I could trap as many as I wished, for the big cats are regarded as a dangerous nuisance because of the destruction they do to cattle. Since building such huge pits was too much for me and I didn't have a trained dog I decided to use box traps such as those I'd used in South America for cougars and in Africa for leopards.

I traveled about, announcing that I was in the market for tigers. Nearly every native village has its professional hunters, called shikari, and although many of these men are frauds and none were as good as the rajah's trappers, they were of great help to me. However, instead of leaving everything to the trappers, I was forced to learn something about the business myself. Without Subrati, I'd have been lost. Not only did he translate for me, but he also checked the trappers and in many cases directed the trapping himself.

We didn't rely completely on the traps. Occasionally a sportsman would shoot a female tiger and then find that she was a nursing mother. When this happened, the natives would bring us word and we'd organize a big beat in the area, hoping to find the cubs. As the cubs were hungry and inclined to wander, we usually succeeded. I got six cubs in this way and raised them on a bottle. They were very tame and playful, although I admit one bit me through the hand while I was romping with him. But it was an accident; he didn't mean any harm. The cubs play very roughly with each other and it's hard for them to understand how delicate a human being is.

Locating the tigers' "beats" was not as hard as I'd expected. Tigers leave scratch marks on trees to warn others away from their territory and they also scent certain places in the area with their urine and musk. The odor is very strong and even a man can easily smell it after some experience. A far more serious problem was getting them to eat after capture, for with the box traps I wasn't able to keep them in a pit for the first few

days until they had quieted down. I covered the front of the
cages with mats so the animals would be as quiet as possible.
Either Subrati or I stood guard over them night and day as the
villagers loved to torment the prisoners to see them rage and
hurl themselves against the bars. I also had the bars put closer
together so the tigers couldn't get their jaws between them and
break their teeth biting the unyielding metal.

When the tigers began to quiet down, I gradually removed
the mats, a little each day. At first, I offered them food only at
night but when they ate readily I fed them in the evenings and
then during the day. In a wild state, tigers are largely nocturnal
and do not eat during the daylight hours but in captivity it's
convenient to have them able to feed at all times.

In all accounts that I've read of tiger shooting or capturing,
the tigers are always described as "ferocious man-eaters." I did
get one man-eater—anyhow, a tiger ate a man and I caught a
tiger in the same vicinity. An old farmer had fallen into the
habit of sitting outside his hut in the evening and smoking a pipe
before going to bed. One evening his family who lived in the
hut with him noticed that grandfather hadn't come in. When
they went out to see what had happened to him, there was his
pipe lying on the ground but the old fellow had vanished.
There were tiger pug marks in the soft dust but no signs of a
struggle and there had been no outcry. Apparently the tiger
had come up behind the man, killed him instantly, and carried
him off. The farmer probably never knew what hit him.

Subrati and I put up our box traps in the neighborhood and
baited them with live goats. As tigers are on the prowl only
at night, there was no use leaving the goats in the traps during
the day so their owners took them away each morning and then
put them back in the evening.

One man was leading his goat to the trap when he heard a
noise behind him. Looking around, he saw the tiger following
him about ten yards away. The man and the goat both began
to walk faster. So did the tiger. Then the man and goat began
to trot. So did the tiger. They reached the trap and both the

man and the goat rushed inside and slammed the door shut behind them. The furious tiger prowled about all night, trying to get at them through the bars, but when dawn came he finally gave up and went away.

After that experience, I had to hire another man with a goat as the first fellow flatly refused to do any more tiger baiting. The new man was an old chap but went about the whole business very methodically. One evening after he'd tied the goat inside the trap, he turned around and there was the tiger watching him. Instead of running, the man carefully closed the trap so the tiger couldn't get the goat and then climbed a tree. He stayed there all night while the baffled tiger nearly tore the trap apart trying to reach the goat.

I asked him why on earth he'd shut the cage as the whole purpose of the business was to catch the tiger. "But sahib, that's a five-rupee goat!" the old fellow protested indignantly. Apparently at the last moment his heart failed him and he couldn't see a valuable goat destroyed. After this experience, Subrati bought the goats himself.

We caught a tiger a few days later in a goat-baited trap. He looked just like any other tiger but the natives were confident that he was the man-eater. Perhaps he was. Certainly no other natives were killed in the district after we caught him.

Getting a tiger out of the box trap, into a transport cage and then into the compound is a terrific task. It means days of dragging the heavy transport cages over jungle trails, down ravines and across rivers. The transport cages were crude affairs made of great logs often tied together with vines and difficult to move. The captive had to be kept dry in case of rain and never exposed to the hot sun. If he became too upset, he would go on a hunger strike. After six weeks in the compound, he could be transfered to the shipping crate. Then came the problem of moving him by truck to Mysore, preparatory to embarkation.

Tigers, like all wild cats, are extremely susceptible to "cat distemper" and should be inoculated against it. As each continent has its own strain of cat distemper, a tiger inoculated with Indian vaccine can still get distemper from an alley cat while the ship is passing through Suez or from a dealer's cage after he has arrived in New York. Giving an infuriated tiger an injection is not easy. If the injection is not given properly, an abscess forms under the cat's skin causing endless trouble, and the animal often goes lame. I usually had to give the injections myself because vets seem to be shockingly nervous about giving an injection to a tiger. They usually just jam the needle in anywhere, squirt in the vaccine, and then run. Such an injection does more harm than good.

Tigers are curious beasts and it's difficult to understand the workings of their minds. My "man-eater" was sent on to Mysore where he was put in a large cage while I went ahead with my trapping. When I went to see him, I found the poor animal in great pain. I'd given instructions to have a tree trunk tied to the side of the cage so he could sharpen his claws on them. Unless tigers have an opportunity to do this the claws often grow too long and, as they are curved, enter the pad of the foot. The "man-eater" had two claws that grew at a slight angle and even with the tree trunk he couldn't wear them down. They had gone into the pads and an infection had started. It was a horrible sight . . . the wounds had become gangrenous and were full of maggots. Subrati and I rigged up a "squeeze cage," a cage with one movable side that can be pushed in so the animal is held helpless. I cut out the claws and doctored the infection with disinfectant. I hate to use a squeeze cage. It drives the animal frantic and he is hopelessly intractable afterwards but in this case there was no other solution. One treatment wasn't enough so we went back the next day, I sick at having to go through the miserable business of squeezing the raging animal between the two planks, tying him in position, and then operating in spite of his screams of pain. To my amazement, the tiger came up to the bars and stuck out his sore foot through the cleaning slot that ran under the bars. Although I must have hurt him, he allowed me to work on the foot without protest. He could easily have reached out with the other paw while I was working but he lay there like a big house cat watching while I cleaned and dressed the wound. After that, whenever he saw me coming with the medical kit, he'd lie down and put his paw out for treatment. He was not tame, however. Except for medication he was as savage as any of the other tigers.

Although tiger trapping is supposed to be dangerous, there was only one time when we found ourselves in a ticklish situation. On visiting the traps one morning, we found three tiger cubs in one trap. Delighted, Subrati and I ran up to examine them when there came a blood-curdling roar and the mother rushed out of the underbrush. We ran for our lives, each going in a different direction. Having chased us away, the mother returned and marched up and down around the trap, pausing to lick the cubs inside and purr over them. I'm sorry to admit that she had to be shot by a planter friend; there was absolutely no other way to collect the cubs or even to get close enough to the trap to liberate them.

After four months' trapping, we'd gotten eight tigers as well as some other small animals and birds, so we returned to Mysore with our catch. This lot, together with whatever Behrend's Indian agent had managed to collect, would make a nice shipment. I intended to send Subrati off to B.A. with the cargo while I stayed in India collecting. Behrend had wired, asking especially for as many young elephants as possible, and I hoped that the Indian agent had managed to pick up at least a few from the lumber camps where scores of domesticated elephants are employed in the teak forests.

We arrived in Mysore to find matters in a hell of a mess. The Indian agent—actually the man was a Persian and an Indian only by adoption—had continued to do absolutely nothing except spend Behrend's money until at last Behrend had sent him a blistering cable and threatened to cut off his funds. Then the man had gone to the nearest snake charmer, bought half a dozen cobras, put them in rickety crates that wouldn't hold a palsied

Pekinese, and sent them by air to the Rome Zoo as part of an exchange program Behrend had worked out from B.A. Now no collector ever buys snakes from a street snake charmer; the reptiles nearly always have their fangs extracted which means that they won't eat and they almost certainly have a mouth rot, for pulling out the fangs leaves raw sockets which immediately infect. Also, no one in his right mind ships cobras—with or without fangs—except in an absolutely snake-proof box.

The plane carrying the cobras was over the Mediterranean when the pilot noticed something weaving about his head. He glanced up and saw a cobra with spread hood reared over him. The man was afraid to stir but the co-pilot frantically radioed Rome to have someone from the zoo meet the plane. They flew the last 1,000 miles with the cobra still in the cockpit, the snake rearing up and hissing every time either of them made a move. When the plane finally landed, both pilots were a wreck. The keeper from the Rome Zoo easily caught the snake with a noosed pole.

At first, the airlines even wanted to ban all shipments of poisonous snakes. This would have been a major disaster for collectors as snakes are very delicate, highly susceptible to changes in temperature, and many die on a long sea voyage. Finally they relented but insisted that collectors sign a release against all accidents. This shot up the cost of shipping poisonous snakes to a staggering amount and was all the fault of that damn agent.

This was only the beginning of my troubles with the agent. Fortunately, I had a partial hold over the man as I knew of a special deal in which he was engaged that was strictly illegal. Emigrants from India to South America are not allowed to take any money out of the country, so these people would turn over their rupees to the agent and then receive local currency when they arrived in South America. Of course, the agent charged them for the service and in addition gave the emigrants exchange according to the legal rates while actually obtaining black-market exchange rates for himself.

I'd spent the money I'd gotten from the sale of the nutrias

during my four months of tiger catching. The European zoos had sent me small sums on account for the South American and Russian cargos but I didn't have enough to ship my tigers and other animals to B.A.

Zoos frequently do not pay C.O.D. for animals. The payments may be spread over months and often part of the payments may be in other animals which the zoos do not need. These animals must then be sent to other zoos or to local dealers who in turn make other arrangements. As a result, the final payments may cover a period of years.

As Behrend refused to send me money except in small sums, I finally demanded that the agent turn over some of the money he was stealing from Behrend. He retorted, "If you try to sue me, it will only lead to endless litigation and besides you know what a foreigner's position is in our courts."

This was the reply that I'd expected. I replied, "True enough, but I'm stuck here with six tigers and 200 other animals and they'll die on my hands unless I get money. Unless you give me enough to ship them, I'll report you to the police for the emigrant swindle."

The agent knew that I wasn't bluffing and grudgingly gave me a few thousand rupees. I thought that I'd won, but he got his revenge later.

I was still trying to find a ship bound for B.A. that would accept my cargo when Subrati, through the grapevine among animal men, found that there were three baby elephants for sale in Tripura. I flew up there, leaving Subrati in charge of the animals.

The elephants were owned by the lovely young maharani of the district. I went to the palace with five rickshaws . . . one to ride in and the rest for style. The maharani received me in the throne room with her advisors. Negotiating for elephants took about three hours. During the discussions, the maharani played with her pet dwarf. As she took no part in the conversation, I supposed that she didn't understand English but when a price was finally agreed upon, she asked me in perfect English if I'd like to see the crown jewels. I assured her that it would be a great honor so she sent the dwarf as my guide. He turned out to be a smart little fellow and a great conversationalist. He showed me several million dollars' worth of gems, all carefully watched by armed guards. Why anyone who owned all that wealth should spend so long striking a bargain over three elephants, I can't imagine.

My next problem was how to get the elephants to Mysore. I'd intended to ship them by rail but at the last minute found that I couldn't get them through Pakistan. Finally, I resolved to fly them out. As far as I knew, elephants had never been flown before but I saw no reason why it couldn't be done.

After a lot of trouble, I finally found an ex-R.A.F. pilot who had an old York cargo plane and would fly anything anywhere for a sum. He had an Indian co-pilot to make it legal for an Englishman to be conducting a business in India and seemed to know his job.

When the time came for the babies to be loaded into the York, they refused to move. Their mothers were with them and both mothers and babies were weeping over the separation, actual tears running down their cheeks. I won't attempt to excuse my part in the business except to say that I'd already paid for the plane and the babies and I just couldn't take the loss.

None of us could move the babies and at last one of the mahouts said, "Sahib, stand aside. We will manage it." The mahouts gave their orders and the mothers pushed their babies into the plane, still crying bitterly. It was the most remarkable example of men's power over animals that I have ever seen in my life.

I got in with the babies, the doors were closed, and the plane took off. As soon as she tilted up to rise, all three elephants and I were thrown into the back of the plane, landing in a heap on top of each other. The babies weighed about 600 pounds each and with that weight in the tail, the plane couldn't level off. For a while it was touch and go whether or not we'd crash. Luckily the pilot was finally able to get control. We arrived in

Mysore without any more trouble but when the elephants and I disembarked, I noticed that the native co-pilot was pale and shaken.

"It was a close call on that take-off," I said smiling.

"That didn't bother me," he replied sadly. "But when I heard what language the Englishman was using, I thought we'd all be struck by fire from heaven."

When I returned, I found that Behrend had been sending the agent furious cables and had again threatened to cut off funds. So the wretch had finally ordered four baby elephants from eastern Pakistan, to be shipped by rail, but their boxcar had been left in the sun at a siding all one afternoon and they had died. The agent had another elephant, a little female, but she was so sick that I refused to handle her. This drove him into a fury. Naturally he wanted to turn the animal over to me so that if she died, I'd be responsible and he could subtract her value from the money he owed Behrend. I told him to get a vet to look at the poor little thing, although I knew she was beyond saving. He continued to insist that I take her and then went into a fury. "You are a rajah, sahib, in your country or you couldn't afford to come over here!" he shouted. "Therefore, you can afford to make up my loss, and don't forget that if I went to the United States where you hope to sell these elephants, I would be laughed at because of my dark skin." It was impossible to follow this kind of reasoning, so I left him screaming and went back to my hotel.

In the next two weeks Subrati and I managed to collect seven baby elephants, all of them brought in either by plane or rail from various parts of India. My original three had become quite reconciled to their new life and were very tame. They ran around the compound like dogs and our only problem was to keep them from getting too near the tiger cages. We also had the baby tigers who needed a romp every day, so we were constantly busy. Only one of the elephants caused us any trouble . . . a little female from Tripura named Gertrude. She was the meanest, nastiest, foulest-tempered little fiend I ever saw. She'd butt the other babies and torment the little tigers who were tied to stakes in the compound. She fought like a fury when we caught her, and specialized in sulking. Baby elephants are generally the nicest of all animals but Gertrude was certainly an exception. I looked forward to putting her on a ship and sending her off to a zoo.

While driving back from the railroad station one afternoon, my taxi was held up by a policeman and a little boy rushed over to the car and offered me a pariah dog puppy. These pariah dogs are found all over India and although they have some value as scavengers, they are also a menace. A pack of them will often drag down a sheep or a goat and they have even been known to kill children. They are simply mongrels—domestic dogs gone semiwild—and of no value but this little fellow was particularly appealing. He wagged his tail hopefully at me and looked so lonely and eager to please that I gave the kid a rupee for him. When I arrived at the compound, Subrati took one look at my new purchase and then groaned, "Do we not have enough animals now without dogs which are unclean and I am forbidden to touch?" The pup wasn't weaned and I had to feed him every two hours with an eyedropper, day and night. But Ali, as I named him, was the nicest pet I've ever had. He was full of fun and used to play with the elephants and even the baby tigers. Gertrude hated him, as she did everybody, but Ali never seemed to realize it. He ran up to her on their first meeting and Gertrude picked him up in her trunk and slung him as hard as she could across the compound. Luckily, Ali lit on a pile of hay and came dancing back, evidently thinking this was a new game, but I interfered. The next time he might not happen to land on some hay.

I was lucky enough to find a steamer sailing from Madras bound for B.A. She was the *Betty Ryan*, owned by an English family, but of Argentinian registry. The ship was due to anchor in the river early the next morning and sail at 10 o'clock the same evening—ample time for me to get the animals aboard.

Subrati had his exit permit from India ready so he could go with the cargo to B.A. while I was planning to continue trapping in India. I had the bills of lading, export permits, and all the rest of the papers required. I walked back to my hotel that evening at peace with the world.

When I reached the hotel, I found it surrounded by police cars. I thought there'd been a riot and rushed inside. The police were talking to the hotel clerk and I asked what had happened.

"You know well what has happened!" shouted a policeman. "You poisoned a valuable elephant!"

The agent was there. The little female elephant he had was dead and he claimed I had poisoned her. "In front of me and my servants, this man said, 'The elephant is sure to die,'" the agent bellowed. "Now she is dead. How could he have known she was going to die if he didn't have a hand in her death?"

"True, very true," agreed the police, gravely shaking their heads.

There was even more damning evidence than that. A post mortem had been performed on the elephant and traces of arsenic had been found in her stomach.

"Search this man's rooms and you will find that he has arsenic!" trumpeted the agent. The police rushed to my rooms. Ali put up a spirited defense but he was overpowered and crawled back to me, limping from a kick. To everybody's surprise, no arsenic was found.

Although I didn't know it at the time, arsenic is a standard drug for the treatment of sick elephants. When the baby elephant had collapsed and couldn't stand, the agent had finally called in a vet. The man had given the baby a dose of arsenic, hoping to save her. Anyone working with elephants carries some of the drug and the agent was sure that I'd have some— which would, of course, have convicted me. He overestimated my knowledge of elephants.

Even though no arsenic had been found, I was dragged to the police station with Ali under my arm. The ship was arriving the next day and I was frantic. The police chief listened to my story thoughtfully. Then he said, "It seems unlikely that you would want to poison an elephant that you could sell for a large sum in South America. If you will post a bond for the elephant's value, I will let you go."

There was nothing else to do. I posted the bond and returned to the hotel. At least, everything was ready for loading on the *Betty Ryan* the next day and nothing more could go wrong.

# Chapter 11

# The busiest
# day of my life

In ADDITION to the 10 elephants and 6 tigers, I also had 4 leopards, 7 bears (sloth and Himalayan), 6 Negali antelope, 4 black buck, 40 monkeys, 3 pythons, 4 cobras, a pair each of fishing cats and leopard cats. I also had 300 birds, including sarus cranes, shama thrushs, green hunting cissas, and giant and lesser hornbills. This made quite a shipment but I had everything arranged and I was sure that Subrati could deliver the lot to B.A. without accident.

My only fear was that the ship might be delayed. I was up before dawn and hurried to the wharfs. There, thank God, was the *Betty Ryan* steaming into the harbor. I went out to her in a tug and talked to her captain. He was a friendly fellow and rather pleased than otherwise at the prospect of such an unusual cargo. Everything was going smoothly and I returned to the docking area to make final arrangements for loading the animals.

The customs officer asked to see my shipping order. I explained that the cargo had been cleared through the Argentinian consul.

"Then ask him to issue you a shipping order. Until I have that, the cargo cannot enter the docking area," the officer told me.

I went to the embassy. The consul agreed that the cargo had

been cleared but the shipping order had been sent from Argentina and hadn't arrived as yet.

"But what will I do?" I demanded.

"We can only hope it will arrive before the ship sails," said the consul.

I was still arguing with the consul when Subrati rushed in.

"Sahib, the man who supplied food for the elephants won't let us take them out of the compound until we have paid his bill."

This was easily managed as I had a letter of credit drawn against the shipment. Begging the consul to let me know the instant that the shipping order arrived, I hurried to the bank. The manager examined my letter of credit and then said, "Before I can honor this, the cargo must be in the loading area. Is it there?"

"No, and can't be before I pay the food bill," I explained.

The manager shook his head and returned the letter of credit. "I am sorry but I can't give you the money until the cargo is on the docks and has been approved by the customs officials."

By now, I was growing desperate. There is a law in India, as in the whole of the sterling area, that the counter value of any export must be deposited in the currency of the country of final destination of the consignment before the consignment can be shipped. In the case of wild animals this is especially difficult as the value of the animals must be determined by a customs appraiser and there is no such thing as a rigid price on wild animals. The theory behind this regulation is that a valuable commodity is being taken out of the country so an equal sum must be left behind by which the economy of the country can profit. Posting enough money to cover the value of the cargo had taken almost my last rupee but I'd been counting on my letter of credit to see me through.

I also had to raise enough for the feed bill somewhere. I went to the agent and demanded the sum. He laughed at me. I had papers proving his dealings in the emigration racket and I swore that I'd take these to the police. He dared me to try it. I didn't care what happened now so I went to the police station, asked to see the chief of police, and laid the papers on the desk before him. As he reached out to pick them up, the agent dashed in, panting and terrified.

"A slight mistake, sir," he said, snatching up the papers. "A little business misunderstanding between my friend and myself. Here is the money you wished, my dear Peter. Accept it with my compliments."

I apologized to the puzzled police chief and went to the merchant who'd supplied the feed and paid his bill. It was 10 A.M. and I'd expected to have the animals loaded by now, but I was helpless until the shipping orders arrived from Argentina.

At 11 o'clock, the consul sent a messenger to me saying that the shipping orders had just arrived by plane. I instantly gave orders to start moving the animals. The baby elephants went first, trotting along in a line like school children. As we reached the street, a policeman stopped us.

"It is against the law to walk elephants through the streets except at night because of the danger to the populace," he explained.

"But these are babies!" I protested.

"The law says nothing about the age of the elephants. You must wait until after sundown."

That would be too late. Subrati came to my rescue.

"I will hire trucks and move them that way, sahib."

The trucks were hired but I didn't have enough left after paying the feed bill to pay for the trucks. Still, once the animals were in the loading area, my letter of credit would be good. I saw them on their way and then rushed back to the bank. I found that it had closed and wouldn't be open until the next morning.

Fortunately, I had a number of Indian friends so I went from one to another of them, borrowing money. At last I had enough to pay for the trucks and returned to the docking area. Here I found Subrati almost in tears.

"Sahib, they say my 'export' papers are not in order so I cannot sail with the animals."

"But we've already had your papers checked and approved," I protested.

"There is one stamp missing," the passport official told me. "He has eight stamps but he needs a ninth. It is a new law, just passed, so the man who approved the papers hadn't heard about it."

I went with Subrati to the government offices to get the stamp, meanwhile assigning my number-two man to load the animals on to flats so they could be floated out to the *Betty Ryan* anchored in the bay.

While we were at the office, one of my men rushed in to say that they couldn't get the elephants off the trucks. "We have pulled, shoved, tried to bribe them with sweets . . . nothing will move them, sahib," he protested. I raced back to the wharf. Gertrude was, as usual, being particularly obnoxious and had thrown the rest into a panic. I was in the middle of this difficulty when one of my men dashed up to say that the trucks carrying the cages with the rest of the animals had gotten lost somewhere on their way to the docking area and couldn't be found.

I left the men to deal with the elephants and went off to look for the trucks. I found them after a two-hour search. They'd gone to the railroad station by mistake. When we returned to the docking area, the elephants still hadn't been unloaded and Subrati hadn't returned. We finally got them off the trucks by main strength and then I went to look for Subrati.

He was in a long line outside the government building where he'd been for the last four hours. At the rate the line was moving, the office would be closed long before he could get to it. However, I knew that the ship would put into the port of Colombo, Ceylon, before going on to B.A. Colombo is only a day's run from Madras so I could cable Colombo to have a trained animal man join the ship there and go with the cargo to B.A. I'd been in correspondence with Aubry Weinman, the director of the Colombo Zoo, and I knew he had two men with South American visas. I cabled Weinman and he cabled back that the two men would meet the ship at Colombo and go to South America with the animals.

An hour after this exchange of cables, I got a call from the shipping company. I went there at once. They had found out about my arrangements and wouldn't allow any of the animals to be shipped unless a trained man was to accompany them from Madras. "We can't have a cargo of animals on a ship with no one to take care of them," the clerk pointed out.

I knew that Subrati would never get the extra stamp he needed in time. "Very well, I'll go," I said.

"Then you will have to be cleared, so you can leave India," the clerk said.

I had my passport but no exit permit and no medical certificate. I took a taxi to the government building where the exit permits were issued but it was closed for the day (it was now after 5 o'clock and the ship sailed at 10). Some of the clerks were still about and I bribed one to give me the home address of the passport official. I went there and he good-naturedly returned to the office and gave me the export permit.

Now I had to find the doctor for the medical certificate. Time was ticking away and I was half mad with anxiety. Finally I found the doctor in one of the remote sections of the city but he was eating dinner and wouldn't be disturbed. I waited until 9 o'clock when he finally finished and consented to sign my papers.

I raced back to the hotel, packed my belongings, and hurried down the stairs. Suddenly I remembered that I'd forgotten something. Ali! I tore back up the stairs and there was poor Ali waiting anxiously. I remembered that while I was packing, he had been following me around, terrified at being left behind but afraid to interrupt me, realizing how frantic I was. Even when he saw me going he hadn't even yelped but stood watching me sadly from the head of the stairs.

With Ali under one arm and my suitcase in the other, I raced back for the waiting taxi. The manager of the hotel stopped me with the bill.

I hadn't a rupee left. "Take this camera," I said, handing him a Bolex I'd used during the trip. "It's all I have."

The manager scratched his head but accepted the camera. I drove to the docking area and luckily Subrati had enough to pay the driver. It was a few minutes before ten. I ran to the docks with Subrati behind me. All the cages were loaded on the flat but not one of the elephants!

"Sahib, we cannot get them on the flat!" wailed Subrati. "We have tried everything."

"We must," I told him. "Put Gertrude on last, or she'll disturb the others. Get eight men to an elephant and carry them on board."

The little fellows were incredibly strong and put up a terrible fight, squealing and kicking, but I had become utterly reckless. We dragged, carried and manhandled the elephants onto the flat and pushed off, headed for the *Betty Ryan*.

We were almost to her when Subrati shouted, "She leaves, sahib, she leaves!"

He was right. The steamer had weighed anchor and gotten up steam. We had missed her by less than five minutes.

I shouted and waved and Subrati danced like a madman but it was too late. A party had been given on board her for the Argentinian colony in Madras and men and women in evening clothes were preparing to leave her in shore boats. They stopped to stare at a raft full of elephants with two lunatics screaming and gesticulating.

"What's the matter?" shouted a man. He was in a tropical dinner jacket and had a beautifully gowned lady on his arm.

I made a megaphone of my hands and explained as well as I could. Everyone howled with delight.

"We can't leave the poor man out here with a Noah's Ark of animals!" called one of the women. "Let's help him get them aboard!"

The captain shouted distractedly from the bridge, "Señora, we are already past our sailing hour. It will take hours to load these animals. We cannot spare the time."

"Nonsense, Captain," called her escort. "You can't leave with us still on board and we won't get off. Come on, everyone! Let's help the poor fellow."

In spite of the the captain's almost tearful pleadings, the guests uproariously set to work throwing lines over the sides and trying to swing the booms into position. At last the poor man gave up and ordered the grinning sailors to hoist my cages aboard. The guests, who had dined very well indeed, lent a hand. Slings had to be rigged for the elephants and they all came aboard nicely except for Gertrude. As soon as she landed on the deck and was released from her sling, she broke away from us and charged around like a miniature bull. Ali went racing after her, barking his head off, and Gertrude stopped to chase him. When the little dog saw the raging elephant coming, he tucked his tail between his legs and fled, crying at the top of his voice. They went round and round the deck, barging into the crew and bowling over the guests like tenpins. I tried to catch Gertrude but meanwhile the tigers were coming aboard to the accompaniment of screams of laughter and the women were reaching through the bars to pet the animals. I had to leave Gertrude to supervise the tigers. The captain was rushing back and forth muttering, "How did I ever get myself into such a situation?" Several of the guests nearly fell overboard, either trying to balance on the rail or being pushed by Gertrude. Altogether, it was as lively a loading as I've ever experienced.

The greatest sufferers were two Indian tally clerks who'd come aboard to check the animals against the list I'd given the Indian government. As cages were being hauled over the ship's sides from all directions, these men were frantically dashing about the ship with their papers trying to keep track of what was going on. For some reason Gertrude took a personal dislike to the officials and charged them on sight. The clerks were terrified of the little elephant and so, in addition to their other troubles, they had to keep a constant lookout for Gertrude.

I was busy trying to keep the guests away from the tiger cages when the two clerks marched up to me.

"It is this sort of thing that makes it difficult for us to perform our official functions," said one man severely. "I must solemnly warn you that I intend to protest—"

"Run for your life! Here she comes again!" shouted the other. Both men started running as Gertrude came charging around the cabin, trumpeting for all she was worth, with Ali at her heels doing everything in his power to make the elephant step lively. The men went round and round the ship with Gertrude after them for the rest of the loading but I couldn't find time to help them.

We finally got the last of the cages on board. The hilarious guests and the gibbering clerks were sent ashore. The captain ordered full steam ahead.

I shouted good-bye to Subrati who was standing waving on the empty flat. Ali and I lay down on the deck, both of us dead tired. Gertrude had been tied up, together with the other elephants, and all the animals were safe. I supposed that I had a cabin somewhere on the ship, but at that moment I didn't care. With Ali in my arms, I fell asleep.

# Chapter 12

# Bali

THE *Betty Ryan* arrived in Colombo and Aubry Weinman had two mahouts ready to accompany the animals to B.A. They seemed to be good, capable men and would have been perfect for the job had not the kindly captain had a barrel of wine available for the crew at all times. Neither of the men had ever tasted liquor and even before the ship left Colombo, both were drunk as owls; in fact, they couldn't even stand. One man was completely unconscious; the other was able to lift his hand and wave to me feebly when I said good-bye. A cable was awaiting me from Behrend (I'd cabled him before leaving Madras) telling me to go at once to Singapore as there was an enormous demand for Malayan animals. I hated to leave the cargo to the care of the mahouts but the captain and the crew assured me that they'd take care of the animals themselves. "Besides, once we get to sea these men will no doubt sober up," said the captain optimistically. As matters turned out, he was too hopeful. Both mahouts remained drunk for the entire voyage but the crew did such a good job that not a single animal was lost. Many months later, I heard that the mahouts had persuaded the Argentinians that they were the sons of a rajah and were living in luxury in Buenos Aires, supported by a group of wealthy planters who were delighted to have members of the Oriental nobility as their guests.

I had to leave Ali on the ship. I couldn't take the pup with

193

me on my travels and Ali had become the pet of the crew. Ali
was having such a good time that he hardly noticed me when
I said good-bye to him. He is still mascot on the *Betty Ryan*
and probably the best loved and fed pariah dog in the world.

My first act was to air-mail Behrend the bills of lading for
the cargo, having discovered from my Kenya experience how
vital those sheets of paper could be. Then I went on to Singapore, cabling Subrati to meet me there. Singapore was Frank
Buck's old stamping ground; the Sultan of Johore was his patron
and nearly all his cargos came from there.

I discovered that conditions had vastly changed in Malaya
since those halcyon days. The country was full of communist
bandits and English troops fighting them. Pictures of Stalin were
openly displayed in every small village and instead of respectful
natives calling any white man "tuan," you were likely to get a
knife between your ribs. Because of the general disorder, trapping was impossible and I doubt if Blackstone himself could
have made sense out of the conflicting shipping regulations.

I went to the old Adelphia Hotel and was put in a dormitory
with six other men, the British troops having pre-empted most
of the available rooms. I was almost flat broke but luckily one
of the European zoos came through with a payment for some of
the South American animals so I had enough to keep me going
for a few weeks. There was an animal market in Singapore and
as soon as Subrati arrived he showed me the place. There were
a few birds, reptiles, and small mammals for sale, enough to
make up a modest shipment, and I cabled Behrend telling him
the situation and asking for instructions.

For a long time I got no answer. Then I began to receive a
most remarkable series of cables from Behrend who was by now
almost insane. The *Betty Ryan* had arrived but because part of
the shipment included antelope that might carry the hoof-
and-mouth disease, the Argentinian Agriculture Department
wouldn't let the ship dock. A warship had even been sent out
to sink her if she came too near the shore. The ship had been
forced to go to Montevideo. Then it was discovered that the

bills of lading hadn't arrived. After a frantic series of negotiations between Behrend and the Uruguayan government, the animals had been landed but held in a compound which Behrend was forced to build. In addition, he had had to post a bond of $10,000 with the Uruguayan government, part of which was taken as a fine for every day the animals remained in the compound. Behrend computed that it was costing him $3,000 a day to keep the animals, counting food, care, and the fine.

Behrend, of course, took for granted that I hadn't sent the bills of lading and his cables were so profane that I'm astonished the telegraph company transmitted them. After two weeks of this came a cable that the bills of lading had been found. They'd been in the Montevideo post office all the time but some postal clerk who collected postage stamps had cut the stamps off the envelope. The post office wouldn't deliver the letter without the stamps so they had thrown it aside.

I thought everything had now been cleared up but instead I received another long series of cables from Behrend which were obviously the work of a raving lunatic. A typical cable would read something like this:

"*Grossmaulige hundschnautze*, why did you cause trouble with that fine agent of mine in Madras? *Verantwortungsloses Nichtsnutz*, you said that German count didn't understand the animal business. He didn't, eh? When an animal died, on shipboard, he had the captain of the ship sign a paper for proof so he could collect the insurance. After a few died, the captain didn't bother to check the dead animals so the count had him sign for a lot that were still alive. Then he collected the insurance and later sold the animals in Marseilles. Ah, but no doubt you got your percentage in this crooked deal, thinking to deceive a *gutmuetiger Trottel* like myself. What are you doing in Singapore, you *geistesschwacher?* Go to Australia. We can't import camels from Arabia into the U.S. because of the quarantine but there are herds of wild camels in Australia, brought there as transport animals which later escaped. Get 1,500 of them at once. Stop in Sumatra on the way. I have an order from the Regent Park Zoo for a pair of hairy rhinos. Pay all costs in Indonesian rupias and exchange them for Straits dollars when you collect the orangutans. A Peruvian priest is sending you 180 military macaws, arriving on BOAC Flight 127, June 10. Exchange these against the Malayan animals you have so do not leave Singapore. Why didn't you send me more elephants? I can sell another twenty. Get them at once as rainy season is starting in India. Do you think I can handle everything here in Buenos Aires? Come at once and help me. You always ask for money. I have no money for you, *Deine Birne ist wohl weich geworden!* I am spending it on animals. Put yourself in the hands of the agent at Madras. He is an honest man."

I would sometimes get three or four such cables in a single day. Meanwhile, Subrati and I were out in the jungles catching stray snakes and birds which we sold to the local native animal dealers for whatever they would give us. I remember that the Singapore reservoir was a very good place for snakes. We'd get mangrove snakes there and occasionally a small python which we'd sell for a Straits dollar (about 33¢) a foot. With Subrati buying the food, we could live for a week on a four-foot python.

Out of the welter of cables I received from Behrend, only one fact stood out. A cargo of macaws was definitely arriving on June 10. There were several "amusement parks" in Singapore that provided night clubs, cabaret girls, Chinese theaters, roundabouts, and so on. I went to the Happy World Park, operated by an elderly Chinaman, and described the macaws. Malayans love strange animals, especially brightly colored birds, and I was able to convince the Chinaman that the macaws would be a sensation. He had an enormous cage built and advertised the arrival of the birds widely in the newspapers and by posters. A big crowd came to the airport to see the macaws land and the Happy World Park was packed with sight-seers.

The macaws didn't come. The pilot knew nothing about them and neither did the airlines office.

Subrati and I pooled our slender resources and cabled Behrend to find out what had happened. All we got was another incoherent series of cables, mentioning everything but the macaws. Months later, I found out the answer. The Peruvian "priest" was an animal dealer who used to don a priest's cassock when making his deals to inspire confidence among dealers. He had had the macaws and received payment for them from Behrend, but had then sent the birds to Europe. Behrend would never admit this in his cables but I discovered it through other sources.

The proprietor of the Happy World Park was naturally furious, having spent large sums to build the cage and to publicize the macaws. I found that none of the native dealers in Singapore would have anything to do with me or Subrati. The hotel demanded that I pay my bill—I'd been living on credit— and I received another long cable from Behrend, denouncing me as a swindling incompetent and demanding that I instantly return to Río Muni to start the gorilla business again. I had exactly 72¢ left. On my way to the Raffles' bar in the hopes of finding someone who would give me a job, I fainted on the street. Subrati found me and took me to the home of a Mohammedan family he knew. The kindly family nursed me for several days as I was in a state of complete collapse. I had spells of delirium when I thought I was back in Switzerland or on the high seas with a cargo of animals, interspersed with fits of despondency so terrible that Subrati watched me night and day.

When I had partly recovered, I swallowed what was left of my pride and went to see some old friends. I explained my situation and they managed to scrape together 200 pounds which they gave me. My first act was to send a cable to Behrend, dissolving our partnership. I said nothing about my 40,000 francs and, of course, never saw a sou of it. Not too long after this I heard that the fabulous old Behrend had died.

My second act was to give Subrati enough to get him back to India, plus back wages and all I could spare. My one remaining ambition was to get away from Singapore. I decided to go to

Bali. I'd heard that Bali was a beautiful spot and I was prepared
to spend the rest of my life there as a beachcomber.

I arrived at Denpasar, the port of Bali, in rags and with only
a few rupias in my pockets. At once, I was enveloped in beauty
as though I had passed from a nightmare into fairyland. I have
traveled to many parts of the world, but in Bali the flowers are
more beautiful, the butterflies more brilliant, and the air fresher
than anywhere else I have been. In the center of the island
stands the great extinct volcano Gunung Agung, "the navel of
the world" as the Balinese call it, its slopes a checkerboard of
terraced rice fields, reflecting the blue sky overhead. In the rice
fields, the peasants sing as they work in their round, yellow
straw hats and around them flocks of white ducks wander along
the banks, never going far from their "standard," a pole with a
cluster of duck feathers tied to the top which the ducks regard
as the leader of the flock. On the green slopes graze the famous
cattle, brown with white "stockings" on their feet, descendants
of the banting cattle. The nights are soft and star-filled. When
the sun sets over the bamboo forests, the demons begin to move.
Then the people squat beneath the torches and the village orches-
tra, composed of xylophones and bamboo clappers, plays while
the virgins in their gold headdresses dance to preserve the balance between good and evil.

I spent weeks wandering from village to village . . . always
courteously received, always welcome. I lived drunk on loveli-
ness. I swam on the perfect beaches covered with sand as fine
as velvet, watched the white mynah birds in the palms or the
red jungle fowls in the bush without having to wonder how
much they would bring in London or Buenos Aires. At night
I slept wherever I happened to stop. Time meant nothing to
me. I had no watch, no calendar, and one day was like the next.

My wanderings brought me to the Holy Hill, Iseh, which
looks towards great Gunung Agung. Here I was told another
European lived: a man who painted pictures, talked Balinese
like a native, and had married a Balinese girl. He would prob-

ably turn away a ragged tramp like me but I cared little for that. I had found my earthly paradise where I hoped to spend the rest of my life and no rebuff meant anything to me any more.

The artist did not turn me away. He fed me and put me in his guest house, an exquisite little bamboo toy with a great window facing towards Gunung Agung and a big, comfortable bed. For three days I did nothing but sleep and eat, waited on by lovely bare-breasted girls who walked as straight as guardsmen and held contests to see which could bring me the most appetizing dishes.

On the fourth day, I left my cabin and went out to meet my host who had left me strictly alone. He was an olive-skinned, thick-set, friendly man, a fine artist and, to my way of thinking, the world's most interesting personality. His name was Theo Meier and he was the only perfectly happy man I have ever met. He had come to Bali years before, fallen in love with it, married a beautiful girl who had been one of his models, and settled down on Iseh. He was a friend to everyone—to the bandits in the mountains who came in the evenings to play chess with him, to the new leaders of the Indonesian Republic who came to talk politics with him, to the peasants who came to his little dispensary to have their cuts treated and ailments cured, and to any down-and-out wanderer who needed help and found his way to Iseh.

In the evenings, Theo and I would sit on the terrace of his house, overlooking the valley that lay between Iseh and Gunung Agung. A river ran through the center of the valley and the slopes were covered with the terraced rice fields. The sun would set behind the pastel-colored clouds and Gunung Agung would stand out against the sky, black as an ebony tombstone until the last light faded. Then would come the chorus of thousands of frogs from the rice fields as the stars appeared. Sharply at midnight, the bigger frogs would start up with their deep bass "Male-akidik . . . male-akidik." Theo told me that a wife always knew at what hour her husband came in; if it was after the big frogs started, he was in trouble. The ghosts appeared as soon as it was properly dark . . . we could almost see their fitful white forms floating under the trees. We never saw any demons, for Iseh was a holy hill where they dared not come but Theo said there were plenty in the bamboo forests and he had often seen them there.

Theo's "house" was really a collection of little bamboo huts, all separated from each other. He had his studio that overlooked the valley, his bedroom and living room where he and his wife lived, a kitchen, a bath, the guest houses and the houses for the servants. Theo did much of the cooking himself. He presided over the stove like a priest over an altar and wouldn't hear you if you spoke to him. His meals were wonderful and varied. We had Balinese, European, Asian, South American, and African dishes. I am fond of cooking too and I was able to give him a few recipes, but not many.

Occasionally Theo would give a party. The guests were of every nationality: European, American, Chinese and Indonesian. Theo always received his guests on the porch where there was a table with a big silver bowl full of tobacco. You rolled your own cigars in maize leaves. There was palm wine in smoked pumpkins, open at the top like punchbowls. This wine was brought in fresh every day by a man who carried two big pumpkins on either end of a long pole hung over his shoulder.

On great occasions, we had arak made from distilled rice, served in a silver punchbowl with a water buffalo embryo floating on the surface. The fiery liquor slowly disintegrated the embryo, so everyone got a small bit. The arak was served in green vase-like cups by the beautiful girls, turned golden-brown by the torches which were the only light. Then there was a salad of dragonflies and grasshoppers, roasted on a grill, that tasted like roasted peanuts.

Theo treated all his guests alike, whether they were prudish lady tourists who sat frozen with horror at the sight of the semi-nude girls, or visiting rajahs who arrived with huge retinues, or starving beachcombers or prominent Indonesian politicians. One of the guests was Sukarno, president of the Indonesian Federation. He is a strikingly handsome man who always wore a Mohammedan black velvet cap. He speaks four languages fluently. I remember how he shook his head when I told him that I was an animal collector.

"I can't approve of your profession," he said bluntly. "I've spent so much time in prison that now I can't bear to see even a potted plant."

When the guests had gone, Theo and I would sit on the terrace discussing everything from religion to the habits of animals, for Theo was an excellent field naturalist. Often these talks wouldn't break up until dawn when the cocks began to crow in the distant villages and the brilliant stars faded in the sky. The days followed each other in easy succession and I have no idea how long I spent in Iseh. It may have been weeks or, more likely, months. As far as I could tell, Theo was perfectly willing to have me spend the rest of my life there.

But eventually I began to have some qualms of conscience about imposing on this generous man indefinitely. The European zoos had sent me the rest of the money for the South American shipment but when that was gone, I would be pennyless. One evening on the terrace I said to Theo, "I never want to leave Bali but how can I live here? I can't write or paint and there are no animals on the island I can sell. What can I do to make a living?"

Theo considered before answering. "You might open an aquarium," he said at length. "There are wonderful fresh and salt water fishes in the coral reefs and the Balinese love to see aquatic life. So do the tourists. Before the war, two Germans had an aquarium here and it was very popular. You could probably buy the building and their old tanks for very little."

The more we considered the plan, the more excited we became. The next morning both Theo and I hurried down to Denpasar to inspect the ruins of the old aquarium. There wasn't much left. The bamboo walls had rotted away and the glass in the tanks was broken, but that seemed a small matter.

"You can get more glass in Singapore," Theo assured me.

"Rebuilding the bamboo walls won't be much of a problem. Also, you can probably sell fish to hobbyists in Europe and America as a sideline. I know that the fishermen will sell you a lionfish for five rupias and lionfish are worth $150 in Germany or the United States."

The lionfish, also called the scorpion fish, is one of the most spectacular of all salt water tropicals. The fish is about six inches long and has long "streamers" which are really spines containing a deadly poison, nearly as potent as the poison of a cobra. The fish is pink, striped with brilliant reddish and brown bars, edged with white. In spite of the danger involved in handling these fish, they are so dramatic with their long streamers and marvelous coloring that any aquarist would be eager to own one. There were, of course, many other valuable but harmless fish in the reefs around Bali, exquisite butterfly fish, lovely angelfish, graceful damselfish, and the fantastically colored tangs. There were also plenty of fresh water fish, ranging from the rasboras to the lively little barbs.

However, I had my doubts about going into the tropical fish business. I knew that in Brazil the exporting of tropical fish is completely controlled by one big New York company and not a fish leaves without the consent of this concern. The company has a string of planes flying back and forth, carrying cargos of fish to the retailers, and they jealously maintain their million-dollar monopoly. I suspected that the same might be true in Indonesia.

But this wouldn't interfere with an aquarium. I found that some of the tanks could be made to hold water and that the aerating pumps and filters could be repaired. Two thousand dollars had come in from the European zoos, more than enough to buy and repair the aquarium. I closed the deal and set to work.

With the help of two young Balinese fishermen, I went out to the reefs after fish. Most of the small, beautifully colored reef fishes cannot be caught by seine nets because they live in holes along the coral heads and, of course, a hook and line must not be used as the hook would injure the fishes' mouths. We went after them with masks, swimfins and hand nets.

I rented a thirty-foot boat and installed a number of tanks in her, each tank equipped with aerators, filters and water circulators. As in all animal collecting, getting the fish, although a problem, was the least of our difficulties. The real knack was keeping them alive afterwards. A cake of ice in a blast furnace is a stable commodity compared with a cargo of live fish. If the batteries that operate your filtration system give out, your fish will die in a matter of minutes. If a storm keeps you at sea a few extra days or, if you must anchor in a choppy sea, the delicate fish can die. The water constantly swishing about in the tanks makes fish used to the comparative calm of ocean depths "seasick."

When we reached the reefs, we'd use glass-bottomed boxes to study the underwater formations. Different types of reefs meant different fish in residence. Staghorn coral usually meant angel- and butterfly fish. Damsels were found only on the outer reefs at twenty foot depths or more. The tangs, tiggerfish and squirrelfish were found in comparatively shallow water.

I had one fisherman from Ceylon who was a Buddhist and had some curious but rather appalling ideas about fishing. He brought up a large lobster and after examining the animal, dove in with him and carefully put the lobster beside his hole again. As I wanted a lobster for the aquarium, I asked him irritably why he'd done it.

"That was one of a mating pair," he told me simply. "I wouldn't take him away from his wife."

I had to learn the habits of the different fishes. Angels usually swam upcurrent while tangs went in big circles. Most of the smaller fish were never far from their holes. You had to guess which hole was home and then cut the fish off from his escape. While chasing them, you had to remember not to touch the fire coral which burns like acid, and to avoid the deadly red sponges which sting like nettles. Some of the jellyfish were harmless, others could cripple a man with their stings. There were sea urchins with quills like porcupines and sting rays that lay buried in the sand but had a poisoned dart on the end of their tails.

Sharks, barracuda, and octopuses never caused us much trouble. The small octopuses were never a danger, but if you met one with tentacles six feet long, you avoided him. The sharks never attacked us; they seemed curious more than aggressive. Sometimes a barracuda would rush at you as though he meant business but he always turned away at the last second. The natives told me stories of men who had been killed by sharks, but it seemed to be a rare occurrence. I suppose that as with tigers much depends on the individual animal and the circumstances of the meeting. If the shark is hungry and used to catching prey in a certain area, he may attack a man, especially if he comes on him unexpectedly.

Once caught, the fish had to be sorted out according to size and temperament before putting them in the tanks. The sargassum fish, who looks like a collection of red seaweed and has an enormous mouth can swallow a fish bigger than he is. They have to be kept by themselves. Then there are others who exude a poison that will kill every fish in the tank; and some so delicate that they faint when captured and will "drown" because their gills no longer operate. These must be kept in darkness until they quiet down.

I also got to know something about the fresh water varieties. Often in some dirty pool by a roadside, I'd see $500 worth of fish: danios, rasboras, barbs, banded coolies, glass catfish, panchax and even guppies which are a Central American fish but had been liberated in waters off Singapore and are now common in many parts. Of course from Siam there were bettas, the famous "fighting fish," of all hues and descriptions. Two male bettas will fight to the death if put together in an aquarium and "fish fights" are often staged in hotels and bars as a tourist attraction. Some Indonesian fanciers breed these fish for ferocity as though they were fighting cocks but such "purebred" fish aren't of any use to the collector. They lack the ornamental flowing tails and fins which make bettas valuable in Europe and America.

There are two big fish collectors in the Far East. One is Rabaud who flies to Singapore twice a year from New York with all his equipment. From the local collectors, he will buy 20,000 rasboras, 30,000 barbs, 90,000 danios and so on. He also picks up a few rare specimens like archerfish which shoot a tiny drop of water into the air so accurately that they can knock down a flying insect, or mudskippers which can crawl about on land, using their fins as legs, and can even climb trees. After making his collection, Rabaud then returns to New York by ship. The tanks, now full of water, would be too heavy for air transport.

The other big collector is Gagelmann, sent out by Aquarium Hamburg in Germany. Gagelmann always travels on the *William Ruys*, a luxurious passenger ship. By special arrangement with the shipping company, he has his tanks permanently installed on the ship and, as soon as he unloads one cargo of fish in Hamburg, he returns on the *William Ruys* for another load. Thus, except for brief stopovers in Hamburg and Singapore, he is constantly at sea. He told me that he has had only one serious accident. The *William Ruys* has a sister ship, the *Oranje*, and when they pass each other, both ships come as close together as possible to exchange news. Once in the Red Sea, the two ships bumped and all of Gagelmann's fish flew out of the tanks. The shipping company made the loss good but the disaster threw the European tropical fish market into a panic for several weeks during which fortunes were made and lost overnight by speculators.

I decided not to try to compete with these two men. I did not have either the capital or the experience. The fish business is a law unto itself and you must be an expert in it to hope to succeed. It's like the butterfly business; an amateur can't hope to get anywhere.

I soon had the aquarium rebuilt and my few usable tanks stocked with fish. Already the aquarium had caused a good deal of interest and people were coming daily to ask when it would be opened. With high hopes, I flew to Singapore to get the glass.

As soon as I arrived, I cabled Subrati, asking if he'd like to go into the fish-catching business. He arrived in Singapore two days later. Meanwhile, I had gotten a room at the Adelphi Hotel and ordered the glass from a local dealer. It was not to arrive for a few days and while waiting, Subrati and I amused ourselves picking up small mammals and reptiles. We did it just as a means of passing the time.

One afternoon I was passing through the hotel lobby when I heard an outburst of ohs and ahs, and cries of "Woo! Woo!" A girl was walking across the lobby towards the "horsebox," the booth where plane tickets were sold. She was the most exquisitely lovely girl I'd ever seen. None of the cheerful beauty of the girl I'd loved in Switzerland, but exotically sexy, though she maintained a touch-me-not attitude towards the crowd. She stepped into the horsebox, relieving the other girl there. She was obviously the new clerk.

Soon the horsebox was surrounded by a crowd of men asking for timetables, folders, general information, and trying desperately to make dates. I fought my way to the front. On closer inspection, the girl was even prettier than she'd seemed from a distance. She was naturally graceful, just seeing her bend down to take a folder from a pigeonhole was a pleasure. The crowd was trying to push me away from the booth but I clung to the edge and stared and stared. Her body was perfect, full, rounded hips which swayed slightly as she moved and she was wearing a well-fitted blouse that showed off her luscious figure to perfection.

An Indian had forced his way through the crowd to see what all the excitement was about. He took one look at the girl and then asked sneeringly, "What are you, some sort of Eurasian?"

"Yes, I am a Eurasian," said the girl quietly and turned away to wait on another customer.

The Indian laughed loudly. "I thought that's what you were!" he said proudly as though with great shrewdness he'd detected the girl in some despicable crime. He looked at the rest of us contemptuously and then forced his way out of the mob.

I didn't care what the girl was and apparently neither did anyone else. When my turn finally came, I asked for a folder or a timetable or some such thing and then begged her to have dinner with me. She quietly refused and then turned to the next man.

I was discouraged but not beaten. I couldn't do anything with that mob around the booth but I resolved to wait for the girl outside the hotel. For a few shillings slipped to a bellboy, I found out when she was off duty and took up my stand by the hotel steps. To my disappointment, I found out that there were a couple of other men standing there who obviously had the same idea. While I was waiting, Subrati came up to tell me that there was a fine ten-foot python in the reservoir and we'd better hurry and catch it before someone else did. The girl wouldn't be out for some time so I reluctantly left my post and went off with Subrati to catch the snake.

# Chapter 13

# Mercia and Siam

SUBRATI AND I caught the python without much trouble—he was a nice little fellow, about eight feet long—and I hurried back to the hotel. As we had no compound, I had to keep the animals we caught in my room and while I was hurrying across the lobby with the python, I ran into the pretty girl. It was an embarrassing moment as I know that most women don't like snakes, but the girl only stepped quickly out of my way, looked at me curiously, and then went out of the hotel where she was instantly besieged by the crowd of men gathered there. Thinking that I had lost all chances of making a favorable impression on her, I went up to my room and put the python in a bag. Unlike mammals, reptiles are very easy to keep in captivity, at least for a short time, and I had a number of other snakes in bags around my room like sacks of laundry, waiting to be air-mailed to various parts of the world.

The next evening I happened to meet the girl again in the hotel lobby. She smiled and asked, "How's the boa constrictor?"

"He's not a boa. He's a regal python," I told her.

She laughed. "You're like the scientist in Africa whose wife rushed in to tell him that their child had been eaten by an alligator. He said indignantly, 'My dear, it must have been a crocodile. There aren't any alligators in Africa.'"

Apparently she did know a little something about animals.

"Why don't we have dinner together and I'll explain the difference between a boa and a python," I suggested.

She hesitated. "I'll have dinner with you, but don't talk about snakes. I hate them."

This was a disappointment but the dinner was a great success. The girl's name was Mercia and she knew Singapore as well as I knew Basel. She took me to a little Chinese restaurant where they served satee, which is meat on sticks roasted over charcoal and then covered with chili and hot peanut sauce. They also had real Danish beer. There were a number of independent chefs, each with his own stall and each having some specialty. One man handled the meats, another the salads, another the vegetables, another the desserts, and so on. The waitress would shout out your order and then go around with a tray and collect the various dishes. You could get virtually any dish that you cared to name; all were delicious.

The restaurant was open all night and Mercia and I sat there until dawn talking. She told me the history of her life and although I thought it was the most pathetic story I'd ever heard, Mercia recounted it in a cold, matter-of-fact way; obviously not making the smallest bid for sympathy. My face must have shown how much her story affected me, for Mercia said curiously, "What's the matter with you? You're a European and can't understand how I feel about these things."

Mercia's earliest memory was being in a Singapore institution with scores of other children, ranging from babies to adolescents. "I must have been five or six at the time," she told me. She could recall no other existence and was neither happy nor unhappy. Or to be more accurate, life was simply a long, dull ache of steady routine. Some of the children had parents who came to see them occasionally and Mercia envied them inordinately. To have a father and mother seemed to her the greatest luxury in the world.

One afternoon, an older boy stopped to stare at her. He asked her name and when Mercia told him, the boy said carelessly, "You must be my sister."

Mercia was stunned. She'd taken for granted that she was alone in the world and to find that she had a relative was joy almost too great to be borne. To his intense irritation, she clung to the boy, crying with happiness, and asked, hardly daring to hope, "Does that mean we have a father and a mother?"

The boy laughed bitterly. "Of course, but they won't have anything to do with you or me. We're blacky-white so they're ashamed of us. That's why we're here where nobody can see us."

The boy then told Mercia about their parents. Their mother was a beautiful Eurasian woman who had been married to an English rubber planter. The marriage didn't work out. The couple separated and the children's mother had married again. The new husband didn't want the children so they were put in the institution.

"Where's Mother now?" Mercia had asked.

The boy shrugged. "Perhaps she's still living with the Englishman. I don't know and I don't care. She hates both of us."

"But what about my father?"

The boy laughed. "He hates you worse than Mother does. He's married a white woman and he's afraid she'll find out he lived with a half-caste."

Mercia brooded over what he'd told her for several days and then collapsed from what was termed "brain fever." She cried constantly, had such terrible nightmares that she was afraid to sleep, and couldn't eat. A doctor was called in but his only comment was, "All these Eurasians are emotional."

Mercia lived, but she became completely changed. She was moody, given to fits of violent tempers ("I still have them," she told me casually), and took to stealing make-up to try to lighten her complexion. Scolding, privations and even whippings had no effect. She was regarded as incorrigible and the other children avoided her.

When the war came and the threat of a Japanese invasion was imminent, the children were packed into two ships bound for Australia. Mercia's ship was the *Devonshire*. Off the coast of

Java, the ships were attacked by Japanese planes. At first the children were delighted and ran back and forth shouting "Dit-dit-dit-dit!" in imitation of the machine guns. Then the other ship was hit by a bomb and began to sink. The planes swept over the *Devonshire*, strafing and bombing. Several of the children were killed and the rest went mad with panic. "We thought they were killing us because they were Asians and we had white blood," Mercia explained. The *Devonshire* remained afloat and managed to reach India where the children were landed.

The children were sent to whatever schools, private homes, and institutions would accept them. Mercia was sent to a school for English girls but the headmistress refused to take her. "I cannot have the tone of the school lowered by accepting a Eurasian child, wartime or no wartime," she told the placement official. A court order had to be gotten before the headmistress reluctantly yielded.

"The white girls weren't unkind to me," Mercia said while we sat in the almost deserted restaurant supping our kirsch as the dawn lightened the dark shadows in the narrow street and the first birds began to sing in the mango trees. "They simply ignored me. I learned to accept it."

Mercia had no money but occasionally she would be able to earn a few annas doing odd jobs around the school. When the other girls brought fruit in the market, the fruit was peeled for them by the merchants. Mercia would then buy the peelings and suck them, pretending that they were real fruit. Her most painful time came after the war when the other girls went Home (Home was always England) during the holidays. Mercia helped them pack and listened to their chatter about seeing their friends and relatives again. Mercia had never been to England herself but she always proudly referred to it as Home.

When Mercia was eighteen, she left the school and went out into the world on her own. She had no training that fitted her for any business or profession so she took whatever jobs she could find. She was a receptionist, a clerk, a saleswoman and a tourist guide. Her remarkable beauty was both an advantage and a handicap. In dealing with men it gave her an enormous power which she used with cold calculation, but in Singapore society it was taken for granted that a handsome Eurasian girl would become the mistress of some wealthy white man, so Mercia's attempts to support herself were regarded with exasperated amusement.

Mercia discussed her beauty exactly as though she were analyzing a piece of marketable merchandise. "I must have security," she told me matter-of-factly. "That's what these stupid men who are always trying to get me to sleep with them don't seem to understand. Why should I sleep with them? Even if they paid me a hundred pounds a night—and most of them expect me to do it for nothing—it wouldn't be worth it. I'd be depreciating my only asset."

Mercia was saving her money so she could learn French. "A French-and-English-speaking girl, especially if she is pretty, can always get a good-paying job with the airlines," she assured me. "Of course, I can speak kitchen Malay but that's only useful as long as I stay in Malaya and I want to get away."

We had been talking in English. I told her I could speak French and offered to exchange lessons in French for lessons in Malay. Mercia knew a little French and she carefully tested my ability before consenting to the exchange. ". . . But after all, you aren't charging me anything and you'll probably buy most of my meals into the bargain," she added reflectively. Mercia was always perfectly frank and to me this was one of her greatest charms.

We saw each other regularly after that, but somehow Mercia's French progressed much faster than my Malay . . . she was really serious about the business. I was hoping to get her to go to Bali with me, as my secretary or some such thing. I finally offered her a job at a much better salary than she was getting from the airlines company.

Mercia didn't jump at the suggestion as I'd hoped. She considered it very carefully.

"The salary is all right," she said at length. "But I'd want a contract for at least a year. Also, I'd want my rent and board paid—I hear things are expensive in Denpasar—and a bond posted covering my return flight fare to Singapore in case I don't want to stay."

"My heavens, it would be cheaper to marry you," I protested jokingly.

Mercia looked at me gravely. "Yes, much cheaper. Would you marry me?"

I'd already entertained this idea. She was the loveliest girl I'd ever seen. She was clever, capable, and had a good business head. I've always lacked these qualities and admired them. I didn't care about her being a Eurasian. In fact, it gave her additional glamour. But most important of all, she was so beautiful that I didn't care what happened if I could only wake up in the mornings and find her lying in bed beside me.

"Very well, let's get married," I said eagerly.

We went at once to the government clerk and asked for an emergency license. At first he wouldn't give us one, saying they were only issued if the woman was obviously pregnant or if the man was a sailor. I tried to argue but Mercia whispered, "Get out and leave him to me!" I got out and a few minutes later Mercia emerged with the license.

We were married immediately. For the next ten days I forgot all about aquariums, plate glass and even Bali. We went to Bedok, a suburb of Singapore, for our honeymoon. Bedok was a real Malayan village, with houses on stilts. We rented a small place and Subrati stayed with us; he and I were still animal collecting although during this time I left most of the work to Subrati. I was perfectly happy. Mercia and I spent most of our time on the beach. Often we would spend the whole night there under the palm trees, cooking little meals for ourselves over driftwood fires and watching fishermen catching crabs in their scoop nets by the light of the moon.

I was troubled by Mercia's attitude towards Subrati. I had always regarded Subrati more a friend than a servant, but Mercia had been taught that servants must keep their place. Subrati, however, just shrugged. "What can you expect from a woman, sahib?" he told me philosophically. "I was married once but praise Allah my wife and the children are dead. They were too much trouble anyhow. Now I stick to animals. All women are crazy."

My most serious shock came when Mercia said she couldn't go to Bali. "Who would I associate with?" she asked desperately. "The Balinese men do not allow women to mix socially, and the women would not accept me." In the next few weeks I began to understand how rigidly lines are drawn in the East. Although I had been welcome at any club or swimming pool in Singapore, I found that I couldn't take Mercia. If I met any of my European friends on the streets, the men would speak to Mercia but the women refused, pointedly putting their hands behind them and turning away. These same women were very "friendly" to Indians but, as one of the *memsahibs* explained to me, "We are forced to be polite to the Indians now for business reasons. But we still will have nothing to do with Eurasians."

This attitude of the English has always struck me as unfair for, after all, it was they who created the Eurasians. Mercia's registration cards were always carefully marked for race with an "E" instead of a "C" for Caucasian. But she was no darker than a Spanish or Italian girl and, in fact, lighter than many people of pure Nordic blood—for example, much lighter than Adolf Hitler who was a very swarthy little man. However, this prejudice will continue until this generation of English colonials die and go to hell.

There was also a definite series of gradations in Eurasian society. There was an old, aristocratic set of Eurasian families—like the creoles in South America—who traced their ancestry back for many generations and always married among themselves. Mercia's father was an Englishman and her mother a first-generation Eurasian, but the aristocratic Eurasians considered themselves superior to her. They would speak to her in public but not invite her to their homes. Mercia would speak to first-generation Eurasians (father white, mother pure native) but we could not have them as guests or go to their houses. Of course, as far as the natives themselves were concerned, Mercia modeled herself on the *mem-sahibs*—ignoring them completely whenever possible.

Mercia fought fiercely to advance herself in this caste system but any attempt by those below her to improve their position threatened all her hard-won rights and threw her into a frenzy so violent that her mind almost seemed to be affected. I think the English *mem-sahibs* found themselves in a similar position. Most of them came from very humble walks of life in England and everything depended on their maintaining their position above the natives and the Eurasians.

Mercia had had such a hard life that she tended to show a certain aloofness towards people which I knew the Balinese would resent. Under such circumstances, life on the island would be impossible. Sadly, I sold the aquarium and canceled my order for the glass. I returned to animal collecting, the only business I knew.

Now that I was on my own in the animal collecting business, I began fully to realize for the first time how dependent I'd been on Behrend. In spite of his shortcomings, the old scoundrel was a genius in making arrangements. Everything I'd done so far had been because Behrend had set things up for me. Now that I had broken with him, I felt lost. I wrote dozens of letters every day in order to build up my own business but I had little ready cash and the collectors did not know or trust me.

I would have been completely lost without Mercia. I soon learned to leave all business arrangements to her. Everyone was fascinated by my wife. Also, she was willing to bargain with a native dealer for a day if she could beat him down a few Straits dollars in his price. Publicity is vitally important to an animal collector, for unless the zoos and big dealers have heard of you, they ignore your letters. Mercia was marvelous at publicity. There was no newspaper photographer so blasé that he didn't want pictures of Mercia. The only problem was how to include the animals.

Mercia was willing to pose with any animal except snakes. As snakes were our biggest item, I tried hard to find some way to overcome her prejudice. I had several dozen mangrove snakes that I wanted to sell. These are shiny, bluish-black reptiles with neon-yellow bellies and chins. We needed publicity to move them, and as mangrove snakes are only slightly poisonous, I decided that they were the ideal snake to use for breaking Mercia into the reptile business.

For some press photographers I got Mercia to pose reclining on a couch in a skin-tight, green bathing suit. She had given the men a very convincing story about how she loved being married to an animal collector and was passionately fond of all animals. When the movie cameras were set up, I came up quietly with a basketful of mangrove snakes and dumped them on top of her. I'd counted on Mercia's not screaming or showing any panic with the photographers there. She was too good a business woman for that.

Mercia didn't disappoint me. She continued to smile sweetly with the snakes crawling all over her. The photographers got their pictures and as a result of the publicity I was able to sell the snakes for a good price. When Mercia saw the profit we'd made, she agreed to pose with any snake if I'd only tell her ahead of time, not dump it on her unexpectedly.

I'd always been casual about money matters; my bank account was in my coat pocket. Mercia stopped all that. She kept track of every rupia. At the end of the first few weeks, she came raging in to me flourishing her account book. "How can I tell what's going on in this madhouse?" she wept. "Look at my books: 'Soap 2 rupias, laundry 6 shillings, rats for python 4 Straits dollars, rent 80 guilders, hay for tapir 150 Hong Kong dollars.' I'm going mad!" I told her not to worry but Mercia did worry. Her early insecurity had taught her the value of a stable income.

Mercia was really fond of me although I got on her nerves.

Once she returned from a shopping trip and seeing Subrati with a very long face, asked him what the trouble was. Subrati shook his head sadly and replied, "Sahib too much beer." Mercia took for granted that I was lying drunk somewhere and scoured the town for the next four hours. When she finally found me, the mystery was explained. I'd bought a little bear and Subrati thought that I'd paid too much for him. In her relief not to find me unconscious in a gutter, Mercia gave me a very unpleasant ten minutes.

As Bedok was too far from the docks, we moved to Singapore and stayed in a hotel but then we had no compound for the animals. Mercia used to smuggle small animals up to our room under her blouse and this gave rise to the rumor that she was pregnant. Mercia encouraged the belief and used to stage fainting spells in the lobby. After she had been revived with cold water and smelling salts, she would weakly thank the clerks and stagger out the door, returning an hour or so later with anything from a bagful of snakes to a pair of mouse deer hidden about her person. No one dared to interfere with her.

Of course, it was impossible indefinitely to conceal from the management that we had animals in our room but everyone was very good-natured about it. Mercia took this indulgence as a matter of course. If I or my business was touched, she was like a tigress defending her young but it never seemed to occur to her that other people had rights. Once we had twelve mangrove snakes in the bathtub and as the snakes seemed quiet and content, we went out for lunch. When we got back, the snakes had vanished. We started to look for them, Mercia bursting into rooms without bothering to knock, confident that if a woman was inside, she could out-argue her and if it was a man, he wouldn't object. In one room, she found a Chinaman sitting quietly on top of the wardrobe with his legs folded under him and four of the mangroves crawling around the floor. Mercia, who had lost all her fear of snakes, started collecting them without bothering to speak to the Chinaman. He watched her for a while and then mildly inquired where the snakes had come from. Mercia instantly went into a rage. "Don't you dare question me!" she screamed at him. "Besides, what are you doing on top of that wardrobe? Come down and help me!"

"Aren't they poisonous?" asked the Chinaman nervously.

"They're only semi-poisonous. Now get down off that wardrobe!"

The man actually obeyed her and helped carry the snakes back to our room. Mercia was still fuming. "Imagine his making all that fuss about a few little snakes!" she told me indignantly.

A few days later, after we'd shipped off the mangroves, we awoke one morning to find the room full of shed snakeskins. They were twined around Mercia's combs and brushes, among our clothes, and tangled about the faucets in the bathroom. Mercia was furious. "What's the matter with this hotel that they can't keep snakes out of people's rooms?" she demanded. "I'm sending for the manager!" The manager arrived and promised a careful investigation. The investigation showed that Subrati had brought in a load of mangroves while we were out and put them in the bathroom. The snakes had escaped but before leaving had paused long enough to shed their skins wherever they could find something to rub against. Subrati told the whole story frankly and after listening to him, the manager turned to Mercia who had been raging up and down the hotel like a fury.

"Madam, I'm sure the snakes only came to your room to say good-bye for they are now all over the hotel. The guests are all out in the street waiting until the creatures can be captured."

This was the only time that I can remember when Mercia was at a loss for words.

There weren't enough animals in Singapore to make collecting profitable and it soon became obvious that we'd have to move to a better territory. There was a considerable demand for Siamese animals so I decided to try my luck there. Mercia and I, together with Subrati, flew to Bangkok. As we had to save our money, we moved into a small hotel, the worst accommodations I have ever known. Our room stank like an out-house, the mosquito nets were torn and dirty, the bed was a cot covered with some filthy sheets, and there was a cracked chamber pot, no other furniture.

I went out to see if I could pick up some animals in the market. There I met a young Swiss who told me that he was in the animal business. Over a glass of warm beer, he explained that he'd heard of a wonderful opportunity.

"There's a Swedish engineer in a place called Suratthani who's made a fortune out of wolfram," he confided to me. Wolfram is a mineral used in the manufacture of tungsten steel. "He's crazy to go into the animal business and he'll put up all the cap-ital needed."

I took the Swiss to meet Mercia. She was wild with enthusiasm over the project—by now, we were both ready to be enthusiastic over any project that would get us out of Bangkok—so I took the railroad to Suratthani with the Swiss. I liked Suratthani on first sight. There was a lovely little village built on both sides of a river full of valuable crocodiles, miles of jungle in every direction, and the natives assured us it was an excellent place for king cobras—worth $200 each in the U.S. or Europe.

We met the Swede, a big, good-natured man who'd been working for a European mining company in Siam. He'd had a fight with the boss and quit.

"I've always wanted to go into the animal business," he told us. "I'm ready for anything. But I haven't a tical. In fact, I hope you fellows can lend me enough for supper tonight."

The Swiss' jaw dropped. "We've been counting on you to put up the capital."

The Swede roared. "I'm working as a coolie right now, try-ing to get enough rice to eat."

I was the only one who had any money, a few hundred Swiss francs. This situation seemed so funny to us that we all had an-other drink. Several drinks later, we decided to form a corpo-ration. Leaving my new partners to celebrate, I returned to Bangkok.

I was somewhat concerned about what Mercia would think of this new venture as she was so conservative in business matters but I needn't have worried. Mercia was hysterical when I arrived and willing to do anything to escape from the hotel. It was a commercial hotel and the traveling salesmen had their sales talks on records which they played day and night over loudspeakers set in the open windows. Mercia hadn't been able to get any sleep but that was the least of her problems. There was no lock on her room door and men had kept bursting in on her at all hours.

"I tried to take a sponge bath with the bed propped against the door, but they must have heard me splashing for a lot of them burst in and stood giggling and snickering at me," she sobbed.

By the greatest of good luck, there was a check from the Bristol Zoo for 300 pounds in payment for a jaguar I'd sold them months before. With this money we left for Suratthani with Subrati. We rented a small native house on the outskirts of the village and together with my two partners, we started catching animals.

There were black leopards, tigers, gibbons, the rare spectacled langur, and plenty of king cobras. The first day we were there, the natives told us of a pair of king cobras that were nesting near a little waterfall in the jungle. We rented an elephant to go in after them. Mercia stayed in Suratthani but my partners and Subrati went along.

There was no trouble about finding the pair even in the waist-high grass. They reared up nearly as high as a man. We went after the female first, still riding on the elephant, using a fifteen-foot pole with a sliding noose on the end. We got the female without any trouble and popped her into a bag. Then we went after the male.

He was the biggest king cobra I've ever seen, a little more than sixteen feet long. As I advanced the pole towards him, he dodged the noose and charged. He struck the elephant on the foot before I could get the noose around his neck. Subrati slipped off the pad and grabbed the giant snake by his little mouse head just above the hood. We got him into the bag despite a tremendous struggle, the poison dripping from his fangs.

The elephant stood trembling and the mahout said quietly, "He will die."

"Nonsense," said the Swede. "A cobra bite can't kill anything as big as an elephant."

The mahout repeated dispassionately, "He will die," and sat down to wait. The elephant stood shaking for about twenty minutes. Then he sank slowly to his knees, groaned a few times, and fell over dead.

The Swiss said in an awe-struck voice, "Good God!"

There was nothing for it but to walk back to Suratthani. The mahout made us go first as he said the country was full of king cobras and no one in his right mind ever went on foot. Forcing our way through waist-high grass in cobra country was an unpleasant experience especially with the death of the poor elephant still in our minds. We saw several other cobras but they slipped away into the grass before we could catch them.

The mahout charged us 8,000 ticals (about $400) for the elephant. However, there were still plenty of king cobras around and we spent days catching them. They are very aggressive creatures and will charge a man at astonishing speed. Luckily, they generally rear up before striking which gives you a chance to jump out of their way. The Swede didn't like cobras and used to take along a shotgun for protection. He killed one that attacked him—a fine fourteen-foot female—and Mercia was furious at the loss. She wouldn't allow the Swede to go out after that, but went herself with a noose pole, even though she still disliked snakes, especially poisonous ones.

None of us three men cared much about money so Mercia kept the accounts, doling out to us whatever sums she considered necessary for liquor and tobacco. As a business manager, Mercia was wonderful, and I was happy to find that she was remarkably good with baby animals too. Only a woman can be really successful in raising baby animals. A collector has too many other things to do. The babies require constant care and, what is equally important, affection. Without love, they pine away and die.

Mercia raised several young leopards on bottles and was the best person I've ever seen with baby gibbons. Gibbons are apes, like gorillas and chimps, and so belong to a higher order of primates than do monkeys. They are extremely intelligent and in captivity are absolutely dependent on human love.

The natives shot gibbons for food and would sometimes find a baby clinging to the dead mother's breast. Mercia raised the babies on goat's milk. The gibbons used to sit in a circle on Mercia's desk, watching while she made out the accounts. They were fascinated by the pencils and papers but after a scolding or two, never touched them. They were perfectly tame but we had to keep them chained most of the time as they were insanely jealous of the village children and would make murderous attacks on any child who went near Mercia. Whenever she could, Mercia would take a troupe of five or six for walks along the edge of the jungle, Mercia keeping to the paths and the gibbons swinging through the trees by their long arms. Except possibly for chimps, gibbons are my favorite primates. They have only one bad habit. Every morning at dawn they set up a loud "hoo-hooing" that carries for miles and makes sleep impossible.

Even after several months of married life, Mercia remained a mystery to me. She would go into violent fits of rage over some unimportant detail and then accept a real annoyance without protest. On one matter, she was an absolute fanatic: clothes. I'd always traveled with only three suitcases but with Mercia's luggage we had forty-six pieces. The cost of taking so much luggage greatly increased our traveling expenses and inconvenienced us but Mercia, who was so careful about money, refused to move without all her paraphernalia. She guarded her clothes carefully and if there was so much as a run in a stocking, she was heartbroken. She did all her washing herself to make sure the clothes weren't injured. We had a big red-faced monkey who was very tame and we kept him on a chain but he was always escaping. For some reason, the instant he was free, he'd go for Mercia's washing, pulling down the clothes and tearing them to shreds. I'd have thought Mercia would have murdered the creature but she never even scolded him, spending hours mending the clothes (she was an excellent seamstress), washing them again, and hanging them up. "Poor thing, he doesn't know any better," she told me when I questioned her. "Also, a big tame monkey like that is worth a lot of money."

In addition to the gibbons, there were a number of other primates, especially rhesus monkeys. These monkeys are so common that there is no use collecting them except in wholesale lots for hospital research or some such purpose but a native boy brought in a little rhesus he'd caught when the mother had put the baby down to get some grubs from under a log. We gave him a tical or two for the baby and, as the mother was hanging around our camp, tried to return the baby to her. She refused to accept him and we had to bottle-raise the orphan. A few days later, the mother kidnaped a kitten which she nursed as though it were her own baby, while curiously continuing to ignore her real child. I'm afraid the kitten had a short life. I saw the mother rhesus trying to train it to swing from branch to branch and then beating the poor thing severely when it refused to learn.

At the end of six months' hard work, mixed with some real dangers and plenty of disappointments, we had collected about $75,000 worth of animals. Subtracting expenses, shipping charges, permits, etc., each of us was expecting to realize a profit of about $10,000 . . . no fabulous sum but we were all content. Then came my meeting with Theo Meier in Bangkok and the news that all export of animals from Siam had been forbidden. And then, mercifully, Pat Stracey's letter giving us permission to collect the Indian rhinos arrived.

These rhinos were the ones that caused me such grief to say good-bye to at the Basel Zoo. We had been through so much together in Assam, floating down the Brahmaputra River and sailing to Genoa on the *Alcione*. But they did save our lives and established me as a recognized animal collector.

# Chapter 14

# Orangs and dragons

MERCIA CONTINUED to be a sensation in Switzerland, where we had brought the rhinos. Although it was her beauty that first attracted people, it was her wit that held them. She handled all my business affairs for me. The animal dealers had never before seen a lovely, intensely feminine woman who had a steel spring mind when it came to money matters; the combination left them breathless. Mercia was equally successful socially. She was what actors call "a quick study" and could pick up a language, mannerisms, and style almost instinctively.

Naturally, Mercia loved Switzerland. For the first time in her life, she no longer needed to feel self-conscious. Once she realized that she was simply accepted for what she was, she gradually lost her nervousness but the corrosive effect of her miserable childhood and her Eastern training did not disappear overnight. Mercia had a hard, practical way of approaching any issue which was very unlike my easygoing enthusiasm. When a group of dealers asked me to get a big consignment of Indonesian animals, I was ready to start off the next day, and it was Mercia who had to argue terms with the dealers and make sure that I hadn't taken on an impossible assignment.

One of the main problems was the time limit put on the delivery of the animals. I hadn't realized how restrictive this item could be. I knew that zoos do not like to leave cages empty for long periods of time any more than department stores like to

224

leave their counters bare. If other animals are put in the cages intended for the new stock, the question then arises as to what to do with them when the ordered consignment arrives. Also, if the zoos pay something in advance, they do not like to have large sums tied up and not showing any tangible returns for a year or more. So for the dealers to require a specific date for delivery didn't seem to me unreasonable.

Mercia pointed out several factors that I'd ignored. The rainy season was coming on which ruins trapping; the animals must be shipped during the European summer to avoid chill; a war might break out; collecting licenses in various areas might be revoked, or a sudden fluctuation in the local currency might ruin the venture. She got the contracts rewritten to juggle the time element somewhat to allow for possible miscalculations.

To my regret Mercia refused to leave Switzerland. She was far too happy there. As for me, I often didn't know what to make of my beautiful, temperamental wife. She was quick to make decisions, absolutely fearless, and possessed of a driving ambition, all qualities I intensely admired. Without her, I might well have ended up a beachcomber in Bali. Yet I often felt unable to keep up with her fierce, driving power and this worried me. But she was so lovely that if I were without her all the beauty seemed to have gone out of the world.

Still, I had a living to make and I was mad to get back to Indonesia. It was one of the last great animal areas in the world. There were orangutans, the fabulous Komodo dragon, the rare clouded leopard, the giant pig of Borneo, the terrible salt water crocodile and, most interesting of all to me, the maleo: a bird that lays its eggs in the sand and leaves them to incubate as do certain reptiles. Already I felt that I had been in Europe far too long. So I left Mercia with my mother and caught a ship for Ceylon.

I took along a cargo of African animals which I hoped to exchange in the Surabaja Zoo in Java against some of the Indonesian stock. I made sure of including some white-faced chimps which I knew are always wanted in the East. I arrived

in Ceylon with my cargo and put the animals in the Colombo
Zoo, under the care of Mr. Weinman, who has always been
such a good friend to me. I cabled the Surabaja Zoo and got
an enthusiastic cable in reply, offering me a pair of orangs for
each chimp. Everything seemed easy and I couldn't imagine
why more collectors didn't go to Indonesia as there was a tremendous demand for Indonesian animals all over the world.

In addition to the African animals, I had a few orchid bulbs
which a fancier had asked me to give to a Dutchman living in
Surabaja in exchange for some Java specimens. I thought that,
in addition to doing the men a favor, the bulbs would be a good
introduction and the Dutchman could give me an idea of conditions in Indonesia, for I'd heard rumors that the new republic
was in a somewhat confused state.

At the last moment, I decided not to arrive in Java with my
animals until I'd first studied conditions. So I went on to Surabaja taking only the bulbs and a pair of tame hyenas, leaving
the rest of the African animals in Ceylon.

In Surabaja, I met the Dutch orchid collector, a very elegant
gentleman indeed—tall, thin, with a waxed mustache, dressed in
spotless white and carrying a swagger stick. He took me to his
home and after much shouting and pounding on the door, it
was finally opened by an old native woman in rags with only
two teeth in her head, one on the upper jaw and one on the
lower.

"What do you mean, you pig's backside, disturbing me at
this hour?" she shrilled. "You know I sleep in the afternoon.
Is that the Swiss? How many bulbs did he bring? What condition are they in? I want to see them before he enters this
house."

"Later, later," said the Dutchman nervously pushing past her.
I was astonished that the man permitted this old servant woman
so much latitude, although I knew that men who live in the
tropics often have an old ayah to whom they allow astonishing
privileges. However, it turned out that the woman was his
wife and owned the house.

The place was a madhouse. Although there were electric refrigerators, fans, lights, and even an air-conditioning system, nothing worked. The only light was a single candle and we ate food cooked over a smoky charcoal grill. The house was alive with animals. There were pariah dogs everywhere, all of them crippled. The old woman picked up any injured dog she found on the streets and brought it home which at least showed that she had a kind heart as far as animals were concerned. There were also dozens of parrots and cockatoos flying about, none of them housebroken. The house was never cleaned and the dogs licked the plates which were then put away for the next meal.

I love animals but that house was a little too much. There was one particular cockatoo who took an especial dislike for me. The bird lived behind the toilet and used to rush out and bite me every time I sat down. I really got to hate that cockatoo. But the old woman loved all her pets. She would sit in the middle of the floor with mangy pariah dogs licking her face, parrots crawling all over her, cockatoo droppings all around her. She would grin with delight and gurgle baby talk to them.

I'd been afraid that my hyenas wouldn't be welcome, but in that household all that was needed was a couple of hyenas to complete the ménage. The hyenas became the old lady's favorites. They ate far better than I did and slept with the old hag in her bed, the only comfortable one in the house. That was one privilege I didn't envy them. She smelled like a goat.

Both the husband and wife were continually after me about the orchid bulbs which I decided to keep hidden until after I'd closed my deal with the Surabaja Zoo. I went to the zoo the next day. They had no orangs and no definite idea of how to get any. The director was very annoyed to find that I hadn't brought my African shipment with me. I gathered that once the cargo had been landed in Java, I'd have had a hard time getting it out again. The director was an important political figure and the zoo seemed to be the headquarters of the anti-European movement. Big rallies were held there with screaming mobs shouting, "Down with the white man! *Merdeka* [freedom]!"

Discouraged, I went back to the house of my Dutch orchid collector and told him that I was returning to Ceylon. He demanded the orchids which I turned over to him although I never received any bulbs in exchange. I'd planned to take the hyenas back with me, but the old wife refused to be parted from them. She clung to the animals, sobbing, "Mama won't let you go, my darlings." Mama didn't let them go, either. I couldn't pry her loose. Meanwhile, I received a peremptory order from the director of the zoo to turn the hyenas over to him, threatening to confiscate them as I had no permit to keep wild animals in Java. I solved the problem by presenting the hyenas to the old lady and leaving her to fight out the issue with the zoo director. A pair of hyenas were certainly an appropriate gift for that old witch. "Sweets to the sweet." I hope the hyenas ate the whole family, starting with that damned cockatoo that lived back of the toilet.

I returned to Colombo and sold my African animals to a Japanese dealer for a very good profit. The Japanese pay more for animals than any other nation—including the wealthy Americans. They must be passionately interested in wildlife. I was still determined to collect in Indonesia but I'd learned a few things during my stay in Surabaja. The Indonesian Republic is very reluctant to grant permits to Europeans or Americans but they will deal with another Asian state. As Ceylon was one of the Bandung Conference states, I obtained an order from Mr. Weinman for a pair of orangs for the Colombo Zoo. Armed with this order, I returned to Java.

This time I went to Bogor and found the officials in the conservation department very reasonable and knowledgeable men. They gave me a permit to capture two orangs, to be delivered only to the Colombo Zoo, and added, "If, after getting your pair, you find any baby orangs in the native villages, buy them at once. Don't worry about the permits . . . we'll issue them to you later. The villagers can't keep the babies alive more than a few weeks. The little apes pick up human diseases too easily, so they'd be lost anyhow." This was exactly what I'd found with young gorillas in Africa. I thanked the men sincerely and, feeling much better about my chances in Indonesia, made plans for my trappings.

Orangs are found principally in Borneo. The island of Borneo is divided in two, one section being British and one Indonesian. There had been an uprising against the Indonesian governor by a local leader who hoped to establish his section of the island as an independent nation. This revolt had been downed but conditions were still so uncertain that it would have been no use for me simply to land in Borneo and hope to do any trapping. I had to have some influential contact on the island.

I started calling on everyone who might possibly be able to help me. After following out several false leads, I met a Dutchman whom I'd known at Theo Meier's home. He introduced me to Dr. Debrunner, a Swiss, who was head of Shell Oil in the area. Dr. Debrunner was more than kind to me. He arranged to have me go to one of the oil-well communities in the interior of Borneo. After that, I was to be on my own.

I took a steamer to Balikpapan and from there went on to Samarinda in the interior. From there, I took a Shell Company plane to one of their oil fields. The field turned out to be two oil wells in the midst of one of the most magnificent jungles I have ever seen. The country was like a huge botanical garden. The wells were drilled on the edge of a vast river system, much like the delta of the Brahmaputra or the mouth of the Amazon. There were rivers, streams, waterways, and drainage-overflows in every direction. The Shell manager at the station was the only white man for hundreds of miles. He told me that all travel was by boat, for the jungle was so thick that you couldn't cut your way through it with a bolo.

I got four dugouts and some native paddlers. Then we set out, taking along a tent which the Shell manager had loaned me and a big net that I'd bought from Europe. For days we paddled through the waterways, keeping an eye out for signs of the great red apes. In some sections were vast plains of high grass, like the delta of the Río Plata in Argentina, without a sign of a tree. In others, there were forests of the enormous pĕdada trees, so huge and with such thick foliage that nothing could grow below them. In the pĕdada trees were families of the rare proboscis monkeys, reddish animals about the size of a baboon with very long noses. They are very hard to keep alive, eating only the leaves of certain trees, but a pair had been kept successfully at the San Diego Zoo in California. I spent days trying to catch them but it was no use. They went so fast I couldn't even photograph them. As they ate the leaves of the trees around them, there was no way of baiting them. The trees were far too big to cut down and the trunks too thick to climb. As far as I know, the only way to get one is to shoot a mother with a suckling infant, and this I wouldn't do.

After several weeks, we came to a patch of firm ground in the great swampy area, not just one of the "mangrove islands" made by the intertwining roots of the mangrove trees. This area was covered with tall trees, but none as big as the pĕdada. We camped here and set about our usual business of looking for orang signs.

We spread out to cover as large an area as possible and were starting to move through the jungle when I heard one of my men shouting wildly. I ran to him and found him pointing up. There was a big nest, much like one of the gorilla nests I'd seen in Río Muni. Orangs also build these nests, so we knew that there were orangs somewhere in the area.

One of my men climbed the tree and called down that the nest, from its size and the large branches that had been used, must be the nest of an old male. Orangs, unlike gorillas, do not live in family groups. The adult males are solitary creatures, keeping away from the females and young except during the breeding periods. Judging from the condition of the leaves on the branches, the nest was about a week old. Orangs generally built a new nest every night wherever they happen to stop, so

I was afraid that this fellow would be miles away by now but the men assured me that orangs travel very slowly.

We started off. I kept searching the ground for signs, as I would have if following a gorilla. The natives were greatly amused. "Tuan, the mias, orangutans, swing through the trees," one man told me. "Why, then, do you hope to see marks on the ground?" If the animals were completely arboreal, I felt we were lost, for there was no way of tracking but the natives went confidently on. We came upon another nest, but before we could investigate it, there was a crashing in the distant tree tops. "The mias!" shouted the men and started off at a dead run.

I managed to stop them. There was no need of alarming the beast. Quietly we crept closer and, guided by the sound of the branches, we located him. He was a fine male with huge arms and covered with long reddish-orange hair. Although not nearly as big as a male gorilla—he weighed about 200 pounds and was about 5½ feet high—he was a very formidable-looking animal. I was astonished at how slowly he moved, almost like a giant sloth. I could understand now why the natives had been so confident of catching up with him.

I watched him all that afternoon. He never made any attempt to come to the ground and the natives told me that the mias seldom descend even to drink, relying on dew or rainwater caught in the boles of trees. This was so unlike my experiences with gorillas and chimps that I could hardly believe it. The orang was constantly feeding as he went, picking small tender leaves from the branches and occasionally catching an insect on the bark. Sometimes he'd have a sudden burst of energy and go swinging around from limb to limb like a gigantic gibbon, apparently just for fun.

When evening came, he began to build his nest for the night by the simple method of sitting on a limb and pulling down all the smaller branches within reach to form a pile around him. Then he curled up in the middle and went to sleep.

I studied the nesting tree carefully. There were five other trees near it but these trees would not have to be cut down;

simply cutting off a few strategic limbs would keep him from reaching them. I pointed out these limbs to my men in the gathering dusk and assigned a man to each limb. Then I sent back to the dugouts for my net. I also had the men make "fake" nets out of creepers so when the time came for the final rush, the old boy would think that he was completely surrounded.

Just before dawn, we quietly took up our positions around the nesting tree. The men assigned to the limb-cutting started to climb with their brush knives in their teeth. When each man was in place, I shouted the signal to start cutting.

The blows sounded like rifle shots in the pre-dawn stillness. Birds began to scream and the men shouted in their excitement. It was light enough to see the old male sit up in his nest, obviously wondering what was happening. Then he tried to reach the nearest tree but as he took hold of the branch, it fell, cut through at the base. He started back, giving a roar of surprise and anger. We were all shouting to bewilder him and instead of trying to escape from the nesting tree, he only climbed higher. The other connecting limbs dropped and he was a prisoner.

We sat down around the tree to wait until full daylight before atempting the actual capture. The old orang sat up in the tree watching us, confident that we couldn't get at him. If he'd come down to the ground while it was still dark and made a rush for it, we'd never have been able to stop him, but he felt safe fifty feet up in the tree.

When it was fully daylight so we could see what we were doing, I had the men surround the tree with their faked nets while I, with ten of the best men, took up my position with the heavy net made of strong hemp rope. When all was ready, I gave the signal to start cutting down the tree. This was the critical moment and I was sweating from nervousness far more than from the heat.

At the first blows of the axe, the orang jumped nervously as he felt the vibrations on the tree trunk. He started down, changed his mind, and went up again. The axe men worked

with a will, cutting the trunk so that the tree would drop into
an open space where my men and I were ready with the net.
The chips flew. Then came a rending noise as the tree began
to totter. The axe men ran for their lives, the tree swayed and
then came sweeping down, hitting with a stunning crash. As
soon as it struck, we rushed it with the net. The orang was still
clinging to the branches as we threw the net over him but once
he felt the meshes, he let go and began to fight.

Although I thought that I was fully prepared for his great
strength, I felt as though we had netted a bull elephant. Time
after time he reared up, screaming with fury, and tearing at
the heavy cords with his huge teeth. Each time we had to jerk
him off balance while continuing to wind the net tighter around
him. At last, he was as helpless as a man in a strait jacket. We
tied him to a long pole carried by four men and hurried back
to the dugouts.

I offered the men a bonus for speed and they made the dugouts fly. Every hour counted. Although of all the great apes
only orangs are sufficiently tractable to be captured when adults,
they are extremely emotional and subject to shock. It was absolutely necessary for me to get this fellow out of the net and into
a large, comfortable cage as quickly as possible.

Although we got back to the Shell station within two days,
the orang refused to eat when we put him in his cage. He sat,
drooping and miserable. I tried every trick I knew but he
steadfastly ignored me. I decided to give him one more day.
Then if he did not eat, I'd liberate him. Certainly a dead orang
was of no use to me and besides I could not watch this magnificent old fellow pine away before my eyes.

Then I got word that some natives in a nearby village had
a pet female orang that they wished to sell. I went there at once.
The female was quite young, weighing only about 80 pounds,
and a perfect pet. To my surprise, she was in splendid condition without a sign of any of the usual ailments of captive apes.
She was quite happy to go with me and I hurried back to camp,

reasoning that if I had to liberate the male, at least I now had a female.

I held on to her hand as she walked over to examine the male, for I was afraid to let her get too near the bars . . . the old fellow was too unpredictable. She went as close as I'd let her and stood making little sucking noises. The old male was sitting in his usual mood of deep dejection, but as soon as he saw the little female, he sat up blinking as though he couldn't believe his eyes. Then he came over to the bar, still obviously unable to believe this miracle. He reached out but I wouldn't let him touch her; she was so small that I was afraid he might drag her against the bars and hurt her. They had a long conversation in orangutan language, she apparently asking him why he was so grumpy and he begging her not to leave him. At last, I gave the female some food, afterwards passing the bowl in to the old male. After a few cautious sniffs, he began to eat. From that time on, we didn't have any trouble with him. I put them together a few days later and the old fellow was very gentle with the little girl. In fact, she ruled the cage, always taking first pick of the food while her gigantic consort stood humbly by until she'd taken all the tidbits out of the plate.

Later, I got four other orangs, all from villagers. One of the babies had a bad case of diarrhea but I cured it with sulfa compounds.

I returned to Ceylon with my six orangs and turned the old male and his little wife over to the Colombo Zoo. I still had four that I could sell in Europe. I decided to send them by plane as soon as they were a little older and meanwhile I set about picking up some other animals for a shipment by boat. I cabled Subrati in India to join me and together we made a nice little collection of animals from local dealers, including three young tigers bred in the Colombo Zoo. A young Dutchman who'd had some experience with animals was returning to Antwerp and, for the price of his passage, agreed to take care of the animals during the voyage. I made arrangements to load the cargo on an English ship that was stopping at Colombo and got a reservation for the Dutchman on the same vessel.

The day before the ship was due, I got a cable from Mercia. She'd decided to come out after all and was flying out to join me. Naturally, I was half frantic with delight, for except when I was actually animal trapping, I missed her desperately. Mercia was very fond of flowers so I lined the hotel room with them, making all sorts of plans for a second honeymoon with my lovely wife.

The English ship arrived the next day and I loaded my cargo. The captain was very unpleasant, deliberately rude and over-bearing. I was glad to see the last of him and pitied the young Dutchman who'd have to put up with this boor during the long voyage.

I was preparing to meet Mercia at the airport when the young Dutchman came to the hotel almost in tears. The captain had decided that the tiger cages were too weak and had ordered the animals off-loaded. He had also tossed out eight weeks' sup-ply of meat for the cats from the ship's freezer and it had all gone bad in the hot sun. The tigers were now on a flat in the middle of the bay under Subrati's care.

I went immediately to the ship. The captain at first refused to see me. When I finally got his attention, I was treated to a blast of profanity, coupled with an absolute refusal to take the tigers. He was a heavy, choleric individual with a drooping handlebar mustache, looking and behaving exactly like an old English colonel from the military school at Poona. There was nothing I could do so I returned to shore.

Here an even worse problem awaited me. The customs men refused to allow the tigers to be landed. They argued "As the tigers have been on an English ship, they are now English tigers and cannot be imported into Ceylon."

I now had three tigers on a flat in the middle of the harbor and couldn't bring them ashore or put them on the ship. I finally got permission for the flat to tie up alongside the dock as long as the cages were not put ashore. Meanwhile, Mercia's plane was due so I grabbed a taxi and raced to the airport.

After the long trip, the passengers staggered off the plane looking more dead than alive, stiff, unbathed, red-eyed and gasping in the heat. All except Mercia. She tripped down the landing steps looking as though she had just emerged from a beauty salon on the Rue de la Paix.

After our first greeting, I told her what had happened. Mercia listened quietly. "An Englishman, you say?" she commented thoughtfully. "Old colonial type? You leave this to me."

We drove to the hotel, followed by another taxi crammed with Mercia's multitudinous paraphernalia. Mercia shooed me out of the room while she changed. A few minutes later she emerged in a pair of high, spiked heels, the shortest shorts I have ever seen, and a too tight blouse. She was a standing invitation to rape but when I protested she only snapped, "Get those cages alongside the ship. We're loading."

I hurried down to the wharf where Subrati was sitting disconsolately by the cages. "Subrati, get the flat moving and back to the ship," I shouted as I sprang aboard.

Subrati shook his head. "Sahib, it is no use. I know that sort of Englishman. Nothing can move him."

I was mad with impatience. "The *mem-sahib* has just gone aboard to argue with him," I shouted.

Subrati bounded to his feet. "Why didn't you say so, sahib? Boatmen, cast off the lines! Get out the oars! We haven't a moment to lose!"

The boatmen threw all their weight on the sweeps while Subrati and I urged them on. We went fast, but long before we reached the ship I could see the crew swinging out the loading booms while the captain goaded them to fresh efforts.

The cages were loaded without trouble, Mercia directing the crew where to stow the cages as they came on board. The captain was following her around, whinneying like a stallion. Mercia introduced me as her husband but the captain only glared at me as much as to say, "What the devil are you doing here?" and continued to pursue Mercia, making little chuckling noises and stroking his mustache.

The Dutchman came aboard and the ship weighed anchor. I wanted Mercia to leave with us but she said, "No, you idiot. This fat fool thinks I'm going with him to Europe. He could still have the animals off-loaded. I'll go ashore with the pilot boat."

I was still concerned about her and, as soon as we returned to the docks, I rented a power boat and followed the ship. When the pilot was dropped, I picked up Mercia. The captain, his face the color of a ripe tomato, leaned over the rail screaming insults at white men who married blacky-whites, the dishonesty of foreigners, and his opinion of the whole proceedings in general. From the stern of my boat, Mercia responded in kind, tracing the captain's ancestry back for several generations and making some succulent comments on his personal morals.

We had no more concern over our cargo. It was heavily covered by insurance and the insurance company would hold the captain strictly responsible for any trouble during the voyage. With a clear conscience, we returned to the hotel and had a cooling drink.

Subrati left me soon afterwards to return to India. His family had arranged for him to marry a beautiful young girl of eighteen (Subrati was well over fifty) and not even the animal business could compete with that attraction, which soon overcame his antipathy to the married state. The little orangs were now old enough to risk the long flight to Europe, and Mercia agreed to go with them. As it would be autumn when they arrived, she knitted pullovers for the babies although measuring them turned out to be a tremendous task. I saw them and Mercia off at the airport. I hated to lose her but I wanted to get back to Indonesia and start collecting again.

I was particularly eager to get a few pairs of maleos, the strange birds that bury their eggs. Maleos are not spectacular birds. Both sexes look alike and somewhat resemble a very small female turkey, but they would seem to be an evolutionary link between birds and reptiles. As far as I knew, there were none in captivity. Since they are not spectacular looking, I couldn't hope to get more than a couple of hundred dollars a pair for them but I didn't care. I wanted to see them and bringing some back would be a great reputation-builder for me.

In a bar, I'd been lucky enough to meet a man who'd been an officer on the *Straat Malacca*, the ship on which I'd returned from Kenya some six years before. He gave me a letter of introduction to an official in the Celebes Game Department. Maleos are found only on the Celebes and there only in one section, very difficult to reach. Armed with the letter of introduction, I took a KPM ship to Macassar, the main city in the Celebes and presented my letter. The official was most friendly but warned me that much of the island was in the hands of bandits and I was foolish to take such a risk for the sake of a few birds. I wasn't eager to meet any bandits but I was determined to get the maleos.

The official gave me a letter to a friend of his at Gorontalo, the area where the maleos live. I flew to Manado and then took a local steamer to Bumbulan, near Gorontalo. The ship was named the *Kakap* and was the dirtiest tub I've ever seen. The passengers and crew didn't even bother to go to the side to relieve themselves and the decks were incredible. In the intense heat, the odor was sickening. The only food was rice and rotten fish. I shared a stuffy, stinking cabin with a jovial native police officer who was bringing his dead grandmother to Bumbulan. Bumbulan had been her birthplace and the old lady had expressed a wish to be buried there. Her coffin was in the already overcrowded cabin and her dutiful grandson had covered it with artificial flowers. The old lady had not been properly embalmed and what with grandmother, the smell of the decks, the rotting fish, and the stifling heat, the atmosphere of the cabin was indescribable.

I will say that never in all my travels have I met a nicer group of people than the passengers on the *Kakap*—or *Kakhus* (Dutch for privy), as I found she was popularly known along the coast.

Everyone was friendly, cheerful, and obliging. I'd have gladly gone through the experience again to be among such open-hearted folk . . . well, almost gladly. Still, I was not broken-hearted when the *Kakap* dropped anchor at Bumbulan, the ship's last port of call.

From Bumbulan, I took a pulling boat to Gorontalo, a few miles down the coast. Here I found a scene of wild excitement.

The eggs of the maleos are believed by epicures to be the best tasting eggs in the world. The birds nest only along this one stretch of beach and the egg collecting concession is sold by the government to a group of Chinese merchants. These men, in turn, hire natives to dig up the eggs, paying them one egg in every three for their work. When I arrived on the beach, it was covered with men frantically digging while the Chinese mer-chants stood over them and kept a careful count of the eggs.

One small section of the beach is supposed to be a reserve where no digging is permitted but no one seemed to pay the slightest attention to this restriction. I met the game warden and gave him my letter from the official in Macassar. He was a very cordial chap who took a keen interest in the birds. "I hope you can get several pairs and start them breeding elsewhere, for they'll soon be extinct here," he told me. "I can't control these Chinese. They all have political connections and dig where they please."

He told me quite a bit about the maleos. They nest from September to November. The hen digs a funnel-shaped nest in the sand and lays her eggs while the cock runs around to keep watch. At the first sign of danger, the cock gives the alarm cry and both run. After laying her eggs and covering them with sand, the female then digs a number of false "nests" to fool predators. Only about six eggs are laid over the whole of the nesting period. They are the size of a turkey's egg, although the maleos themselves are no bigger than a small chicken.

"They say the hen faints with pain each time she lays an egg which is why the cock must guard her so carefully," the warden explained, showing me one of the huge eggs. I don't know if this story is true but from the size of the egg in comparison to the size of the birds, I could well believe it.

The warden told me that when the chicks are hatched, they burrow up through the sand and go at once to water. They take a bath and then run for the bush. The parent birds pay no attention to them; the young are born completely independent and fully able to take care of themselves, just like young reptiles.

I spent several days at Gorontalo, mainly in the bush watching the maleos and studying their habits. They are very nervous creatures, fast runners and good fliers. They are grayish-black and have tiny combs of hard skin. I noticed that they followed little paths like rabbit trails through the bushes and so I put out some snares. After a little trouble, I caught three pair. They ate and drank readily in captivity and quieted down almost at once. Not even catching the Indian rhinos gave me so much satisfaction. I thought, and still think, that the maleos are one of the most interesting birds in the world.

I arrived at Bumbulan a day late but the *Kakap* had politely waited for me, her captain remarking, "We wouldn't leave you here with your birds as you think so much of them." The other passengers, instead of objecting to a twenty-four-hour delay in the murderous heat, were all charming and insisted on giving the birds the coolest section of the deck. We arrived at Manado without incident except that while riding from the port to the town in a bus, we were shot at by bandits. However, no one was hurt.

In Manado, I was picked up by the police. Although I had a permit for the maleos from the Celebes Game Department, Java had revoked it. While I was in Java I'd agreed to show a film on wildlife at the Bogor Institute. A note had been sent to my hotel by the university authorities naming a date but I was away at the time and hadn't received it. As a result, two hundred university students had been disappointed. The authorities considered that I'd deliberately insulted their institution, and revoked my permit.

I pointed out that thousands of the eggs were being dug up

every year by the Chinese merchants with the full consent of the Indonesian government. The only answer was a shrug. I argued that the local populace trapped the birds regularly for food. I begged them to let me take the birds to Java and argue my case there. More shrugs. The birds were killed and eaten by the police and I returned to Java empty-handed.

I had managed to conceal four maleo eggs in my pockets and I hoped to be able to hatch them out. The hatching period is sixty days but although I buried the eggs in sand and kept them warm, nothing happened. They must have been too much shaken in transit. So my great plan to start a new colony of these fantastic birds came to nothing. It is a great pity for, as things are going now, the maleos will soon be gone and hardly even a record of them will remain.

I was deluged with orders for Indonesian animals and although it was almost impossible for a European to obtain export permits, I refused to give up. At last through various contacts, I was able to obtain a few permits and spent the next six months trapping in the archipelago. I was able to get several of the beautiful clouded leopards, which are not really leopards at all but a giant wildcat. They are only about three feet long with thick, soft fur, marked with both spots and stripes and looking as though they had been dusted over with fine powder. We caught these handsome cats in box traps baited with chickens. I also got some of the exquisite mouse deer, no bigger than a small rabbit. The deer were lured in by beating on the ground with sticks to imitate the stamping of the male in rut, the same method used to catch agoutis in South America. Although American zoos would have paid large sums for these wonderful little fellows, they cannot be imported into the United States because they are cloven-hoofed animals and so could conceivably spread hoof-and-mouth and other diseases. Mine all went to Europe. I also got a number of the strange antenna snakes that have feelers like a catfish and live in swamps. Red-faced and stump-tailed monkeys were easy to capture. The natives put out coconuts with a small hole in the top just big enough to admit the monkey's hand, and then scrape the white "meat" inside the nut until it is loose enough for the monkey to grab a handful. The monkeys put in their hands, grab a fistful of the meat, and then cannot withdraw their hands. Rather than release the handful, they allow themselves to be caught.

In spite of this trait, the stump-tails are very clever little fellows and are often trained by the natives to collect coconuts. The monkey climbs to the top of a coconut palm and touches each nut in turn, looking down at his master for orders. When he reaches a ripe nut, his master gives him a signal and the monkey twists it until it drops. A really well-trained monkey is a very valuable possession and really earns his way in life.

I tried to catch some of the giant forest pigs with great, curving tusks that often form a complete spiral. But the natives refused to have anything to do with the animals, not from fear but because they were Mohammendans and the pig is considered an unclean animal. I did manage to get a number of gavials, curious, crocodile-like reptiles reaching twelve feet in length with long noses like the handle of a frying pan. Gavials are quite harmless, living entirely on fish, and are often caught in fishermen's nets.

A very different proposition was the great thirty-foot salt water crocodiles, inveterate man-eaters, that are the largest reptiles in the world. Nearly every croc killed has a collection of women's ornaments in his belly, for the women go down to the rivers to wash their clothes and the big crocs, coming up the streams from the ocean, lie in wait for them. The local sultans offer a bounty for these crocs, depending on how many ornaments are found in their stomachs. The natives have an ingenious way of trapping these monsters. They construct a long runway to the stream, wide at the mouth and gradually narrowing until it is only slightly wider than a croc's body. A goat or a dog is tied at the narrow end as bait. The croc crawls up the runway until he is in the narrow section. He has no room to turn and he is too big and heavy to back up. I could have gotten all of these crocs I wished but there is no demand for them and the cost of shipping such a gigantic animal would be enormous, a big croc weighing well over a ton.

All during my trapping, there was one animal ever present in my mind: the famous Komodo dragon. These great lizards have been called "the last of the dinosaurs." They reach a length of twelve feet or more and may weigh as much as 300 pounds. They were unknown until 1912 when a Dutchman brought back four specimens. They are found only on a chain of four islands, Komodo, Padar, Rintja and Flores, to the east of Bali. At that time, there were none in captivity in either Europe or the United States, although there were a dozen or so in the Surabaja Zoo. The director was asking the fantastic price of $5,000 each for them, F.O.B. Surabaja. No zoo would pay this absurd price so the lizards remained in Surabaja. But I knew that there were plenty more on the islands and I was determined to get at least a pair.

I moved heaven and earth trying to get a permit to capture some of the dragons, but without success. Still, I wasn't discouraged. I sent letters to two of the best known American zoos, explaining the situation and asking what price they would pay for Komodo dragons. Without waiting for a reply, I took a trading schooner that made irregular trips from Bali through the archipelago and after a ten-day trip, I arrived at Komodo Island.

Komodo is volcanic. The center is a vast mass of curious sugarloaf mountains, surrounded by ridges of jagged rock that are almost unclimbable. The rest of the island is mostly jungle, full of coconut and uraka palms and cut up by deep valleys with a few open stretches where nothing but an occasional bush grows. There is a little town on the island, ruled over by a local sultan, and a population of a few hundred Malayans. For a small sum, a native family gave me a room in their house and as soon as I had washed and changed, I went to see the sultan's secretary.

I was assured that as far as the sultan was concerned, I could catch all the lizards I wished for 1,000 rupias each. There are twelve rupias to the dollar at the official exchange and thirty-eight to the dollar on the black market—which is everywhere. At that rate, the lizards would cost me $26 each—fair enough. Of course, any arrangement I made with the sultan wouldn't be recognized in Java but I decided to worry about that when the time came.

The next day I went out, with two natives as guides, to see the lizards. I didn't intend to capture any this trip, I just wanted to see and learn something about them. Then, after finding out what the zoos would pay, I'd make my plans.

We traveled the first part of the journey by bullock cart and then went on by foot. The lizards live in dens among the rocks and by the time we reached the first line of hills, it was evening. I could see the lizards' tracks along the beaches, together with the tracks of crocodiles. The lizards' tracks were just as big but their tails left a wavy line while the heavier tails of the crocs made a straight mark. We saw several wild pigs and the guides told me that these are the lizards' principal food.

We camped along the rocks for the night and as soon as it was light, we crawled up on a high ridge to wait. When the sun had warmed the rocks, we began to see the lizards emerging from their lairs. Although I had seen and handled the eight-foot kabaragoya lizards, I got a shock when I saw these monsters. Most of them were not much over eight feet but they were much heavier than the kabaragoyas, the difference between an eight-foot bull snake and an eight-foot anaconda. I saw one stand up on his hind legs to sniff the morning breeze. He was nearly as tall as a man. Their long tongues were constantly flicking in and out. Probably like snakes they could pick up minute particles of matter carried by the wind and transfer the particles to the taste organs in the roofs of their mouths, "tasting" the air so to speak. The natives told me that the lizards were completely deaf but could smell a man a mile away. Fortunately, we were upwind of them.

I spent all day watching them and would gladly have spent a week. They seemed to grow more active as the sun grew hotter, making occasional short dashes after some small quarry with surprising speed. Like most cold-blooded creatures, their actions seemed entirely dependent on the temperature. If it was cold, they were sluggish. If warm, they were very active. The natives told me that they could catch deer. I believe it; even a five-foot monitor lizard can catch a rabbit by making a sudden dash. For a hundred feet or so, lizards are astonishingly fast. Even a heavy crocodile can put on an amazing burst of speed for a few yards.

I asked if the lizards ever attacked humans. The natives said that they'd never heard of a case; humans seldom went to the mountainous central area where the lizards live. They did, however, often attack dogs that went wild. "On Padar Island, wild dogs are the lizards' main food now that most of the deer have been shot," one man told me.

The natives assured me that catching the lizards would be no problem. A tree is bent down and a noose is tied to the end, attached to a trigger release. A dead pig is used for bait. When the lizard puts his head in the noose to get the pig, the trigger releases the tree and the reptile is caught. The more decayed the bait the better, for although the lizards do often kill for themselves, they are largely carrion eaters. With their remarkable sense of smell, they can scent carrion a long distance off and will head for it immediately.

On the way back to Java, I did a great deal of thinking and when I arrived on the island, I spent several days going through all the records I could find of the Komodo dragons. Finally, I presented myself at the forestry department in Bogor.

I based my arguments for a permit mainly on a government pamphlet, put out by the Indonesian forestry department itself, on the situation in Padar. In the past, the giant lizards on Padar had lived on deer but in recent years, natives had gone to the island on hunting trips with dogs and exterminated the deer population. Some of the dogs had been left behind and the lizards had managed to survive by eating the dogs. Now the dogs were fast disappearing and, according to the forestry pamphlet, the lizards on Padar would starve to death within the next few years. In exchange for a few of the lizards, I offered to trap as many as possible and liberate them on any other island designated by the Indonesian government. I also, of course, agreed to pay any reasonable sum for a trapping permit.

My offer was flatly refused. The lizards were a valuable natural resource, worth $5,000 each according to the director of the Surabaja Zoo. If I wanted any lizards, I would have to buy them at that figure from the zoo.

I still wasn't beaten. It would be perfectly feasible to go to Komodo, pay off the local sultan, and get the lizards from Padar without the consent of the Indonesian government. I was very reluctant to do such a thing. It would mean that Indonesia would be closed to me from then on and besides, I don't believe in such methods. Still, this was an emergency. The Padar lizards were dying and in some cases the end justifies the means.

Then I received a letter from each of the two American zoos. The letters were so nearly identical that I'm certain the zoo directors must have prepared them together. They offered me $750 each for the dragons, to be paid when the lizards were actually delivered at the zoos. Of course, such an offer was ridiculous. The lizards would have to be flown to the United States—they were far too valuable to ship by water—and such a sum wouldn't even pay the freight. The zoos explained that in 1936 a scientific expedition had gone to Komodo, gotten a few of the lizards through arrangements with the Dutch govern-ment, and sold them for that sum. Naturally, conditions were uterly different then and besides the expedition had been heavily subsidized and had sold the lizards for merely a token payment on return.

With the exception of the giant panda, the Komodo dragon is the greatest "drawing card" any zoo can have, so I tell the story to show how little knowledge zoo directors seem to have of actual conditions in the field. But a few years later, the Surabaja Zoo did get $5,000 for a pair of Komodo dragons. The pair were bought by the Bronx Zoological Park and *Life* magazine,

*Life* putting up half the sum in return for exclusive use of the story. This sale has now definitely established the price of these reptiles at the enormous sum put on them by the Surabaja Zoo, although I doubt if any more will ever be sold at such a figure. I believe that if the Indonesian government put a reasonable price on the lizards—say $1,500 each—a small number could be collected every year and part of the sum could be set aside to provide food for the remainder, thus preserving the species and providing a source of modest but regular "dollar income" for the new republic. The Belgian government does this with the okapi and it seems to me a very good system.

I stayed on in Indonesia and continued to do some collecting but the difficulty in obtaining permits was almost insurmountable. Mercia had sold the young orangs in Europe for $3,000 each and there was an international demand for the big, red apes. Unfortunately I couldn't get permission to take any more. Orangs were being constantly shipped from Indonesia but they were all smuggled out, usually by Chinese merchants. It was a fantastic business. Through my various connections with animal dealers, I once had the opportunity to see twenty-eight baby orangs being smuggled into Singapore by night. A junk was waiting offshore and, after an exchange of signals flashed by lanterns, a boat was sent in with the babies. They were quickly picked up by the waiting men and the boat raced back to the ship. The sail was instantly raised and the junk got under way while the shore party leaped into cars, disappearing in all directions. It must have been very much like the old slaving days. As Singapore is a British crown colony, the bills of lading would show the "port of origin" as being somewhere else than Indonesia. The babies were in a terrible state, having been hidden below deck all during the voyage and half dead from damp and starvation. What a pity the Indonesian government does not see fit to organize the exportation of these rare animals instead of forcing it into the hands of smugglers.

I reluctantly came to the conclusion that attempting to trap in Indonesia was not practical. The former colonial possessions that have now gained their freedom are suffering from a violent sense of inferiority. Inexperienced, eager to establish themselves as important people, they take great pride in their "ancestral culture" while at the same time trying to modernize. Although they hate and despise their former rulers, they try desperately to copy them and often succeed only in copying their arrogance and not their ability. Even educated natives fail to realize that the "arrogant" European usually knew his job and worked hard, and they had no idea how much the former colonial powers did until the whole responsibility was dumped in their laps. The lower classes are unchanged; it is the half-educated groups that present the difficulty. Many of these men confuse cleverness with intelligence, stubbornness with firmness, rudeness with authority. Time will correct these faults but time is a precious commodity with the communists pressing in from all sides.

Merca flew out to meet me in Colombo and we discussed our future plans. I'd failed in Indonesia, there was no doubt of that, but the Philadelphia Zoo in the United States had ordered a pair of Indian rhinos and I had obtained the trapping permits from Assam. After getting the rhinos, I'd intended to send them with some capable man to America while remaining in India to pick up some other animals, but Mercia had a different idea.

"Peter, we must deliver the rhinos ourselves," she told me. "Remember the sensation we caused in Europe with the first pair? People have got to know about you. We'll take over a whole shipment . . . not only the rhinos but tigers, leopards, pythons . . . and sell them directly to the zoos without going through a dealer who'd put a markup of two or three hundred per cent on them."

I tried to explain to Mercia how impractical it was to arrive in a strange country with a cargo of animals hoping to sell them. But she was so determined that, against my better judgment, I agreed. With our precious knowledge of the business, trapping the two rhinos turned out to be a routine job. We also picked up 2 tigers, 5 leopards, 2 leopard-cats, 8 pythons, 15 cobras, and 4 kabaragoya lizards which are nearly as big as the

Komodo dragons. We also had several hundred cranes, storks and smaller birds. In addition, I secured several dozen Ceylonese kangaroo rats, one of the rarest of the rat family. With high hopes we loaded our cargo on the *City of Capetown* and sailed for New York.

# Chapter 15

# Elephants and America

WHILE CROSSING the Mediterranean, we ran
into the worst storm I've ever experienced at sea. Wave after
wave crashed down upon the deck and the cages were flung
about like paper boxes. Mercia and I lashed down the rhino
crates, using every piece of rope the crew could spare us, and
I threw open the doors of the monkey cages to give the poor
creatures a chance for life. The monkeys promptly dashed below, most of them ending up in the engine room. I managed to
get the bird cages below decks but the other animals had to take
their chances. One of the leopard-cats got such a soaking that
he was half dead when the storm subsided. Leopard-cats are
savage little customers not much bigger than a domestic cat,
but this one had all the fight knocked out of him. Mercia took
the scarcely conscious animal to her bunk and nursed him back
to health with brandy, massage and hot milk. As soon as he
had recovered enough to stand, he bit Mercia, scratched me,
and wrecked the cabin. We had all we could do to get him back
in his cage.

It took us several days to recapture the monkeys and at first
the captain and the crew considered them a great joke. One
monkey moved into the galley and the cook used to give him
any meat left in the hamburger grinder. The monkey learned to
operate the grinder and ground his own meat. Another group
of monkeys joined some seamen who were painting between

decks. The men left for a coffee break and when they returned, found that the monkeys had taken the brushes and were busily painting away. Unfortunately, the monkeys finished the job by eating the brushes. Mercia and I couldn't catch the monkeys by ourselves and the crew enjoyed them so much that no one would help us, but one afternoon the captain entered his cabin to find one of the monks using his toothbrush as a back scratcher. After that, the captain ordered the crew to see that all monkeys were returned to their cages.

The only animals I lost were the Ceylonese rats. Their cages were smashed and they ran all through the ship. As they were worth $15 each, I tried hard to recapture them but without success. The rats enjoyed life at sea and have since bred and done very well. The *City of Capetown* is now fortunate in possessing one of the rarest rats in the world, although neither the captain nor the crew seemed especially grateful to me.

As we approached the United States, I became more and more apprehensive about selling the cargo. Except for the rhinos, we didn't have a single animal on consignment. I didn't even know if the customs officials would allow them off the ship. Mercia tried to buck me up. "You've studied the market and you know that all these animals are in big demand. As for the customs officials, we can always bribe them."

"You can't bribe American customs officials," I told her miserably.

Mercia stared at me in astonishment. "Can't bribe the customs officials? What a terrible country! Why did you ever bring me here?" and the poor girl burst into tears.

I consoled her as best I could but we were both miserably apprehensive as the ship entered Boston harbor. I knew that even under the best possible conditions, we had a long job ahead of us. We would have to rent a storehouse to keep the animals, arrange for food, write scores of letters and make hundreds of phone calls. The future looked gloomy.

As the ship approached the dock a Cadillac half a block long and covered with gleaming chrome came tearing up and stopped with a scream of brakes. Two men jumped out and ran to the edge of the dock. One of them shouted. "Is Peter Ryhiner, the animal catcher, on board?"

"Here I am," I yelled.

"Have you any animals besides the rhinos?"

"Plenty!" shouted Mercia. "We have—"

"We don't care what you have, we'll buy the whole consignment," one of the men shouted back.

"How much?"

"Put your own price on them. How long will it take you to unload? We haven't any time to waste. Start getting the cages up now."

One man rushed away to find trucks. The other went to arrange for import permits. Mercia sat down weakly on the deck. Finally she managed to gasp, "See, what did I tell you? I knew America would be like this!"

When the ship docked and the two men were able to get aboard, we found that they were from the North Atlantic Fertilizer Company which, they assured us, was the biggest wholesale house for wild animals in the country. This seemed a curious title for an animal import firm but we asked no questions. Mercia asked double what we had hoped to get for the cargo and the men instantly consented. Mercia was heartbroken. "I knew I should have asked three times as much," she whispered to me bitterly. We had one big leopard that was very tame and Mercia tried to correct her mistake by saying that he wasn't included with the other animals but that she'd let him go for a very special price. The men paid it without question. The pythons we sold by the foot, $5 per foot of snake. After glancing at the snakes, one of the men remarked, "They seem to average about fifteen feet each. Shall we settle for that?"

"Oh no you don't!" snapped Mercia. "We'll measure them right here on deck." All the pythons were taken out and measured with a yardstick. Handling an 18 or 20 foot python is quite a problem but Mercia held their tails and I took their heads, Mercia stretching them until their backbones almost cracked.

The check amounted to more money than either Mercia or I had ever seen at one time. After the men left, we sat in our cabin staring at the check and at each other, unable to speak.

We went on to Philadelphia with the rhinos where a big reception had been arranged for us. We were swamped by TV cameramen, newsreels, press photographers and reporters. Mercia posed in a sarong, in a special "jungle costume" with shorts designed to show her pretty legs, and in her Paris gowns. I think she must have changed her outfit twenty times in three-quarters of an hour. In some miraculous way, Mercia had picked up American slang and habits apparently by osmosis, although I noticed that she had talked quite a bit to the sailors between Boston and Philadelphia. She chattered with the reporters about baseball scores, how she was looking forward to seeing everything from the Empire State Building to the Grand Canyon, and how she had dreamed all her life of coming to the United States. As usual, she made a tremendous hit.

Mercia's picture—with or without the rhinos—was plastered over the front page of the newspapers. We began to get letters, phone calls, and telegrams from zoos, dealers, and lecture agencies all over the country. We went to New York and took a hotel room until we could go through the pile. With all these offers plus our profit on the voyage, it seemed to me that we could do a little celebrating, so I took Mercia to the best restaurant I could find. Mercia cares little what she eats or drinks, but she seemed to be having a good time until the check came. She snatched it up and then gave a scream that caused the startled waiter to leap into the air.

"My God, for this much we could live for six months in Singapore! Let's get back to the hotel. We're not safe out of our rooms. What a terrible country!"

The next day we discovered that the two men from the North Atlantic Fertilizer Company had sold the animals for an enormous profit. They'd disposed of the tame black leopard the same day for a profit of nearly $600 to a television program that needed a tame leopard. As far as Mercia was concerned, this was the final blow. She sat in our room moaning, "We've been robbed! Oh, why didn't I know about that TV program!" Her pleasure in the very substantial profit we'd made was completely spoiled.

I tried to explain to her that an animal collector can't possibly keep in touch with current demands which is why collectors nearly always have to sell to dealers who, in turn, retail the animals. Mercia was finally convinced although, as she said quite truthfully, "It's the dealers who make the big profits while running none of the risks. You should be a dealer."

"I'm not a business man," I told her. "And besides, the dealers don't have any fun."

"Fun!" sniffed Mercia. "You call it fun to live in the jungle and clean manure out of cages?"

I did, but I knew better than to argue with Mercia.

We signed a contract with Colston Leigh, one of the biggest lecture agents, for a six months' tour. Mr. Leigh was disappointed that we had no motion pictures but I'm a fairly good amateur photographer so it was arranged that the tour would be put off until after our next trip and meanwhile we would get some pictures of the animal trapping. The terms Mr. Leigh offered us were so favorable that Mercia gave up all ideas of making me an animal dealer instead of a collector. Our only problem was where to make our next trip.

The next day, we were called into the office of Mr. Zeehandelaar, the head of the animal-dealing department of the North Atlantic Fertilizer Company. We discovered that the organization had indeed started as a fertilizer company but now had many interests, of which the animal business was one. Mr. Zeehandelaar explained how he operated.

"As you know, there are enormous profits to be made in the animal business," he began. "Animals that can be picked up for a few dollars abroad will sell for huge sums in the United States. Yet all animal collectors and most dealers are constantly broke."

Mercia and I nodded. Every collector, including ourselves, was living from hand to mouth and we knew that even dealers often went bankrupt, although from the mark-ups they put on animals, I could never understand why.

"The trouble is that the business isn't organized. Now I propose to bring modern American business methods to the animal game. See that blackboard there?" He pointed to a gigantic blackboard covering one side of the room. "There I keep a list, which is changed from day to day, of anyone desiring animals and also what animals they want and what they'll pay. You'll notice the list includes zoos, circuses, carnivals, traveling menageries, Hollywood and TV productions, little roadside zoos and small exhibition parks in various parts of the country, and even private individuals. Now here," and he produced a file, "is a card index of dealers, animal collectors, and so on who have animals for sale, showing what they have and the prices they are asking. As a result of this system, we can supply anyone with virtually any sort of animal at a moment's notice."

We stared with our eyes popping. This was big business indeed.

"But that's not all," Mr. Zeehandelaar went on. "We have salesmen touring the country checking all possible sources requiring animals. If you know where we can get a number of a certain species cheap, the salesmen plug that line. They do a lot of entertaining, get a lot of off-the-record information, and telephone in their reports. Over there we have a teleprinter which brings us the market quotations on animals from all over the world. For example, zebras have dropped considerably on the market in the last few days, while elephants are up. There's a growing trend in elephants, I may as well tell you. All this information is filed on cards which are then run through machines that give us the statistical results."

He took up a list that looked like stock exchange quotations.

"Our latest survey shows us that in spring there will be a demand for young, female Indian elephants all below five feet at the shoulder. Can you supply us by the first of May with ten such elephants? We will pay you $2,200 each for them, landed in New York harbor."

The elephants would bring us a profit of about $20,000, in addition to whatever we made on other animals brought over on the same ship. We were enormously impressed by Mr. Zee-handelaar's businesslike methods and the incredible organization he'd built up.

Although impressed, I was also doubtful. American business methods might work well for selling soap, refrigerators or chewing gum, but animals are a different proposition. To obtain ten baby elephants by May (it was now autumn) of the precise specifications laid down by Mr. Zeehandelaar would not be easy. On my first trip to India, I had gotten elephants but then I cared nothing about size or sex and did not have to have a certain number by a certain date. To make sure of fulfilling the contract, we would have to go on shikar in the Garo Hills to get the animals, and the problems involved in bringing back such young elephants were enormous. They would hardly be weaned. I tried to explain all this to Mr. Zeehandelaar but he stopped me with a good-natured smile.

"Look, what I'm interested in is can you do the job or can't you?"

Mercia and I looked at each other and I could see her lips form the words "twenty thousand dollars." I took a deep breath. "We can do it," I said.

Mercia and I left New York two days later by plane. We flew direct to Karachi and then took a local plane to Jorhat. Here we made arrangements to go out on shikar. I knew almost nothing about the business and badly missed Subrati; for the first time in India, I was without his help.

I discovered that there are two types of shikars; the keddah shikar and the mela shikar. In the keddah shikar, groups of wild elephants are driven into a big corral. In the mela shikar, young animals are noosed from the back of pad elephants in the jungles. The big keddah shikar was not due for several weeks yet and as I had no idea how many young elephants of the right

A Komodo dragon. These giant lizards from Indonesia sell to zoos for as much as $5,000 a pair.

Theo Meier enjoys a backrub in his Bali home.

Capturing a giraffe in Kenya. This method of roping an animal with a noose attached to a long pole worked equally well with zebra, eland and other plains animals.

*Gus Pasquarella*

I am working here with a new gadget which may revolutionize wild animal collecting. These are cartridges for a syringe gun, an air rifle which shoots a hypodermic needle into big game. The cartridge contains a syringe which, on contact with the animal, injects either curare or nicotine into its muscles, paralyzing it long enough for the hunter to secure it properly. For night hunting the fuzzy material on the tail of the cartridge can be dipped in phosphorus.

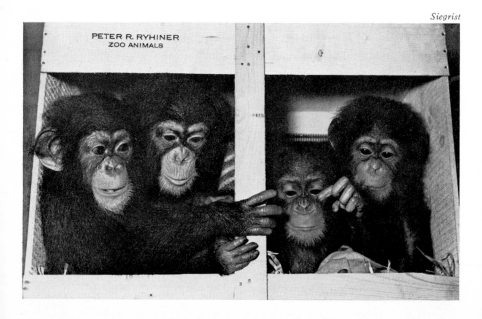

PETER R. RYHINER
ZOO ANIMALS

Far more difficult and hazardous than capturing the animals is keeping them secure and happy in captivity. The jaguar above did $12,000 worth of damage among the other animals and terrorized passengers and crew when he escaped from his shipboard cage. A ship's engineer snapped this picture through a ventilator from a safe hiding place.

←◄

Young chimps, like babies, require lots of love and attention to distract them from the restrictions and boredom of travel. Those on the opposite page kept Mercia busy during the sea voyage from Sierra Leone to Ceylon.

Hugo Mayr of Swissair and myself with Hairy Josephine, the terror of the television studios.

Mercia and I with some of the elephants we collected for Zeehandelaar.

specifications would be caught in it, I decided to go out on mela shikars while waiting.

For this hunt, two kunkis (tame elephants) are used. Two men—the mahout and the phundi (hunter)—ride on each elephant. The phundi has a long, soft hemp lasso. No other tools are needed.

The kunkis follow the herd for days while the men study the herd's habits and decide which young animals they will attempt to capture. The men also keep an eye out for the old herd bull. The herds are composed of females and young bulls, but every herd has an old bull. The bull does not stay with the others but maintains a parallel course two or three miles away. The babies must be captured when the herd bull is as far away as possible. If he is able to join the others, he can easily defeat the kunkis. For some reason, tame bull elephants lack virility. They usually cannot even breed the tame cows, who in season must be staked out in the jungles to be bred by wild bulls.

No one knows when the opportunity will come to capture the calves and the hunt may take two or three weeks. Although the phundis agreed to take me, Mercia had to stay behind. If a woman has her monthly period while in the jungle, a curse is put on the whole expedition and the phundis wouldn't run the risk. Mercia wanted to go as she didn't trust either the phundis or me to get the right calves, but it was absolutely impossible.

Scouts reported the presence of a herd a few miles from our camp and the hunters performed the pudja, an elaborate ceremony which includes the sacrifice of a white cock and two white pigeons to assure good luck. Then we started out on the two kunkis. Our only food was two sacks of rice, but the hunters told me that sometimes it was possible to catch the calves within a day or two, and I certainly hoped this would be one of those times.

We picked up the track of the herd, simple enough to do for their path was strewn with broken branches where they had been feeding and the marks of their huge feet were clear in the soft loam of the jungle. Late that afternoon we caught up with them. There were twelve cows and five young bulls as well as three calves, just weaned. Of course, it was the calves in which we were interested. We had to find if they were males or females.

I was amazed at how close the men could approach the herd on the kunkis. Apparently wild elephants can't distinguish a man on the back of a tame elephant and, what is even more surprising, can't scent him. However, when the men were in sight of the herd, they never spoke and seldom moved. At the first signs of restlessness in the herd, the mahouts quietly swung the kunkis about and moved away. If alarmed, a herd cow can move with astonishing swiftness and the kunkis can't possibly keep up with them.

Two of the calves were females. "It would do us no good even if there were more, for we can only catch two calves," one of the phundis told me when we camped for the night. "That is all our kunkis can handle." We ate our rice cold, for we did not dare light a fire. The hunters told me that sometimes they were able to catch fish on these hunts but they could not shoot for the sound would frighten the herd. Meat cannot be carried as it would go bad in the intense heat, and canned foods are too costly, so rice with some vegetable curry is the staple diet.

We followed the herd for five days, camping in the evenings. The hunters took turns watching the elephants during the night for sometimes a herd moves on without warning. Twice the herd drifted on unexpectedly and both times we instantly had to break camp and follow. While one kunki followed the herd, the other went off to keep track of the herd bull who was following his harem a mile or so away. Until the distance between them widened, we could do nothing.

On the afternoon of the sixth day, the kunki following the herd bull returned and the phundi reported that the bull was in a wallow four miles away, and would probably remain there for the rest of the day. This was the moment for which we'd been waiting. The phundis uncoiled their ropes and the mahouts urged the kunkis forward.

Guided by the knees of the mahouts, the kunkis moved in to cut out a cow with a female calf at her side. As the pad elephants came in on either side of the cow, one of the phundis swung his rope and noosed the calf around the neck. The calf squealed loudly and her mother turned on us, trumpeting a warning to the rest of the herd. The others began to trumpet and came for us. The biggest kunki turned away and met the charge. He had enormous tusks and the cows could do nothing against him. The herd, even the calf's mother, didn't put up as much of a fight as I'd expected. Later, the phundis told me that the females are instinctively cowed by the presence of a big bull with tusks. When the herd was driven back, the phundi on the second kunki also roped the struggling calf and she was dragged off between the pad elephants with her mother following anxiously after us. As soon as we were clear, the baby was tied to a tree and then both kunkis chased the mother back to the herd.

The second calf was captured in the same way an hour or so later. After that, the herd took the alarm and started running, or rather drifting at full speed through the jungle at a pace the kunkis could not hope to match.

The two calves stood a little under four feet and were about a year old. The phundis told me that such small animals are never ordinarily captured as they are only partly weaned and too much trouble to rear. Ordinarily I wouldn't have taken them myself, much preferring babies two or three years old and well over five feet at the shoulder, but Zeehandelaar's instructions had been specific.

We hurried the two calves back to the bungalow where Mercia was waiting. They had to be dragged along between the kunkis which was much too hard on such little things but we were forced to move fast, for the babies had to be fed as soon as possible and we were three days from camp. Mercia was ready for us. Raising the babies would be a major task (the phundis had said flatly that it couldn't be done), but Mercia had made all arrangements. She had gotten several milk buffalos and also had a supply of canned lactogene, a milk formula which I consider is the best substitute for mother's milk with baby animals.

By combining the buffalo milk with the lactogene, plus some cod liver oil extract and a few vitamins, we were able to rear the babies. It was a terrific undertaking. A hollow bamboo had to be inserted in their mouths and the milk poured down it, taking care that the babies didn't choke. At first the babies fought so desperately that they didn't realize that they were being fed, any more than a man being given intravenous injections realizes that he is receiving nourishment. But once they grew tame, they followed us around the camp and even became a nuisance. If we tied them up, they cried so pitifully we couldn't stand it and once loose, they were all over us like enormous dogs that don't realize their own strength. Their diet had to be carefully watched for one feeding of milk that had gone slightly soured could have killed them both. The lactogene went bad very quickly in the intense heat and the buffalo milk wasn't rich enough in itself to sustain them. But at least they were old enough to take some solid food and by supplementing their milk formula with green fodder, we were able to pull them through.

The phundis got four more calves on other mela shikars but then the herds moved away. As we needed ten calves, we had to rely on the keddah shikar for the others.

The biggest keddah shikar is held high in the Garo Hills, almost within sight of the Himalayan range, and the time had now come for the great annual event. Men had been at work for weeks constructing a giant corral of heavy teak stakes, bound together with strong ropes to give additional strength. This corral was circular, about fifty yards in diameter, and the stockade stood some fifteen feet. A trench, six feet deep and six feet wide, ran around the inside as not even the heavy stakes could withstand the attack of an elephant herd unless the force of their charge could be broken in some way. There was a swinging door at the entrance of the corral with two platforms on either side where the men could stand who had the all-important task of handling the door.

A long, V-shaped runway led into the corral, made of lighter stakes and carefully camouflaged with vines and creepers. A few miles away was a salt lick which the herds were accustomed to visiting every few weeks.

A herd with suitable calves was at the salt lick. When I say "suitable calves" I mean from the point of view of the forestry department who needs young elephants to be trained for work in the lumber camps and as pad animals; that is, calves eight to ten years old. The kaddah shikar was not being conducted for my benefit but is an important economic function and has been so conducted for hundreds of years. The demand for elephants has decreased greatly since the days when certain rajahs used to have stables of two or even three thousand war elephants. After the Battle of Dehli in the seventeenth century, the victorious Timur was able to capture three thousand elephants from his defeated rivals. Even within the memory of living man, two thousand elephants a year were sold at the great Sonpur market. But last year, only twenty-five were sold and soon the market will be no more, for tractors are taking the elephant's place. However, there are still certain areas where the lumbering must still be done by elephants, and to satisfy this demand a few young animals are captured every year. I had a permit to get six young female calves, if any under five feet happened to be caught in the drive.

Mercia and I went to the corral, riding there on the back of pad elephants. Scores of men were busy strengthening the stockade and planting decoy trees in the corral so it would not look too barren and cause the herd to turn away. We were told that the shikari were out watching the chosen herd and other men were in trees around the salt lick to give the signal when the herd came in.

I went out to inspect the salt lick. The forestry rangers wouldn't let me get too close but they explained that elephants do not lick salt as do cows or horses. With their trunks they pick up clods of the salt-impregnated earth and chew it. According to the shikari following the herd, the elephants would come in that evening. Then the drive would begin.

Mercia and I took up our positions on the stockade. It was lined with men carrying sharpened poles, torches, and noisemakers for, in spite of the trench and stockades, the elephants would still break through if left to themselves. The herd would have to be kept in the corral all night for the drive took place after dark and the phundis could not go into the corral to separate the calves from the cows until it was daylight and they could see to work.

About 11 o'clock that night, a shikari came in to report that the herd was at the lick. A small army of several hundred men silently spread out to start the drive, carrying horns, drums, and a few old muskets loaded with black powder. Other men lined the sides of the long runway leading to the corral but kept themselves carefully concealed. The men on the platforms tested the swinging gate and a last minute check was made of the stockade. At any moment now, the drive would start.

Then we heard the faint sound of yells, drums, and horns . . . punctured by the occasional boom of a musket fired into the air. The sounds grew louder but we could see nothing in the darkness. Suddenly the men at the wide mouth of the runaway began shouting. That meant the herd had passed them and were in the chute. They could still break out, for the walls of the chute were too light to stand a determined attack, but with men on both sides and behind them, the herd would probably run forward.

We saw the first of the great, gray shapes in the semi-darkness as they drifted through the trees towards the entrance of the stockade. As the herd passed, men appeared as if by magic on the walls of the chute, shouting, waving torches, beating on pans and blowing horns. It was absolutely necessary that the herd be panicked now and driven into the corral as fast as possible.

The first of the herd plunged into the carefully camouflaged entrance to the corral and tore through the planted saplings and bushes. The rest followed them, jostling each other in their eagerness to escape the figures springing up on either side. Behind them were coming the drivers, making more noise than an inferno full of devils but ahead everything seemed peaceful and safe. As the last animal entered the corral, a man slashed the vine holding back the door. The heavy door slammed shut. Instantly, great beams were raised by a score of hands and thrown into place. The herd was caught.

Within a few seconds, the milling animals had trampled the artificial jungle within the corral absolutely flat. Then for the first time they could see the stockade around them and realized that they were trapped. Led by the young bulls, they charged the teak stakes repeatedly. The men on the stockade fought the crazed animals back, prodding them with poles, firing off blank cartridges, waving torches in their faces. The rest of the men had run up to join us with their noise-makers and the racket was deafening, but through all the tumult sounded the furious trumpeting of the captive animals as they rushed the stockade, pushing against it with their broad foreheads or trying to tear the stakes loose with their trunks. Time after time they came on until I thought that they would surely break through, but at last the fury of the attack passed and the herd began milling, some of them even pausing to pick up the crushed shrubbery with their trunks and eat it.

Although the herd had stopped attacking, an even greater disaster threatened. The young bulls started fighting among themselves. Many animals will do this as a nervous reaction to capture. In the confines of the stockade, the beaten animal could not escape his tormentor. The fights grew worse and worse. By morning, the corral would be full of dead or dying elephants.

"The kunkis will have to be sent in, in spite of the darkness," an old shikari told me regretfully. Even as he spoke, the gate of the corral was slowly swung back and the big, bull kunkis drifted in with their mahouts on their necks. The kunkis with long, sharp tusks were more than a match for the young, tuskless bulls. They broke up the fights but it was dangerous work, the elephants and men working by the dim, uncertain light of the flaring torches which cast black impenetrable shadows. The struggle kept up all night, men yelling until they were hoarse, the mahouts forcing the nervous kunkis on with drumming knees, the watchers on the stockade fighting back the infuriated animals with their long poles and the forestry officer shouting orders that the shikari tried vainly to obey.

At last, dawn came and the roping of the calves could be attempted. This was exactly like a mela shikar, two big kunkis going in, each with a mahout and a phundi, to noose the calves. The cows did their best to protect their babies, holding on to them with their trunks and butting at the kunkis but they had no chance against the bulls' tusks. The corral looked like a sea of snakes as the herd raised their trunks to try to get the scent of their enemies. The young males pawed the ground like bulls and threw dust over their backs as they tried to work up enough courage to charge the kunkis. I saw an old cow come up to the stockade and test stake after stake with her trunk, looking for a loose one before the men were able to drive her back with their sharpened poles.

We got two more female calves from this drive, but we were still two short of the ten that Zeehandelaar wanted. How we would get these last two, I had no idea.

It took about eight hours to catch and remove all the calves. I knew that when the last calf was secured the herd would be turned loose, and I wanted a picture of it. We had run out of film so I asked the forestry official if he would wait until I returned. The distracted man, bellowing orders to mahouts, told me that he would. Leaving Mercia on the stockade, I ran to where we had left the film, got some rolls, and started back.

I was still a few yards from the entrance to the corral when I saw the gate swing open and the herd rushed out. I was right in their path. Luckily, there was a tree there and I jumped behind it. The herd rushed past me on both sides; I could have reached out and touched them. I stood there shaking while the great beasts thundered by. I think that I've never been so scared in my life. Fortunately, the elephants paid no attention to me. They only wanted to get away.

The forestry official apologized to me later. "I forgot all about you, I had too many things to think about," he explained. Mercia's only comment was, "Did you get any good pictures? We need them for the lecture."

The baby elephants tamed easily. The mahouts told me that in spite of the frantic efforts the mothers made to save their babies, within a few hours they would forget all about them. "We know this is true, sahib," one of the men explained. "Because sometimes we capture a calf and then find that we don't want it, for example, if the calf turns out to have seventeen toenails, which brings bad luck. When we turn the calf loose, he will instantly rejoin the herd but after two or three days the mother will reject him."

I had no idea how we were to get our last two calves and greatly missed Subrati who had connections throughout India and was able to produce animals in the most mysterious ways. Then we had a stroke of luck. Some cows with their calves were caught in a ravine—a sort of natural pit—and couldn't escape even though the whole herd stayed there for several days trying to help them. The shikari told us of the situation and we went there immediately. By breaking down the sides of the ravine, we allowed the imprisoned animals to escape but we kept two female calves. At long last, I had my ten females, all under five feet at the shoulder.

Most of the babies we kept tied up but the very little ones had the run of the camp. When we ate, they would come running to the table to get their "specials," such as butter-and-sugar sandwiches, and if they didn't get enough, they'd butt at the table and push it over. They were terribly inquisitive little rascals, always sticking their trunks into things, especially the pots on the stove. They were constantly getting burned and would then run to Mercia to be petted and consoled. There was a Hollywood camera crew at the camp on a tour of India and one night the smallest of the babies got cold and went into the tent of one of the photographers. When the man woke up next morning there was the baby lying by his cot, snoring away. We only had one bad-tempered baby, the biggest of the lot, named Marguerite. Marguerite had an even worse disposition than Gertrude. She'd grab you by the leg and trip you up as you went by. Whenever she managed to get loose, which was often for she was terribly strong, she'd butt everyone she saw. She wasn't doing it as a joke, either. She meant to hurt. A mahout offered her a butter-and-sugar sandwich and then, as a joke, ran off with it and hid in a bungalow. Marguerite promptly butted the door down and went in after him. She got the sandwich in short order.

In addition to the elephants, we got together a cargo of tigers, bears, leopards, hyenas, lesser pandas, otters and monkeys. We also had several hundred birds: black-necked storks, adjutants, red-headed vultures, sarus, demoiselles and mourning cranes, and several hundred small birds. We also had 800 monkeys. With our cargo, we went to Calcutta and engaged passage on the S.S. *Manipur*, the pleasantest ship I've ever been on. The captain and crew were more than helpful. They gave us an entire cargo hold and we built stalls for the elephants and cages for the birds and other animals, using hundreds of feet of heavy-gauge wire.

There still remained the problem of export permits and the hundred and one governmental red tape difficulties involved in exporting animals. As it is very hard for a white man to make business arrangements in the Orient, I went to a Parsee to arrange the details for me. The Parsees are members of a strict religious sect who are famous for their business acumen and, as the Indians put it, "don't waste the scrapings of an eggshell." This Parsee was a thin, correct elderly gentleman who spoke faultless if rather stilted English. The terms he offered me seemed unreasonable but I managed to induce him to stop at our hotel room later that afternoon to continue the discussion. When I returned to our room, I told Mercia what had happened. Her only comment was "Leave him to me."

I shook my head. "He's as dried up as a dead branch. This is once when your charm won't work."

"I know how to handle that type," Mercia said calmly. "Doesn't drink, eh? Too bad, but pour some tea into him and I'll take over afterwards."

The Parsee arrived about five o'clock, driving up in a magnificent Daimler with a liveried chauffeur. I took him up to our room. Mercia wasn't about so I gave him some tea. He drank the tea but it didn't seem to soften him in the slightest.

I was feeling rather discouraged when the bedroom door opened and Mercia glided in. I scarcely recognized her. She was dressed in a sari and kept part of the hem draped over her face, not enough to conceal her lovely features but enough to give a modest effect. Obviously overcome by embarrassment, she hurried over to a chair at one end of the room and sat looking at the floor.

I turned to the Parsee. The old fellow was sitting bolt upright and looked as though he'd just taken a bite out of his teacup. I performed the introduction and Mercia murmured something in response, raising her eyes shyly at the last moment to glance at our guest and then dropping them immediately. The Parsee was fascinated. He tried to draw her out but Mercia acted so embarrassed that she could only pick at the hem of her sari and blush.

I excused myself and left the room. We had a little pantry in the entranceway and I poured myself a beer and lit a cigar. From the next room, I could hear the murmur of low voices and it sounded as though the Parsee had finally gotten Mercia to talk. Three beers and two cigars later, the Parsee came out carrying the contract in his hand and choked with emotion.

"You are very fortunate to have such a lovely, retiring wife, Mr. Ryhiner," he assured me. "So many women lose their precious sense of innocence when taken from the shelter of the home and forced to live in the world. But your wife is an exception. She is as sweet and guileless as a child."

"I'm delighted to hear it," I told him.

The Parsee sighed. "Dear little creature, you have no idea how impressed she was by my position in the business world. Of course, she knows nothing of business and took a childlike joy in having me show her our contract. She even, in her pretty, playful way, wanted to pretend that she too could do business and I allowed her to make a few changes, just small matters which she said had occurred to her. I shall enjoy glancing over the dear child's amusing little additions. You are fortunate indeed, Mr. Ryhiner. She is a veritable flower-girl."

"She is indeed," I assured him. We left the hotel and the Parsee climbed into his Daimler, leaning back with a reminiscent smile. Then he opened the contract. As the Daimler pulled away, the roar of its powerful motor was loud but not loud enough to drown the anguished cry from the Parsee when he saw the changes that his flower-girl had made in the contract.

When I got back to our apartment, Mercia had discarded the sari and was sitting in bra and panties with her feet up on a chair, a gin and tonic in one hand and a cigarette in the other.

"Well, the old goat signed," she remarked, nodding towards our copy of the contract. "He tried to do us in and got done in himself. It's his own fault for trying to cheat us on the contract. Pour yourself a drink."

The voyage to America was without incident except that one of the otters got into the barrels of live mudfish we kept to feed them. The otters would eat nothing but live fish so we had had to load fifty hogsheads of mudfish which breathe air and can thus stand overcrowding. That otter killed over a hundred fish before we found him. One of the black-necked storks got sick and was down so long that he lost the use of his legs. I put him in a gunny-sack sling so that he could use his legs without putting his full weight on them. He came through in fine shape. We didn't lose an animal, and our little elephants were healthier at the end of the voyage then when we started.

We arrived in Savannah, Georgia. Zeehandelaar wanted the cargo unloaded in a southern port because he had his animal compound in Florida. Our arrival had been well advertised and we were met by the biggest crowd of photographers and reporters yet. Of course, they all wanted pictures of Mercia. She wouldn't let them take any pictures unless she was posing with some animal as, after all, we wanted to advertise our stock. So she posed with everything from the sarus cranes to the elephants.

A disaster occurred when Mercia was posing with the young tigers. The tigers were half grown but still very tame and to hold them near her during the picture-taking Mercia fed them small pieces of meat. As the photographers kept saying, "Just one more," she began to run out of meat and would only pretend to feed them. One of the youngsters got mad and bit her in the behind. It was an extremely painful bite but Mercia, like the good trouper she was, said nothing. The photographers got their pictures and left while Mercia retired below to give first aid to her injured posterior.

I didn't realize how bad the bite was or I'd have called a doctor immediately. Deep tiger bites nearly always infect because there are bits of rotten meat on the cats' teeth. As soon as the photographers left, we were both busy unloading the cargo and arranging to have it shipped to the various zoos and dealers so when Mercia told me that the bite wasn't bad and that she'd disinfected it, I forgot about the matter.

We were deluged with newspaper clippings about Mercia and the animals. Apparently none of the rewrite men could think of any title but "Beauty and the Beast," so I got a little tired of it but Mercia was delighted. She collected every line written about her and there were trunkfuls of clippings. As she was still very conscious of being a Eurasian, I said teasingly, "Poor little neglected girl, no one will have anything to do with her!" I only meant to show how silly she was to let this old fear still haunt her, but Mercia instantly screamed, "You think that I care about these things? Well, I'll show you!" and she began tearing up her precious clippings. I apologized but Mercia went through the pile like a fury, ripping and tearing right and left. I finally left the room. When I returned a few hours later, Mercia was down on her hands and knees glueing them all back together again. She wasn't the least embarrassed at being caught. She only said, "Don't stand there—come here and help me."

Mercia's tiger bite did infect and soon it was so bad that she couldn't sit down or lie on her back. I called in a doctor who said that she must be kept quiet for at least two weeks. Zeehandelaar most generously sent us to the Driftwood Hotel at Vero Beach while Mercia was recuperating, explaining, "She got this wound in the line of duty." This I thought was a very nice way of putting it.

We both loved the hotel. It is made of driftwood, put together by a remarkable man named Waldo Sexton who is also the proprietor. It reminded me of some of the better hotels in southeast Asia, except that it has modern plumbing.

We had been at the Driftwood about two weeks when I got a call early one morning from Dick Speyr who runs the wild Animal Compound at Vero Beach. Dick had bought some of our animals. "One of the elephants has broken her leg-chain and escaped," he told me. "Can you come at once?"

I promised that I'd be right over. When Mercia heard what had happened, she only said, "I'll bet it's Marguerite."

Still in my pajamas, I drove to the Wild Animal Compound. The escaped elephant was Marguerite, all right. She had managed to work her leg-chain loose and the night watchman found her grazing on the lawn. Unfortunately, he had shouted and thrown stones at her, so naturally the elephant bolted into the swamps.

Dick was very upset. Marguerite was worth about $4,000 but that was a minor matter. To have an elephant loose in Florida could be serious. No one knew what damage Marguerite might do, for although she was young, she was extremely powerful and bad-tempered. Dick instantly notified the police and posted a $50 reward for information leading to her capture.

Within minutes, the news was on the radio and in special editions of the papers. The police threw up cordons around the area and established road blocks on Route 1 to warn motorists that there was an elephant loose in the vicinity. The schools declared a holiday and the high school children went out to try to find her. I didn't think this was such a good idea, although it was extremely unlikely that Marguerite would actually attack people, but as a precautionary measure, Dick had a warning sent out to leave the elephant alone if she was found. The youngsters were told to go in large groups and if they saw the elephant, simply to watch her from a distance while getting word to us.

Dick and I sat in his office awaiting word, for it would have been fatal for us to be away in the swamps if she was found. All day long, the radio sent hourly bulletins on the progress of the search, but no one saw any signs of Marguerite.

At five o'clock, we got a call from a group of men who had found Marguerite feeding on the edge of a farm. Marguerite had promptly charged them. The men climbed trees, all except one colored fellow who with amazing courage grabbed the elephant by the tail. Marguerite went tearing off with the man hanging to her. Then the man began to lose his pants and had to let go.

Dick and I drove to the spot at once but it was dark by the time we got there and tracking was impossible through the swamps. We went back to the Wild Animal Compound to wait.

The next morning, the Coast Guard was called in. They sent helicopters to fly over the surrounding country but the 'copters found nothing. At our request, the high school children were not called in. There was too much chance of their being hurt. Night came without any word from the searchers.

At 11 o'clock the next morning, we got a phone call from a fisherman. He'd seen an elephant swimming down the river towards Fort Pierce. He explained that he'd thought nothing of it at the time, as anything can happen in Florida, but when he got back to town and heard that we'd lost an elephant, he'd decided that it might be the same animal.

I hired a boat and started down the river with Beck, a young

German who'd been helping me with the animals. A few miles above Fort Pierce, we found Marguerite standing on a sand bar looking very sorry for herself. The three days' search was over.

There still remained the problem of how to catch her. We had an elephant hook and a leg-chain. Both Beck and I jumped into the water and while I held Marguerite's attention, Beck tried to get the chain around her leg. Marguerite charged us both repeatedly. The bottom was covered with sharp shells and I'd made the mistake of kicking off my shoes so it was all I could do to move around. Marguerite was in a terrible mood and all her training of two months had been forgotten. She was trumpeting like a steam whistle, grabbing for me with her trunk, and trying to trample Beck. Beck had to dive to reach her foot and Marguerite kept kicking him off, so time after time he came up gasping for air with the chain still in his hand. I tried to hold Marguerite with the hook but even on firm ground that would have been difficult and in the fast-running water it was impossible. All I could do was keep her from grabbing Beck with her trunk and holding him under.

Beck finally fastened the chain in place. Then we got a rope around her neck and dragged her ashore with the steam launch. Once she was on dry land and had a butter-and-sugar sandwich, she quieted down.

The hunt made headlines all over the country. Of course, Marguerite was represented as a gigantic bull with tusks ten feet long and Dick Speyr was delighted with the publicity. He said that he was willing to let an elephant go every day of the week for the same news coverage, but I begged him to control himself. I was exhausted and my feet cut to hamburger. I've caught elephants in Africa, India and Ceylon but Florida is the worst place to catch elephants that I've ever seen.

# Chapter 16

# Elephants wholesale

FOR THE first time in our lives, Mercia and I had no money troubles. The profits we'd made on the last two shipments—the first cargo to America that we'd brought over on our own, and now this second cargo—left us fairly affluent. All my life, I'd dreamed of having my own zoo. I have many ideas about running a zoo. People ought to be told more about the animals. Parents bring their children, glance at the various animals, and then don't return for another year, having "seen everything." This means that to hold popular interest the zoos must keep bringing in new, dramatic animals and conduct big publicity campaigns. Then once the public has seen the new animals, the whole process must start over again.

Some of the most interesting animals are not spectacular, the maleos, for example, and if they are simply exhibited in a cage, the people merely look at them and pass on. I feel the public must learn to know more about the animals' habits. On a monkey island, there is always a "head monkey" who rules the band. Why not explain this important fact in a sign and then mark the head monkey, perhaps with a collar, so the people can recognize him? Then there are several of the younger males who are seeking supremacy. The squabbles between the monkeys are not aimless but are the younger males' attempts to "feel out" the old leader with the hope of deposing him. All this should be explained. The leader generally has a wise old female who acts as his second in command. Mark her also, say with a red collar. Explain how she stays near the leader, warning him in times of danger, and rules when he is busy elsewhere. Once the public understands the situation, the island is far more than just a collection of monkeys but a tiny civilization with a ruler, ambitious statesmen, loyal followers, and "the masses" who will follow the strongest leader.

Various species of hoofed animals are not particularly interesting until you realize that goats have hoofs specially adapted to climbing the side of a perpendicular cliff, that a stag sheds his tremendous antlers every year and then grows new ones— one of nature's greatest miracles—that reindeer are especially adapted to living in the artic regions while the Indian sambur, who looks much the same to the public, can only live in tropical jungles and that the broad, soft feet of the dromedary which enable him to walk easily over soft sand are adapted, in the case of the Bactrian camel, to walking over soft snow. For this reason, the slave traders who used to raid the Caucasus mountain always used camels, waiting until there was a fall of fine, soft snow so the horses of the Caucasians would be useless.

Wild horses are easily domesticated but zebras, although they will interbreed with a horse and produce perfectly healthy and potent offspring, are very difficult to tame. Of the zebras, the Grevy's zebra has occasionally been tamed but the Burchell's zebra, virtually never. The water buffalo is probably the most important domestic animal in the world, providing both meat and milk as well as serving as a beast of burden. The economy of parts of the Orient are almost completely dependent on him. Explain this, and the water buffalo becomes one of your most important exhibits, rather than just another "animal."

Animals should be encouraged to breed in captivity. Breeding captive animals is a very difficult and elaborate affair. If I were a zoo director, I would take the public into my confidence and explain the problems involved. Professor Hediger and Dr. Lange at the Basel Zoo spent months getting my Indian rhinos to breed. First, they were kept in separate but adjacent pens so familiarity wouldn't lead to indifference and still the animals would not be strangers to each other. They were allowed to use the same wallow but at different times, so they grew accustomed to lying in each other's scent. During the actual mating, the male must gore and lift the female with his horn to arouse her, but when the pair are confined in a small area he may injure her. Keepers with fire hoses had to stand by to separate them during this period. The male as well as the female seems to have a heat cycle and the breeding must take place when the two cycles coincide, otherwise the male may kill her. Hediger took a real chance, when he decided to put the two adult animals together, but it was a calculated risk and successful. For the first time in history, the Indian rhino was bred in captivity. All this information was published in a scientific pamphlet, but wouldn't the public, who after all had paid for the rhinos, be interested in the matter? Wouldn't they feel a personal interest in the calf after it was born if they had followed weekly bulletins in the papers describing how the experiment was progressing?

I also feel that captive wild animals should be trained, not necessarily to perform silly tricks but to show what they can do. A cheetah will course a mechanical hare or even chase a bundle of rags pulled along on a string. Such exhibitions are actually being given at John Hamlet's Birds of Prey, Inc., at Ocala, Florida. The people can see the animal's incredible speed. Elephants can be used to pile logs or carry loads as they do in India. Seals can leap ten feet out of water and pass through a hoop or swim to a man and drag him ashore by his coat; in fact, they have been used to save swimmers and carry lines to ships in distress. An eagle sitting in a cage is nothing, but eagles can be trained to fly free and return to the keeper's whistle. Chimps are natural clowns and enjoy performing while even lions and tigers prefer going through simple routines in a big enclosure to pacing endlessly in a cage. It is better for them, too, giving them some exercise and making them use their wits. In a wild state, animals have to exercise and think. There's no reason why they shouldn't do it in captivity.

I had many such ideas which may or may not have been practical. I was always trying to keep pairs of animals and launch a big breeding campaign. At any rate I now had enough money to start my own zoo and test my theories. There were many places I thought of establishing it: southern Florida with its many attractions or in Connecticut close enough to New York so people could drive there in an hour or two. But meanwhile Mercia and I decided to take a long vacation. We felt that we'd earned it.

We took a luxury liner to Europe—first class for the only time in our lives—and settled back to relax. The second day at sea, we got a cable from Zeehandelaar: "Urgent. Get 14 elephants. All females. Two, 5 feet 6 inches at shoulder. Rest not more than 4 feet at shoulder. Must arrive in southern port U.S.A. on or before May 1."

Even Mercia was staggered. "My God, next he'll be asking us to send him embryos in bottles!" she exclaimed. We'd had enough trouble trying to keep five-foot elephants. Four-foot ones would be tiny infants, completely unweaned.

Zeehandelaar wasn't crazy. As he said himself, he was a business man supplying a demand. The zoos and circuses wanted baby elephants because they are so cute. There were very few available for not many collectors can keep such tiny things alive. Also, spring was the ideal time to sell them. The circuses were starting out on the road then and the people began crowding into zoos, eager to see some new, appealing attraction. "Children's zoos were very popular and every one of them wanted to feature a baby elephant for the children to play with. Young male elephants are too aggressive so females have to be used. It was all very logical.

All very logical except for the problem of getting the elephants. Finding ten that came up to such rigid specifications had been terribly difficult. Getting fourteen would be almost impossible. Anyhow, I was out of the animal collecting business. I was going to open my own zoo.

Mercia was busy figuring with a pencil on the back of the cable. She finally announced. "Peter, with the profit on the elephants alone, we could clear $20,000 in three months. Then there's the profit on any other animals we bring . . . and now we know the American market. It's too good a chance to miss . . . just one more trip."

I refused. I didn't believe it was possible to ship such tiny animals and I was full of plans for my zoo. Mercia, on the other hand, had always regarded my idea of a zoo as completely impractical—which perhaps it was. There was a huge market for animals in the United States and it seemed to her absolute madness to stop now. After all we'd endured in Singapore and Siam, here we were receiving cables begging us to get animals, and at fancy prices. We quarreled all the way to Southampton and continued to quarrel in our hotel room in London.

During one of these quarrels, Mercia threw a heavy ash tray at me. I ducked and it went through the window. It landed on the pavement with a crash and a crowd gathered. The manager of the hotel came up to our room to protest. I apologized, explained that it was an accident, and he left, warning us that if another such "accident" occurred, we'd have to leave the hotel. Mercia's only comment was, "Well, you shouldn't have ducked."

I went to the Regent Park Zoo, partly to see some of my animals there and partly to think things over. The zoo gives little shows with trained animals, a very good idea, and in one of the acts some young chimps sat around a table drinking tea and eating with spoons and forks in a very human fashion. Near me was standing a woman with a little boy. Obviously hoping to drive home an oft-repeated point, the woman said to her son, "Now, dear, you see what perfect manners those apes have . . . why can't *you* be more neat?" The boy answered indignantly, "But Mummy, they're professionals!" This little incident put me in good humor again. I thought things over. After all, it would be only one more trip. When I returned to the hotel, I told Mercia we'd make one last trip.

We flew to Assam and, having an order for two more young rhinos, set about catching them, now a routine job. We got the pair, but matters became increasingly strained between Mercia and myself. Although she wanted the money that animal collecting brought in, she was sick of the difficulties and uncertainties of the life. In America, she had seen how comfortably women can live and she desperately wanted a home of her own, yet she considered my plans for a "model zoo" completely impractical. At last, after many stormy scenes, Mercia sailed for Europe with the rhinos while I stayed on to get the elephants.

As far as animal collecting was concerned, things had been going fairly smoothly, but now my luck turned. The worst floods on record hit Assam. The rivers were impassable, the jungles under three feet of water, and trapping impossible. I had two months left to get the elephants. And there was no escape clause in my contract with Zeehandelaar.

The floods hadn't reached Mysore so I flew there. I went at once to the animal market; the same market where, years before, I'd first met Subrati. While I was looking in the cages, I heard a voice say, "Sahib, for a few rupees I will show you all the rare animals." I turned around and there was Subrati.

We stared at each other and then embraced. Finally Subrati recovered enough to ask after the *mem-sahib*. I told him of the great success Mercia had made in Europe and America. "I doubt if she will ever come animal catching with us again, Subrati," I ended sadly.

"Ah, that is too bad," said Subrati politely. "Still, such trials are sent us by Allah and must be endured."

"But what are you doing here and where is your beautiful young wife?" I asked.

"Alas, sahib, she has run away. She is a very modern girl and so beautiful and popular that she has no time for an old animal man like me."

"That is sad, but you remember that at the time I warned you not to marry such a young girl. Now she has left you."

"True, sahib, just as your wife has left you."

Although Mercia and I had never mentioned a divorce, I knew that she was too ambitious to spend the rest of her life tied to a man who thought of little besides animals. "Subrati, there is truth in what you say," I admitted. "Now let us forget about women and go into the jungles after animals."

"Sahib, it will be like old times again," said Subrati joyfully and so it turned out to be.

With Subrati on the job, getting the elephants was no problem at all. With his numerous contacts, Subrati could accomplish more in a week than I or any foreigner could in six months. Behrend always depended on native collectors to get his animals whenever possible and although he was cheated time after time, he still claimed that this system paid off in the long run. I had often wondered why he had trusted so blindly to the Boer in Kenya, the agent in India and the "priest" in South America, instead of sending some reliable man (such as me) to do the whole thing for him. Now I knew. Only a man born to a country has the contacts and confidence of the people. Luckily, Subrati was absolutely reliable. Finding such men in any country is rare.

Instead of rushing madly from camp to camp, I now had time to work a little with the elephants and talk to the mahouts. They told me many amazing things. The old saying that "an elephant never forgets" is quite true about certain things, even though a cow doesn't seem able to remember her own calf three hours after the baby has been taken away. In Assam, I got a young calf and the mahout told me a strange story of how it had been captured. Twenty years before, a young cow elephant had been caught in a keddah shikar and worked as a pad elephant for five years. Then she was "kidnaped" by a wild bull. During a recent mela shikar the mahout had seen the cow with a wild herd. He recognized her by the training scars on her legs and besides, a mahout never forgets an elephant. He shouted "Bet!" (lie down) and the cow knelt down in the middle of the herd even though she had been running wild for fifteen years. The mahout rode his kunki over to her, dismounted, climbed on the cow's neck and rode her out of the herd, the kunki following. After the cow came three calves, all different ages. They followed their mother back to the camp and it was the youngest of these calves that he offered to me. I bought her. Later, I heard that Nehru had bought another of the calves and sent it to the Tokyo Zoo as a gift to the children of Japan.

Wild bulls will often run off with tame cows. Subrati found a nice little female calf in the Khasi Hills but when I came to buy the animal, she was gone. The distracted mahouts told me that the kunkis, both cows and bulls, had been hobbled and put out to graze when a wild bull in "musth"—a condition of frenzy—charged out of the jungle. The mahouts ran for their lives at the sight of the maddened brute but the bull paid no attention to them. His first act was to drive off the bull kunkis which he could do easily enough for he had enormous tusks. Then he assembled the cows and marched off, followed by his new harem. "He did not have to drive the cows before him, sahib," one of the mahouts assured me. "Once they saw his magnificent tusks, they all followed him moaning with delight." The calves had naturally followed the cows, the calf that Subrati had had, going with the rest.

I wanted the calf and the mahouts wanted their kunkis back so we joined forces. I couldn't find a rifle but I managed to borrow a shotgun loaded with buckshot. I know this seems like a very inadequate weapon with which to face an infuriated bull elephant in musth but we would be riding kunkis and I'd never seen an elephant attack a man mounted on a kunki. I was sure the noise of the gun and the sting of the buckshot would frighten off the bull.

The cows were still hobbled and moved slowly. Also, they had big, wooden bells around their necks that could be heard for two miles or more if the wind was right. By late afternoon we heard the sound of the bells and spread out in a semicircle, preparatory to surrounding the herd.

I was ahead on the leading kunki, our biggest bull. The mahout guided the animal expertly among the trees and then I saw the wild bull. He was leaning against a cotton tree, paying no attention to the cows grazing around him. I could see the dark fluid running from the musth glands to the corners of his mouth. He seemed sick to me, rather than savage and I would have given a great deal to know how the musth affected him. Curiously, even to the mahouts who know so much about elephants, musth seems to be a complete mystery. They only say that it makes the animals savage and even tame kunkis must be chained during this period.

While we were watching him, the bull saw some of the kunkis approaching his harem. He gave a low, guttural growl; I know of no other way to describe it although the noise was too shrill to be a true growl but far deeper than a trumpet. Then he charged through the trees. His trunk was curled up and his ears laid flat against his head. Although he had to zigzag to get through the jungle, he went like smoke. As he vanished, I heard one of the kunkis scream with fear and then I heard the men shouting.

My mahout urged our kunki forward. As we crashed through the underbrush, I saw one of the kunkis running, with the wild bull goring him in the behind. The man on the kunki's back was hanging on for dear life and all the other men were shouting. I threw up the shotgun and fired both barrels at the wild bull's rear.

I heard him scream as the buckshot hit him. He left the kunki and began spinning around, trying to reach the wound with his trunk to find what had happened. I reloaded the shotgun as rapidly as I could; no easy job with my kunki trying to run. The mahout did all he could do to control the animal, but when I finally got the gun loaded, the bull had disappeared. We drove the cows back to camp without trouble.

According to the newspaper accounts, I had defeated a rogue

elephant with a shotgun. Of course, the wild bull wasn't a true rogue. Rogues are insane. All bull elephants go through a definite heat cycle, as do bull rhinos, called musth. This cycle seems somehow to be connected to their sexual lives; a young male doesn't develop musth until he reaches puberty and is ready to breed the cows. However, a bull will always breed a cow whether he is in musth or not. During musth, a dark brown fluid runs out from two glands near the eyes into the animal's mouth. The taste of the fluid seems to madden some bulls, while with other bulls, musth makes comparatively little difference in their dispositions. While I was in Assam, a perfectly tame kunki bull in musth killed his mahout and then attacked a passing bus. He overturned it, reached in through the window with his trunk, and pulled off a man's necktie. He then went running off, waving the necktie in the air. After the musth had passed he returned quietly to camp and took up his usual position in the work lines.

With Subrati helping me with the elephants, I was able to work with some other animals as well. I rented a beautiful little forest bungalow where I lived with three native servants and my chowkidar or watchman. The bungalow was built by the side of a river, full of floating water plants with purple flowers. In the evenings I could sit on my porch and watch the elephants come down to drink. At night tigers would pad silently by in the moonlight and once I was awakened by hyenas fighting under my window. While Subrati was out collecting the elephants from the field camps, I did some trapping and also had time to conduct some experiments with the animals.

The jungles were full of magnificent birds; hornbills, fairy blue jays, golden orioles, wild doves. I trapped some with birdlime, imported from Italy, as the local birdlime got on their wings. I soon learned to study their droppings carefully after capture to see what they'd been eating so I'd know what food to give them. All the members of one species of birds do not always eat the same food. Birds, like all wild animals, are creatures of habit. If they are used to eating one type of food, they will not switch to another, even though the new food is just as good as the old. They don't realize that it's good to eat. A hawk, used to killing partridges, may starve to death in a hen-house because he doesn't realize that the chickens are just as good. I've seen a buteo hawk catching rats in a chicken yard, ignoring the fat pullets simply because he was used to living on field rats and had never seen a chicken before.

The small birds I kept in padded cages so they wouldn't bat-ter themselves against the bars. For most birds I believe in small cages. In a large cage, a flying bird builds up too much mo-mentum and when he hits the side, he may injure himself. I made sure that the perches were the right type for each species. The perches must fit the birds' feet. Some birds like rigid perches and some prefer movable. I also had to be careful how I intro-duced new arrivals into a cage. After making sure that the new birds were not infected with mites or carrying any disease, I usually put them in the cage at night so that when the other birds awoke in the morning, the newcomers would be already estab-lished. In a wild state, each pair of birds have their own area marked out and will fight any intruder to the death. Once established in a cage, they consider the cage their territory and defend it against any of their own kind although they usually ignore other species. This, of course, is true only of certain birds. Some varieties prefer to nest in colonies, like the weaver birds, and these enjoy company.

I also managed to get a number of the beautiful golden-caped langurs which are rare because the natives of South India think that their flesh is a cure for tuberculosis. My langurs developed the unfortunate habit of eating their own dung. I thought for a long time this was due to some dietary deficiency and kept changing their food but the langurs persisted. At last, I came to the conclusion that in a wild state, the golden-caped langurs never see their own dung. As they live high in the trees, the dung drops to the ground and vanishes. In a cage, they are fascinated by the strange stuff, handle it, taste it and finally develop a liking for the substance. I solved this problem by putting the cages on stilts and using wire bottoms. The dung fell through and was lost, as occurs in nature. I think that putting the cages on stilts also made the langurs happier. On the ground, they felt nervous and unprotected but once in the air, they felt safer even if it was only a matter of raising the cages a few feet.

I got a few black leopards, "black panthers" they are usually called although they are only a color phase of the ordinary leopard. I caught them in box traps using goats as bait. The owner of one goat took his animal home after the leopard didn't come for several nights but the next morning, the leopard was in the trap. He'd smelled the goat and gone in anyway.

Newly caught cats are always a problem. They are not a naturally restless animal as most people suppose who see their endless pacing, but in a wild state they will usually kill in one spot, carry off their prey and eat it in a second, and frequently go to a third place to defecate. When this pattern is broken by capture, they become restless and moody. I do not believe in feeding cats always at the same time, day after day. The cats have nothing to look forward to except feeding period and as it approaches, they begin their nervous pacing. This pacing can become a habit and the animals often wear off their skin by rubbing against the bars as they go back and forth. I prefer to feed them several times a day at unexpected periods. It keeps them more alert and breaks up the monotony. Of course, the perfect solution would be to have them tame so they wouldn't have to be confined. The rajahs have often tamed cheetahs, the long-legged hunting leopards, trained for coursing antelope, and these animals are as happy and attentive as dogs. If the animals can't be completely tamed, then the next best solution is to have a regular training period in a big cage as is done in a circus. Anything of this nature keeps them from falling into a state of dull, routine existence.

I found a Dutch ship going from Calcutta to the United States that would take animal cargo. We had a quick crossing and for the second time in a year, I unloaded in Savannah, Georgia. Zeehandelaar flew down from New York to meet the ship. He had a contract with Barnum & Bailey's for six of the young elephants but Zeehandelaar took all fourteen to the circus' winter quarters in Sarasota, Florida. He paraded the whole lot into the circus grounds, all marching in a line holding each other's tails with their trunks. They looked so cute that John Ringling North bought ten. The other four Zeehandelaar quickly sold to various tourist attractions in Florida.

This had been the biggest shipment of elephants of any size or age in history and both Zeehandelaar and I were well pleased with the result. The lecture season with Colston Leigh was just beginning and I had to fly to New York the day after landing the elephants to be in time for our first engagement, Mercia having flown over from Europe a few days before. I had nothing prepared but as usual, Mercia carried everything off perfectly. She was beautiful, clever and amusing. I merely stood about in the background. Mercia had the films we'd taken in Assam and they were surprisingly good; but I think most of the people came mainly to see Mercia.

After the show, Mercia told me that she'd had a hard time getting the rhinos to Europe. There'd been what Mercia called a "mutiny" on the ship. Actually, she'd had a row with the sailors and they'd refused to clean out the cages or bring up food for the rhinos. Mercia had done everything herself, hosing out the cages in all sorts of weather and dragging the heavy bales of hay up to the deck. "I didn't really mind except on my birthday," she said rather pitifully.

I wanted to punch the nose of every sailor on that ship, yet at the same time I knew how Mercia would scream orders at anyone she considered an inferior and naturally the crew had resented it. Her insistence on keeping "menials in their place" had caused her endless trouble. Poor Mercia was trying to be a *mem-sahib* in an era when *mem-sahibs* were no more. She wasn't very good at it anyway. With her charm, quick wits and beauty there was nothing that she couldn't have accomplished if only she'd been able to forget the terrible lessons of her childhood. As I had done so many times in the past, I tried to explain this to her and as usual, Mercia was all contrition. "I'm sorry, Peter, it's my awful temper. I'll control it, I promise." So she would— until the next time.

I knew quite well that I wasn't the sort of man who could really help Mercia. She admired strong, resolute men and wanted the feeling of security that wealth could bring her. Except for clothes, which were also a sort of symbol to her, Mercia was the least extravagant woman I've ever known but I don't believe she had ever forgotten the days when she followed the English girls around, sucking the peels from their fruit. She would still cheerfully suck peels to save a few annas but she wanted the feeling that she could buy all the fruit in India if necessary.

I have always been an easygoing fellow and I have cared little about money except as it has enabled me to work with my beloved animals. Perhaps that is why I got along with old Behrend as well as I did. He too was indifferent to money for all his shady deals, and would throw it away with both hands for an opportunity to study some rare bird or reptile. In our marriage Mercia had always been the one who handled the money, who understood clearly that it was ridiculous to spend several weeks and several thousand rupias in a vain attempt to get some maleos worth only a few hundred dollars at best. It was she who carried the lectures, who made arrangements with Zeehandelaar, who had urged me to ride the boom in the animal market instead of starting a zoo of my own based on theories which every experienced zoo director in the business had assured me were utterly impractical. Mercia could and did feel a great affection for me but she could not admire me or defer to my beliefs. She knew that except where handling animals were concerned, her own ideas were far more practical than mine.

We spent the winter touring America on our lecture circuit. We had a question and answer period at the end of our lecture, and once I made a fearful mistake. A lady asked me what I thought about the popular children's zoos. I told her frankly, "I think they're a very mixed blessing. They do bring children into close contact with animals but they also encourage the idea that animals are simply toys for the children. Animals are very important people in their own right and not just animated teddy bears. Personally, I think that watching a mother bear take care of her cubs in a large enclosure, teach them how to climb a tree, cuff them when they're naughty, and make sure that they don't stay in the pool too long, is far more interesting than putting a collar and chain on one of the cubs and letting children feed it peanuts."

After the lecture, Mercia nearly wept. "What a thing to say when we're deluged with fond mothers showing us pictures of their children with baby elephants or holding hands with a little chimp. Children's zoos are our best market and you're one of the few men who can bring back animals small enough to be exhibited in them. People don't want to be educated, they want to be amused."

I apologized and was more careful in the future. As usual, Mercia was right. After all, if I felt that the children's zoos were wrong, why was I bringing back animals to put in them? Actually, I didn't really think that they were wrong, I just wanted to see more emphasis put on the animals and less on amusing the children.

I learned quite a lot about animal dealers while I was in America. Many dealers are really clever showmen. There's one dealer who, when he has some animal to sell, say an orangutan, will appear in a city wearing a topi and a bush jacket and announce that he is just off the ship after spending months in the wilds of Borneo. "I got a magnificent orangutan," he tells the reporters. "A very valuable animal. Had a terrific battle capturing him," and so on. The public reads the papers and soon a subscription is started to buy the orang for the local zoo. The zoo gets the orang, the dealer gets rid of his orang, and everyone is happy. There's another dealer, a woman, who has live parakeets sitting on her hat. The birds aren't tied and often fly about but are trained always to return to her hat. She also has a special handbag, the lower part of which is an aquarium with live fish swimming around in it. Very ingenious.

Mercia fretted a good deal because I couldn't think up similar clever ways to advertise our business. "All you ever did to make yourself different was grow a beard," she joked. "You've got to make people remember you. Think of Zeehandelaar marching all those elephants down the main street of Sarasota. In this business, you've got to do more than get the animals . . . you have to get them across."

She was right but I'm not good at salesmanship. Few animal collectors are. That's why we sell to the dealers who know about such things.

We did get a pet gibbon and a fishing-cat which we carried around with us as an advertisement. The animals were well behaved but it was a major problem getting them into hotels. Mercia used to smuggle them in under her coat as she'd done in Singapore. Once she was caught and the manager pointed to a sign that read "No dogs or cats allowed."

"But these aren't dogs or cats," Mercia protested.

"That thing's a cat," said the manager, pointing to the fishing-cat.

"But your sign means domestic cats," cried Mercia. "I won't be thrown out on a technicality!"

She wasn't, either. We got the room.

I got a telegram from Zeehandelaar asking for twenty more elephants, all under four feet. I refused. Mercia and I had been moving farther and farther apart as it was without having me leave for a long spell in the Indian jungles. Mercia was a sensation on the lecture platform and was being entertained by Texas oilmen, Chicago millionaires, New York socialites. All a very heady draught to swallow for a little girl from Singapore. She had never been particularly interested in animals but had always regarded animal collecting as a means to an end. Now she felt that she had achieved that end, social recognition and the opportunity to acquire wealth. I always wanted to be with my animals but Mercia had had her fill of worrying over a slow loris with indigestion and mucking out cages. I couldn't blame her and yet animals were my life and I couldn't change. Neither could Mercia. Mine was too limited a horizon for my pretty, talented wife.

The night that I made my decision not to accept Zeehandelaar's offer, Mercia told me that she wanted a divorce.

It was a terrible shock. I was still deeply in love with her. Besides, Mercia and I complemented each other perfectly. She had a good business head, was clever at publicity, and could handle the social end of the concern. Together, we'd made a perfect team.

As always, Mercia was perfectly frank. "Peter, I'm sick of the animal business and you can't think of anything else. Even suppose I stayed in America while you went collecting, I'd only see you for a few weeks out of the year."

"You could go with me," I suggested.

"Spend the rest of my life being insulted by petty native officials and live in jungles full of snakes and mosquitoes? I want to stay here where I'll be treated like a human being. Besides, the animal business is through. Oh, I know there's a big boom in it now but after all, how many baby elephants can America absorb?"

"There are other animals."

"It's getting almost impossible to export them. Look at what happened with the Komodo dragons. Nothing but red tape and endless headaches."

She was right as usual. Even India, Africa and South America were making it increasingly difficult to export animals.

"But if I open my zoo, we can live here together and I won't have to collect," I pleaded.

"Peter, you're not a business man. How many people would come to see the kind of zoo you have in mind? In America, things are different. People here go in for quantity. There's a very successful zoo in the Catskills. They advertise 'More kangaroos than in any one place in Australia.' They have 120 kangaroos in one pen and the zoo is crowded every day. The owner sells packages of food so people can feed them. That means he doesn't have to pay for feeding them and he makes a profit on the food besides."

"Well, I could do that," I argued.

"I can just see you! One week later, you'd be trying to raise some rare pollywog that no one cares about, or else headed for China to get a giant panda even though you know that the communist government won't let them be exported."

It so happened that I *was* planning how to get a giant panda out of China. I began to tell her the details but Mercia shut me off.

"See what I mean? It's not practical. The gorillas, the maleos, the Komodos . . . you never learn. Peter, you'll never be a business man and I tell you that the animal collecting business is dead. Dead, dead. Drop it, and go into something else before it breaks your heart."

"I can't, Mercia," I said miserably. "It's my life."

"I know it is, Peter, but it's not mine. It's not any woman's. I want a home and a family and some sort of security. I've never had security and I want it more than anything else in the world."

So we decided to part. I took Mercia out to dinner that night, hoping that after a good meal and a few drinks she might soften somewhat. I ordered cold filet of river trout; blinis, sour cream, caviar, melted butter; tournedas au fois gras; sabaglione; fromage et fruits; espresso café and mirabelle glacé. I was particular about the wines, Niersieiner Special 1947, Pommard Nuits St. George 1945, Veuve Cliquot 1942. After I'd finished, Mercia glanced at the waiter and said indifferently, "Bring me the vegetable platter and a glass of water."

She wasn't trying to be unpleasant. She just didn't care. When I remonstrated with her, Mercia said irritably, "What do you think a dinner like that costs? That's the trouble with you, Peter, you never think about money."

To Mercia money was a shield against the world and she knew too well what the world could do to you if ever you lost the protection of that shield.

Mercia agreed to postpone the divorce for a few months. Meanwhile, I was determined to show her that I wasn't as incompetent as she thought. Zeehandelaar wanted twenty elephants. He'd get them. In addition, I'd bring back a collection of other animals that would make me famous—I might even manage to get a giant panda. Then, like Frank Buck, my name would be a household word. Everyone would come to see my zoo and financially I would be as stable as even Mercia could wish. Also, I intended to concentrate on publicity.

I flew back to India and found Subrati ready for me. He was jumping with excitement.

"Sahib, I have made a great discovery, the greatest in the history of animal collecting. In East Pakistan near a little village called Kulna there is a white python with blue eyes. The villagers worship it as a god but I have gathered together a few men who will, for a great sum, capture the snake and bring it here."

"Naturally these men wish to be paid in advance," I said sarcastically.

"Oh naturally, sahib."

"Have you seen this snake?"

Subrati hesitated. "Well, no, sahib."

"Have you talked to anyone who has actually seen it?"

Subrati hesitated even longer. "No, but the existence of the snake is well known."

"As a local legend?"

"Exactly, sahib."

I put one hand on his shoulder. "Subrati, I never heard of a white python and if there were such a creature, it would be an albino and its eyes would be red. India is full of such tales. Do not the Nagas have two sacred king cobras twenty feet long who guard a queen hidden in the hills? Has anyone ever seen the queen or the twenty-foot cobras? No, and no one ever will. Once I would have set out with you for this village of Kulna but now I am a practical man. My fingers have been burned too often to put them near the fire again. We have an order for twenty elephants as well as many other animals. Let us set to work."

While Subrati began collecting the elephants, I went to Nepal where, I had heard, a man had two young giant pandas. It is impossible to say what a giant panda is worth; a collector could put his own price on one. They are not only one of the rarest but also one of the best known and most appealing of all wild animals. There are none in captivity, for the communists will allow no one to get in or out of the area where the strange creatures live. However, animals are occasionally smuggled across the border into Nepal. I've heard of snow leopards being gotten in this way. I'd talked to people who had actually seen the two baby pandas and I had every reason to believe that they were there.

I went from village to village, trying to track down the animals. I heard rumors, went on several false leads and was even told polite lies—the courteous Nepalese never like to disappoint a traveler. But finally I found the man and he did indeed have two pandas, both very tame. Unfortunately, they were the lesser panda, a fairly common animal about the size of a raccoon.

In order that the trip would not be completely wasted, I went out with some Sherpas to get bear cubs. The Himalayan bear is a fairly small fellow, about the size of the American black bear, with a yellow V on his chest. They have two or three young and sometimes we would find the babies playing about in the open. Then the Sherpas would grab them and run before the mother got back. As babies, the cubs were wonderful pets but I put them in cages when they got big. I don't think that any adult bear can be trusted. Although they always remain natural clowns and don't seem dangerous, they are far more uncertain than the big cats.

With the help of Subrati, I caught the elephants and got them to Calcutta. There was one tiny lady only 3 feet 4 inches high at the shoulder and very furry. She even had bangs like a little girl. I named her Josephine. Josephine was the smartest, cutest, most playful little elephant I'd ever seen. I decided to keep her for myself and perhaps build her up to be a big TV and movie star, like Mr. Muggs the chimpanzee. It would be wonderful publicity for me, too. Mercia had always thought I didn't have a talent for that sort of thing but I was going to show her.

I returned to America with twenty-one elephants, counting Josephine, and turned twenty of them over to Zeehandelaar. I also disposed of the bears and other animals for a good profit. Then I went to New York with Josephine riding behind my car in a specially built trailer.

I'd done a lot of flying to India, mostly by Swissair, and Hugo Mayr, the American manager of Swissair, helped me put Josephine across. A big reception was arranged for us at Rockefeller Center and Jayne Mansfield, the beautful and talented actress, was to meet Josphine. The reception wasn't a success. Josephine was usually dog-tame but she hated perfume and Miss Mansfield reeked of it. Josephine instantly knocked Miss Mansfield up against the wall. Miss Mansfield was very nice about it but as far as advertising Josephine as "the kiddies' friend" (which had been my idea), the reception was a flop.

I was feeling pretty discouraged when Marté Latham ran up to me. Marté is not only a very attractive woman but also an ace animal collector, specializing in unusual animals with plenty of publicity appeal. She had just gotten back from South America with some giant earthworms a yard long. The worms were a highly important scientific discovery. Previously they'd been known only by Aztec drawings and were considered a myth. The customs officials at the airport had made her change the worms' earth to make sure that it didn't contain any injurious grubs and the American earth which Marté had substituted killed the worms. So when the reporters arrived to photograph the giant, unknown worms, they were all dead and the story flopped.

Marté was at loose ends as a result and eager to help out on the Josephine campaign. I was delighted to have her help. Marté got the idea of having Josephine and myself register at the Delmonico Hotel, Josephine signing the register with her trunk. Marté called the hotel's publicity man who thought this was a great idea, so Marté, Josephine and I took a taxi to the hotel.

A battery of photographers and reporters were waiting for us. Unfortunately, Marté stepped into the ladies' room to fix up for the event and liberally sprinkled herself with perfume. When Marté joined us, Josephine promptly charged her. In spite of everything I could do, Josephine sent poor Marté head over heels and the only picture the photographers got was Marté going over backwards with her skirt flying up in a most embarrassing manner.

To maintain the illusion that we really were staying in the hotel, Josephine and I had to ride up in the elevator to our "room." While the photographers took pictures, we marched into the elevator. Then the elevator boy got frightened and dashed out, the door sliding shut behind him. I didn't know how to open the door and Josephine was terrified. She charged around the car, batting the walls, while from outside the elevator starter shouted directions to me for opening the door. Meanwhile, a rumor had gone around that a gigantic elephant was running amuck in the hotel and a panic began. Women were screaming, men shouting, and the delighted photographers took pictures of the whole affair.

I finally got the door open and emerged just in time to hear the manager firing the publicity man. Marté washed her hands of both me and Josephine so I was left on my own again.

I got plenty of publicity although not the type I wanted. However, Josephine and I were asked to appear on the Garry Moore Show. I made sure that no one would have any perfume before signing the contract. This program, I felt sure, would make Josephine a national personality, for really no one could resist her charm . . . except possibly Miss Mansfield and Marté.

I telegraphed Mercia to be sure to watch the program and went to the studio with my little girl trotting along beside me with her bangs nicely brushed and a pink ribbon around her neck. Everyone at the studio loved her and the audience broke into sighs and ohs when she appeared on the stage. Josephine performed her little repertory of tricks and then I gave her a pitcher of milk which she drank with her trunk. Unfortunately, Garry Moore took this moment to laugh at her. Josephine hated people to laugh at her and she immediately lifted her trunk and squirted Mr. Moore from head to foot.

Josephine and I were asked to leave the studio and I departed very downcast, although it wasn't really Josephine's fault. No elephant, even a baby, likes to be held up to ridicule.

On the street, we ran into a long line of women waiting to see "Heartline," a very popular TV show. At that moment, a police car went by with sirens screaming. Poor little Josephine gave a terrified trumpet and started running. She went through the line of women like a miniature tank and I never saw such a mess. Women were leaping over each other, crawling around on their hands and knees, and lying flat on their faces screaming for help. Josephine ran full tilt into the plate-glass window of a store. The whole window reverberated and I held my breath, waiting to see it come crashing down into the street, but it held. Then Josephine turned and dashed back into the studio with me after her.

Mr. Moore was just introducing the next guest when Josephine and I crossed the stage. He managed to save himself by a quick spring but the guest wasn't so fortunate. I don't know who he was but he certainly took a tumble. Then I managed to collar Josephine against one of the cameras and dragged her out to a taxi, kicking and trumpeting every inch of the way.

Four women attempted to sue either me or the studio. Naturally, Josephine was represented as a gigantic tusker with homicidal tendencies. None of the women had so much as a scratch so none of them collected. Still, I was told that I couldn't keep Josephine in New York any longer. Luckily, Gus Busch of

Budweiser beer wanted to buy her. "That animal has spirit," he told me. "And I like spirit." So I sold Josephine, not without many regrets. She was the nicest elephant I've ever had—but so few people understand elephants.

I did have some other tame animals, especially the little bear cubs, and I tried to interest the studios in them. I'm sorry to say that I had only to mention my name to have receptionists scream with fright and studio managers threaten to call the police. To top my sorrows, I received a telegram from Mercia, "You got plenty of publicity. Please, Peter, stick to animal collecting." A few weeks later, Mercia went to Switzerland where she obtained a divorce.

Zeehandelaar called me. He wanted another twenty-five elephants. America seemed to have gone elephant-crazy. What they were doing with all the animals I couldn't imagine. I still can't, unless they were canning them. I also got a letter from Subrati, written in the beautiful clear hand of a professional letter writer. Subrati had met someone who knew an old woman who had heard a rumor that somebody's grandfather was reported to have said that as a child he'd seen the white python. It was as tall as a tree, could fly through the air faster than a lightning bolt, and talked fluent Urdu. Subrati considered this conclusive proof that the snake actually existed. It was Subrati who'd sent me on that wild goose chase to Nepal after the two giant pandas. I loved the old boy, but sometimes he could be irritating.

Then I got a letter that really aroused my interest. It was from a motion picture company who were making a picture in India and wild animals were to play a prominent role. They wanted me to act as technical advisor. I was delighted. I've always believed that the motion pictures are the best way to interest people in animals and if I made good at this assignment, there would probably be lots of other openings for me. Mercia was right when she said that it was becoming increasingly difficult to get animals out of India. The restrictions on exporting animals were growing steadily more severe, and every year it was harder to find cargo ships that would carry livestock.

Also sooner or later there had to be an end to America's ability to absorb huge quantities of elephants.

I had another motive in making the change. As an animal collector, I had already reached my zenith. I was importing larger cargos of animals than any collector had ever done in history. But the risk, constant uncertainty, and enormous overhead convinced me, as it had long ago convinced Mercia, that the business wasn't really practical. I had been lucky but I was living on borrowed time. There was an unlimited future in the motion picture business and I was sure that it was work that I'd enjoy.

So I accepted the offer and flew to Assam where the picture was to be made. The camera crew and director arrived a few weeks later and we set about making the picture.

The picture was supposed to portray an expedition struggling through the wilds of Assam to rescue a beautiful white princess or some such thing. I was to provide the animals who attacked them en route. The hero had to shoot a charging elephant but as the hero turned out to be terrified of elephants, I had to hire a professional shikari to double for him. I thought this would solve the difficulty but it was only the beginning of our troubles. After setting up the cameras, taking light readings, and posing the shikari, the elephant was then supposed to charge across a predetermined path and be shot at exactly the right distance from the camera.

Naturally, a wild elephant couldn't be used and none of the mahouts had any intention of allowing one of their valuable kunkis to be butchered in this fashion. I finally solved the problem by getting a mahout to stand by the camera and call his kunki to him. Then another picture was taken of the kunki lying down. The mahout ordered him to stand and this portion of the film was later run backwards so the kunki would seem to be falling.

The script also called for the hero to be attacked by a rhino. As no tame rhinos were available, this was more difficult. We went to the Kaziranga Wild Life Sanctuary and I finally managed to find a man who'd double for the hero and allow a rhino to charge him. We had a terrible time finding a suitable rhino. Every one we found was either in too high grass or the light wasn't right on him or there was no place to put the cameras. But at last we found a pair grazing under the proper conditions and the cameras were set up.

The hired double approached the rhinos and did everything to make them charge. He waved his hat, he shouted insults at them, he danced up and down. The rhinos kept on grazing. The camera crew got discouraged and sat down to watch the performance when suddenly both rhinos charged the unfortunate man. He ran for his life with the two huge beasts right at his heels. As the director had deliberately picked an open stretch of ground so as to be sure of getting good pictures of the rhino, there wasn't a bit of cover and I was certain the poor fellow would be killed. By a miracle, just as the rhinos caught up with him, the man fell into a ditch and both animals passed over him.

I sat down sick with relief. The double crawled out of the ditch covered with mud and in a half-fainting condition. At this moment, the director made a megaphone of his hands and shouted, "Do it again! We weren't ready!"

The double positively refused to do it again and as we couldn't find another man in Assam who'd make the attempt, that sequence had to be left out of the picture.

We did manage to stage a terrific hand-to-hand struggle between a man-eating tiger and the hero. I thought it was wonderful and even the director was pleased. Unfortunately, that sequence also had to be left out of the picture. We'd made one slight mistake. We forgot to take the collar off the tiger.

Ever since the days of the Frank Buck movies, animal fights seemed to be an intrinsic part of jungle movies. In the wild, animals rarely fight. When a predator kills its prey, it does so quickly and neatly and fights between tigers and leopards, leopards and pythons, or wild boars and buffalos never occur. Such fights have to be staged by putting the animals together in a pit and even then they usually simply avoid each other.

The director was determined to have animal fights but here

I mutinied. I would have nothing to do with such senselessly cruel performances. So I was fired. Later, I heard that the director tried to stage a fight between a tiger and a sun-bear. The animals refused to fight and had to be dragged together with piano wires. The results were so ludicrous that the scene could not be used but the director got another idea. A leopard and a python were secured and both animals drugged. Then the python was wrapped around the unconscious leopard while the camera men stood by. As the effects of the drugs wore off, both animals made a frantic effort to escape from each other. By running the film backward, the python seemed to be wrapping himself around the cat.

The picture was never completed. The director wanted a sequence showing an elephant falling off a cliff. He bought a tame but magnificent old tusker much beloved by the entire village where his mahout lived. The villagers were delighted to think that this wonderful old fellow, their especial pride, was to be honored by having his picture taken by a big Hollywood company so they all turned out on the day of the shooting. When they discovered what was to be done with their mascot, they staged a riot and the director and camera crew barely escaped with their lives. The authorities rescinded the company's permit to photograph in India and they were forced to return to the United States.

I cabled Zeehandelaar that I'd get him the elephants and picked up Subrati in Madras. I immediately warned Subrati that if he so much as mentioned that legendary white python, I wouldn't be responsible for my actions. Then we set out to get the elephants.

We got the elephants but from then on complications deluged us.

New shipping rules, the usual last-minute emergencies and changes of plan, feeding problems—everything went wrong. All this made overhead on this trip so heavy that I decided to dispense with insurance. After all, I had brought over nearly 100 elephants and never lost one. This lot were older and stronger than most of my cargos and in the last year, insurance rates had gone up nearly 100 per cent. I decided to take the chance.

In the Mediterranean, we ran into a sudden cold spell. I covered the cages with everything I could find, finally using my own clothes and the blankets from my bunk but eight of the babies came down with colds. Fortunately I had plenty of penicillin and we injected millions of units into them. In spite of everything we could do, three died. Then another slipped during a heavy sea and fell on her side, injuring herself internally. We lost her also.

The loss of these four animals wiped out much of my profit on the trip and more besides, for the blow to my reputation was even worse. What dealers had been calling (somewhat sarcastically, I'll admit) the "Ryhiner spell" seemed to be broken. Zeehandelaar was also badly hit. He'd sold all the elephants ahead of time, guaranteeing delivery by May 1, and so lost some of his best customers who'd already launched big advertising campaigns, trusting on his assurance and my skill.

Worse was yet to follow. Barnum & Bailey's decided to abandon the "big top" and the threat of having their herd thrown on the market depressed prices. Although few customers want big elephants (at the time of writing, some of the B & B elephants are still unsold), the bottom fell out of the elephant market. There was no more demand for them, and I had been specializing so much in elephants during the last few years that my contracts for other animals had been allowed to lapse.

Other dealers were now saying grimly, "Well, we knew something like this would happen to Ryhiner. He's finished." It looked as though they were right. I had to make some sensational find to redeem myself. But what? While I was wondering, I got another letter from Subrati. Through the grapevine telegraph that operates among all animal men, he had heard of my disaster.

"Do not worry, my son," he wrote through the professional letter writer. "You were never meant to deal in animals as though they were bags of meal. Let us go back to the old days when animal collecting was an adventure for both of us. Remember, there is still the white python."

I made up my mind. Cabling Subrati to meet me at Dacca, I took a plane back to India in search of the white python.

# Chapter 17

# The white python

ON PREVIOUS trips, I'd always been bringing animals from India to the United States. On this last trip, it occurred to me that there was no reason why I shouldn't bring animals from the United States to India as well. After all, I was spending rupees in India and I might as well earn them over there.

I managed to pick up some cacomistles, or ring-tailed cats, in the Southwest, some sea lions in California and some raccoons from the East. I was able to sell them all for a good price to the Madras Zoo. The raccoons especially made a sensation. The zoo built a de luxe cage for them and crowds came daily to marvel at these exotic animals and watch how they carefully washed their food before eating.

I met Subrati in Dacca. This time he had a collection of testimonials from people concerning the white python. They didn't sound very convincing.

"My cousin's aunt saw the white snake while she was returning from filling her lota by the banks of a stream."

"My grandfather's brother-in-law recalls having seen the god. The god was eating a fish at the time."

"A priest used to put out garlands of flowers and bowls of milk for the snake, but it was angry and would not accept the offerings."

And a few:

"I saw the snake with my own eyes. He lives under a waterfall and seldom comes out by day. He is about as long as a man is high and white as silver. He is very nervous."

"I watched the snake for some time one evening. He was swimming in the stream, catching fish. He is very white and has blue eyes like a European, but I do not believe that he is a god but simply a new kind of snake."

There might be something there, after all, but I was still skeptical. In the first place, I doubted that an albino snake could exist in the wild. Young pythons are hunted by hawks, wild dogs, wolves and other predators and a white one would show up too easily. Also, pythons don't catch fish, although a python might conceivably eat a dead fish if he found it on the bank. The whole story sounded highly unlikely and I was even more suspicious when Subrati said that it would be very unwise for me to question any of the villagers who claimed to have seen the snake or attempt to go after the animal myself.

"Most of the villagers do not worship the snake as a god but they have a reverence for him," Subrati explained. "He is the deota [mascot or totem] of the place. The goddess Hali is supposed to return as a white snake every thousand years. If you ask about him or go in search of him, the villagers will say to each other, 'What will happen if this foreigner takes away our deota?' Then the old men will warn of disasters and the others, while not believing, will grow uneasy. Some of the wiser ones will say 'If the white man comes so far to catch this snake, he must be very valuable. Let us demand a lakh [100,-000] of rupees for him.'"

Subrati was seldom wrong in such matters so I told him to go ahead. He left for Kulna while I returned to south India to resume animal collecting.

Even since my last trip, restrictions on the exporting of animals had greatly increased. I had an order for 800 rhesus monkeys, a very common animal. Rhesus are used extensively in research work, especially to establish blood types, and played a prominent role in the discovery of the Salk vaccine. There are more monkeys than there are humans in India and the monkeys consume about the same amount of food. They are really a plague and the exportation of a few thousand of them every year not only helps to keep the monkeys in check but also provides a valuable source of dollars for the new republic.

A few weeks before I arrived, a shipment of 600 rhesus had arrived in London and been loaded into a truck. As it was winter, a heating unit had been run from the truck's engine to the cab but something had gone wrong with the unit and the monkeys had been killed by carbon monoxide gas. A hysterical group of ladies belonging to some animal league or other had cabled Pandit Nehru demanding that all shipments of monkeys be stopped. While the Indian government was debating this problem, shipments of monkeys from India were temporarily halted. This was a severe blow to research laboratories all over the world and monkeys were being smuggled into Pakistan and then shipped out from there but this process made them almost prohibitively expensive. I had to notify the laboratory who'd ordered the monkeys that I'd be unable to supply them and this was a heavy blow to me, both financially and in prestige.

I did manage to pick up a few animals, but hardly enough to justify the trip. I got a letter from Subrati who'd engaged three shikaris to go with him after the white python. I couldn't imagine why he needed three shikaris for such a job and wrote him so. I also wanted to know what he was paying them. I had to write three times before I got an answer to that one. I could have hired men to extract the back teeth of an infuriated man-eating tiger for less than what those shikaris were charging. Also, Subrati and his shikaris had been in the jungle for three months without seeing any sign of the snake.

Then I got a letter saying that one of the shikaris had seen the snake but it had gone into a rock crevice and escaped. Subrati needed a little more time. I had a strong suspicion that I was being swindled, not by Subrati but by the shikaris. They were probably having a good time off in the jungle with plenty of beer and girls while I paid their expenses. Subrati was so bemused by the white snake legend that he didn't know what was going on.

I sent a message to Subrati telling him to call off the hunt and meet me in Calcutta. I went north with my cargo and when I arrived in Calcutta, I found a message waiting for me from Subrati. The white snake had been captured.

I dropped everything and went at once to the village near Kulna. Subrati had the snake all right . . . an eight-foot rock python, snow white with blue eyes. I'd never seen or heard of such a thing before. As far as I know, neither had anyone else.

Subrati was so proud of his capture that he had the snake in a cage with a wire front so everyone could see her. (The python was a female. By putting a fine wire in the snake's anal opening and feeling how it turns, it is possible to determine the reptile's sex.) The snake had badly rubbed her nose against the wire and my first act was to treat the sore with sulfa powder and then put the snake in a wooden box with air holes so she couldn't hurt herself. I was still in a trance, refusing to believe my own eyes. I'd all but convinced myself that there couldn't be such an animal and yet here it was.

Subrati described the hunt to me. The hunters had gotten to know the snake's sunbathing and swimming spots by the signs she left behind her: dung, marks in the soft sand or earth, and a shed skin. They had stationed themselves at the different points to watch but the python was amazingly cautious—otherwise she'd never have been able to survive all these years—and knew the whole area far better than the men did. They had seen her several times but the snake had always managed to escape, for snakes can move with amazing speed. When capturing a snake, a man should always grab the reptile just back of the head, otherwise the snake will turn and bite him. This requires considerable skill as the head is the first part of the snake to disappear in a rock crevice or among bushes. Pythons are not poisonous but an eight-foot python can still give you a nasty bite. Also, the teeth of a python curve inward so that after a python has seized its prey, the quarry cannot escape. If a python bites a man, the delicate curved teeth are almost sure to be broken off in the struggle and then the snake may develop mouth rot. Subrati had insisted that the shikaris make sure of grabbing the snake by the neck and the men were only too happy to comply.

But after getting my last message, Subrati had gotten desperate. He'd told the men to grab the snake anywhere they could. The next day, one of the shikaris had seen the snake lying in the water under the waterfall and managed to grab her by the tail.

Ordinarily, unless a python is very big, capturing one is no great problem for a determined man. The constricting power of these snakes is greatly exaggerated. It would take a very big constrictor indeed to kill a man, unless the snake got a few coils around the man's neck, and snakes will not do this deliberately. A big python can kill an animal the size of a goat or a small deer because animals do not have hands and so cannot unwind the python's coils or grab him by the throat. However, Subrati assured me that this white snake had been extraordinarily fierce and powerful. The shikari had been badly bitten before his yells had brought up the other men and the snake was overpowered and put in a sack.

After hearing this story, I immediately examined the snake's mouth. Two teeth had been broken but not at the roots. But the snake had already rubbed off the sulfa powder on the sides of the box and damaged her nose again. I had the inside of the box padded before putting her back.

The villagers were crowding around to see the fabulous white deota and I asked Subrati how they felt about the capture. He said that they seemed to accept it without resentment, being mainly interested in seeing the legendary animal. But I noticed that some people had brought offerings of milk, fruit and flowers for the snake and I decided to leave as fast as possible with my prize.

Subrati had been trying to feed the python fish as the villagers assured him that the white deota ate nothing else. The snake had refused to eat. This might be the result of shock or perhaps she simply didn't eat fish. Snakes, like all reptiles, can go for months without eating but the longer they fast, the harder it is to get them to eat, and a snake that has to be force-fed is a great nuisance. Force-feeding hurts a snake's mouth and bothers him. I always try to get a captured snake eating as quickly as possible.

I put two dead chickens in the box and left the python alone. Most collectors believe that a snake will only eat live food but I think that some snakes often prefer food already dead. The struggles of a live animal bothers them in a cage. The next morning, both chickens were gone and there was a corresponding bulge in the snake's body. At least the python was a good feeder and that problem was off my mind.

I tried several times to get the snake to eat fish. Like all pythons, she would pay no attention to them. This is typical of the problems an animal collector encounters when trusting to village talk. The villagers were right that there was a white python with blue eyes near the waterfall and knew quite a lot about her habits, but they were completely wrong about her diet, although this was one of the few points on which everyone in the community agreed. I've found the same thing to be true all over the world; natives are amazingly accurate in certain matters and amazingly ignorant about others. In America, I've had farmers take me to rattlesnake dens and explain with a great wealth of accurate detail the habits of the snakes, and then assure me that rattlesnakes "sting" with their forked tongues.

After paying off the three shikaris, I gave a handsome donation to the village elders and left the next day with my snake in a sack. I drove to the nearest railway station and got a train for Calcutta. I shared the compartment with an Indian and, having had a busy day, dozed off in my seat. When I awoke, I found that the sack had reared itself up and the Indian was sitting paralyzed with terror. I shoved the snake down to the bottom of the bag and apologized to my fellow passenger. "It is quite all right," he said, mopping his forehead. "I knew you had something alive in that bag, but I thought it was only a dog."

I had reservations on a ship for my other animals and had intended taking the snake along with them but at the last minute, I changed my mind. Calcutta is full of animal dealers who jealously watch each shipment and I had no intention of starting any possible controversy. So I made arrangements for Subrati to take the shipment of animals to the United States while I flew to Madras, intending to take a ship from there.

As I was getting on the plane, a customs officer asked me what I had in the bag. I told him that it was rubber tubing for cameras. The man felt the bag, nodded, and said, "Ah yes, thank you sir." I climbed on the plane with a sigh of relief. I would probably have been put off the plane if they'd known I was taking a live snake along with me.

I got a ship in Madras and arrived in the United States on September 13, 1955, with Serata, as I'd named my precious captive from a Sanskrit word meaning "beauty." There was a national convention of zoo directors at Louisville, Kentucky, and I flew there immediately. Serata produced a sensation. She had grown quite tame by this time and anyone could handle her. I was offered $15,000 for her but I refused.

For the next six months, I toured America with Serata, appearing on television programs, newsreels, and giving talks on her. Serata became probably the best known snake in the world —she was already the rarest. Then Swissair called me to New York. They were putting in a new flight to the Far East and had decided to use Serata as a symbol for this flight. A reception was arranged for Serata in Rockefeller Center. She was exhibited on a purple cushion with gold fringes in the show window of Swissair and attracted such crowds that the police had to be called out to handle them. *The Man in the Gray Flannel Suit* was being shot at Rockefeller Center and the crowds were so great that the actors couldn't get past them to enter the building. The director finally had to ask us to take the snake out of the window, remarking, "Damn if I ever thought I'd live to see the day when Gregory Peck would be outdone by a snake."

So many calls came in about Serata that Swissair had to put in another switchboard. *Life* magazine ran pictures of people looking in the window with the caption "Judging by their expressions, why are these people so amazed?" Then followed a picture of Serata that covered two pages. The president of Ciba, a big chemical concern in Summit, New Jersey, heard that Serata ate six white rats a week. He sent the rats once a week in his Cadillac, driven by a liveried chauffeur. Colston Leigh asked me to continue my lecture series, "But be sure to bring Serata," he added.

Between trips, I kept Serata at the Staten Island Zoo. Carl Kauffeld, the curator of reptiles there, is in my opinion one of the top reptile men in the world and I knew that Serata would be safe in his hands. Carl explained to me that Serata was not an albino. She was a color freak in which the guanophores (white pigment cells) exist to the exclusion of all other pigment cells. This condition is known as "leucistic." Serata is absolutely pure white and no markings of any kind are discernible; with an albino the markings can still be seen as a faint pattern.

Serata put me back in the headlines. Once again orders began to pour in, and today I can go anywhere in the world I wish with more orders than I can fill. The future looks clear for me but I hope never again to have to import animals wholesale. I intend to specialize in unusual species and perhaps some day to open my own zoo under my own special conditions.

# Conclusion

MERCIA HAD often told me that wild animal collecting is a dying profession. Was she right? I honestly don't know.

I do know that every year it becomes increasingly more difficult. In the first place, there simply aren't as many wild animals as there used to be. Civilization is pushing in on all sides. More and more species are being protected, a very good plan, but hard on collectors. When you add to these factors the currency tangles, the difficulties of dealing with the new nations springing up everywhere, the ever-increasing customs regulations, and the rising costs of transportation, there would seem to be no hope for the collector.

Animal collecting is a highly romantic profession but the returns do not justify the fantastic efforts necessary and the great risks. Probably the greatest risk that a collector runs is the chance of coming down with some tropical disease, especially when he has a valuable cargo that must be shipped immediately. Luckily, I have always been very healthy. Except for my leg trouble following the zebra kick and one bout of malaria, I have never been really sick. Other collectors have not been so fortunate. I know of several men who have been ruined because they came down with fever at a critical period and so lost their shipment.

I often think wistfully of the good old days as personified by the life of Frank Buck. Then a collector could go to some part of the world, collect his cargo, and peacefully return with it. Time meant little. Now virtually all contracts for wild animals contain the dreadful line "must be delivered by such-and-such a date." If you fail even by a day, the contract is canceled. Then you must sell to dealers for whatever they'll pay you. As the cost of boarding and lodging a tiger in New York for three months will amount to more than your profit, you must sell the animal quickly and the dealers know it.

In Frank Buck's day, the native populations were friendly. There were no regulations. The cost of obtaining animals was little. Buck bought one tiger for $11.60 from native trappers and they were delighted to get the money. Yet the price of a tiger F.O.B. New York is the same today as it was in Buck's time.

In the old days, animal collecting was a profession handed down from father to son. For many years, the Ruhe family tramped from fair to fair in Europe with cages of canaries strapped to their backs, selling the birds for a profit of a few cents each. During the turn of the century, there was an enormous demand for canaries in the United States. To supply the demand, ships had special cages built in their holds and raced back and forth across the Atlantic carrying hundreds of thousands of the birds. The Ruhes became rich. They began to handle other animals and traveled to every part of the globe to collect rare species. Louis Ruhe became one of the largest animal dealers in New York but he no longer collects animals himself. He has found that it doesn't pay.

I believe that there are only three collectors in the world today who handle big shipments of large animals. Each of them has some section of the world in which he operates. There is never any question of poaching on the others' preserves. Meems, a Dutchman in his seventies, was brought up in the great tradition of animal collecting. He operates in India for Louis Ruhe. Schultz, an old collector for Hagenback, is now over eighty and works Australia and what he can of Indonesia. There is also Terni, a young Italian, who specializes in Asia. Terni comes of a long line of collectors, his father and grandfather having been in the same business. No one man covers Africa; that is done by a number of local dealers in different parts of the continent. The same is true of South America.

But if the collectors are disappearing, who will supply the dealers and the zoos? So far, no one has an answer to this problem although there have been many attempts to solve it. The zoos would like to deal directly with the native trappers and suppliers, thus cutting out the big mark-up by both the collectors and dealers. Although this is an attractive idea, I don't think it can be done.

For example, once while I was in India, I got a cable from the director of a European zoo telling me of a native dealer in Calcutta who had a giant panda. The dealer was asking $15,000 for the animal and I was instructed to buy it at once, returning with the panda on the next ship. I couldn't believe that any dealer could have such a rare animal without my hearing about it through the animal-dealer grapevine and also as it was 110 degrees in Calcutta at the time I doubted if a panda could survive such a temperature. However, I flew to Calcutta immediately and interviewed the dealer. I asked to see the panda but he explained that the animal was in Nepal and the property of an Indian zoologist. The zoologist had gotten the animal in China and smuggled it into Nepal. He would arrive with the panda in the next few days. Meanwhile, the dealer wanted me to give him the $15,000.

I refused to pay anything until I saw the panda. However, I offered to fly to Nepal to get the animal. I insisted that the dealer post a bond covering my expenses so if it turned out to be a wild goose chase, neither I nor the zoo would be the losers.

The dealer assured me that this would be perfectly satisfactory. He would post the bond immediately. The next day, he sent a letter to my hotel reading, "As a matter of principle's sake, I cannot put up the bond." I cabled the zoo that I would wait in Calcutta until the panda arrived. Meanwhile, my own shipment of animals was due to leave so Mercia had to take the shipment back to Europe alone while I remained in Calcutta.

Two weeks passed and then the dealer sent me word that the zoologist and the panda were in Calcutta. I went at once to his home and met the zoologist. Both men refused to let me see the panda until I had paid the $15,000. As I couldn't find the zoologist's name listed on the rosters of any Indian scientific institution and his story sounded very thin, I refused to pay the money.

Two days later, I was called to the dealer's home. He and the zoologist triumphantly presented me with a cable from the zoo director reading "Pay no attention to Ryhiner. I have discharged him as my agent." I telephoned the director and he confirmed the cable. "These gentlemen tell me that you are making impossible conditions for them," he explained. I tried to explain the situation but the director angrily hung up on me.

While I was making arrangements to leave India, I learned through the animal-business grapevine that an American zoo had heard about the panda and offered the dealer $25,000 for it. The dealer had instantly canceled his arrangements with the European zoo. He had then cabled the American zoo, agreeing to the sale if the zoo would also purchase $25,000 worth of other animals from him. The American zoo instantly sent him the $25,000.

The next day I was sitting in the bar of the Spence Hotel when an Indian came over to my table and asked if I wasn't Peter Ryhiner, the animal collector. I told him that I was.

"Ah, then you must know what a giant panda is," said the man eagerly.

I assured him that by this time I was virtually an authority on giant pandas.

"Then you're just the man to help out," said the Indian delightedly. "Come with me."

I followed him into part of the bar. There were the dealer and the "zoologist." My new friend turned to me and explained, "These men have been asking everyone what in heaven's name a giant panda is. I don't know why they're so interested, but at last you'll be able to tell them."

Later, I found that the dealer, who knew nothing about animals, had found an old pre-war price list put out by a European collector and had simply sent it out under his own name. The list also included such "typical Indian" animals as gorillas and jaguars. The American zoo later received a cable from the dealer. "Panda has escaped but will send you $25,000 worth of other animals."

After several similar experiences with local dealers, the zoos tried another system. A group of European zoos clubbed together and sent out one of their own men, an experienced old keeper, to collect animals directly from local dealers.

The keeper-collector traveled about through India, Indonesia and Ceylon where he made a list of the animals available. He then wrote back to the group of zoos who had sent him and the zoos selected the animals that they wished. By the time the purchase money reached him, many of the animals were dead or sold elsewhere but some were still available. The keeper then discovered that regulation now familiar to the reader, that before shipping the animals, he had also to leave in each country a sum of money equal to the value of the animals. So additional funds had to be sent him to cover this expense, the funds being in lira, francs, marks and so on, depending on which zoos wanted what animals.

An Italian zoo wanted two lesser pandas. However, the Italian government had decided that the importation of wild animals was a "luxury item" and wouldn't allow lira to be sent out of Italy. So the zoo paid in Swiss francs, arranging the matter with a Swiss zoo in the group. But as the pandas had been listed as "imports for Italy," the Indian government wouldn't accept Swiss currency as part of the sum to be left in India for the animals. While the keeper was trying to clear up this confusion, the two pandas died. Neither the Indian government nor the Italian zoo would accept their deaths without a veterinarian's certificate and the bodies had been thrown away.

The keeper was held in Calcutta with his cargo for weeks. His feed bills were enormous and many of the other animals died during the long wait.

The group of zoos that had sent the collector were in Switzerland, France, Italy and Germany. Each zoo had to get import permits for the animals they had ordered before the animals could enter the various countries. Meanwhile the keeper was naturally getting other animals whenever he found a bargain and some of his other stock died. This, of course, hopelessly confused the licenses. When he did finally return to Europe, there was a grand squabble among the zoos as to who would get what. It ended with all the zoos losing money.

Then the director of one of the biggest European zoos managed to raise $20,000 and decided to go himself to Africa and pick up a shipment. As he was going to only one country and the entire cargo was to be delivered to his zoo alone, his problem was much simpler. He got the cargo without trouble (getting the animals is always the easiest part of the business) and then started back. The cargo was supposed to unload at Genoa and be sent on by rail but the Italian authorities wouldn't permit the animals to be off-loaded. An epidemic of rinderpest had broken out in the Rome Zoo; 250 animals had been shot and even the keepers were quarantined for a year. The ship went on, but the director now found that he couldn't unload his animals in France, Belgium, or the Netherlands, because the cargo had been rejected in Italy and this made the customs officials suspicious. Finally, the distracted man shot all the animals.

A situation like this is commonplace to a professional collector and the solution was simple. There is a transit station in Hamburg. For a couple of thousand dollars, the animals could have been off-loaded there until the necessary papers were forthcoming.

As a result of these experiences, it is hard to see how either the collector or the dealer can be eliminated. The collector must go out in the field and get the animals. Some of them he will have to get himself, others he may obtain from local trappers or dealers, but in any case he must know the market, must understand the currency exchanges, and must understand the problems involved in shipping. This is a full-time job in itself and can only be done by an experienced man.

The collector will then in most cases have to sell to a dealer. The dealer must have a compound where the animals can be held until they are sold. Often zoos ask that at least a portion of the purchase money be paid in other animals. A zoo would like to buy a tiger but can't afford $4,000 for the animal. However, it can afford $2,000 if the dealer will take a pair of young zebras for the other $2,000. The dealer must know where he can sell the zebras. Many zoos must first exhibit the animals and then rely on public interest to get the purchase money. The dealer must be in a position to extend such zoos credit. In some cases, purchases are made through a park commission. The dealer must know the members of the park commission, and understand their personal likes and dislikes. He must be in a position to ship by truck as well as rail. American freight rates are so high that often it has cost me more to ship an animal from New York to Kansas City than it did to bring the same animal from India to New York. A collector, especially arriving in a foreign country, cannot possibly know all the ins and outs of the business and must sell to the dealers who do.

Many zoos are now trying to exchange animals with each other. An American zoo will offer to exchange a pair of big-horn sheep against a pair of Indian black buck in the Madras Zoo, thus eliminating both the collector and the dealer. When possible, the animals are flown, an excellent plan as it cuts down enormously on fatalities. However, the maze of government regulations, the fact that if the animals arrive weak or diseased there is seldom any redress, and the zoos' reluctance to dispose of their rarer animals, has so far prevented this practice from becoming common.

With the collector slowly being forced out by the bedlam of conflicting regulations, currency restrictions and increasing shipping costs, how will wild animals be collected? Often they are beng supplied by wholesale smuggling, as with the orangs in Indonesia, wholesale slaughter to obtain a few specimens, as with the gorillas in West Africa, and by men who are not animal men in the old sense at all but clever promoters. But eventually, I hope, some sensible arrangement can be worked out among the zoos and responsible men put in control of the various areas.

When this happens (and I hope it happens soon) the old-time, picturesque collector will disappear. Yet I'm glad that I lived in an era when a man could gamble his own knowledge and skill in South America, Africa or Asia and come back with some rare and valuable live cargo. It is still possible, although enormously difficult. In addition to the Indian rhino, there are at least five extremely valuable animals in the world today and to bring them back would be a great triumph for any collector.

The most valuable of this select group is the giant panda, worth easily $25,000 to any zoo. These picturesque animals live in the bamboo jungles of western China. Possibly a collector, crossing the border at Nepal, might be able to secure a pair of these animals. A more prosaic but practical method would be to arrange an exchange with the Peking Zoo. I tried this myself a few years ago. The Peking Zoo offered to exchange a single panda for a pair of gorillas but, the director added, "owing to the giant panda's being uneasy to capture, you must capture it yourself."

Well, if you're interested in importing a panda, first you'd have to get your pair of gorillas. You would probably have to buy them as there is now a man in West Africa who has practically a monopoly on the gorilla business . . . the same monopoly that Behrend and I tried to establish years ago. This man lives in West Africa, gets young gorillas from the natives, puts them through a medical examination, and sends them abroad. A pair would cost you about $10,000. You would then have to get the gorillas into communist China, turn them over to the Peking Zoo, and start out after the pandas. Of course, you would be completely in the hands of the Chinese government once you crossed the border, and if they decided not to honor the agreement, you'd have no redress. After getting the pandas (if you did) you would have to sell them in Europe; you couldn't sell them in the U.S.A., because they would be "imports from a communist nation."

The Sumatran rhino is another extremely valuable animal, worth perhaps $15,000. They are hairy with two horns and "half plated," that is, the hide hangs in greater folds than the African rhino but not to such an extent as does the hide of the Indian rhino. They are comparatively small and very rare. A few years ago, two were smuggled out of Sumatra by a Chinese who sold them for $1,600 to a dealer. The dealer tried to bring them back by ship. One died in the Red Sea and the other in Suez. Of course, the dealer should have had them flown back regardless of the expense. With such valuable animals, there was no sense in taking chances. Under present regulations, probably the only way of getting a Sumatran rhino would be to buy a smuggled animal.

The okapi, found only in the Belgian Congo, is worth $10,-000. The okapi was first discovered in 1900 (before that, they were regarded as a native legend) and the first one exported in 1919. The Royal Zoological Society of Belgium has complete control of the animals. Government trappers go out every two years and catch ten or twelve young okapis. These calves are kept in dark stables, as okapis are used to the twilight of the jungles and strong light kills them until they become used to it. To obtain one, you must have a letter from a recognized zoological garden and $10,000. Then you're put on a waiting list. In two or three years, you'll get your okapi.

Occasionally, an okapi calf is smuggled out of the country, generally through Uganda. A notable explorer succeeded in accomplishing this feat a few years ago and the animal is now in a European zoo. Selling a "hot" okapi is generally quite a problem as naturally the Belgian government is bound to protest and diplomatic difficulties result. In this case, the zoo buying the okapi was in a country that didn't worry about diplomatic relations with Belgium. Smuggling rare animals out of a country is generally impractical as the animals can't be hidden once they're in a zoo. Many years ago when the Dutch were in control of Indonesia, a number of orangs were smuggled out and sold in the United States. The Dutch government protested and both the zoos and the collector were heavily fined. However, the present Indonesian government has more to worry about than counting all the orangs in captivity over the world, so smuggling is widespread.

The Siberian tiger is worth about $5,000. These huge animals, weighing up to 600 pounds and more, are the largest members of the cat family and the lineal descendants of the prehistoric saber-toothed tigers. The Siberian tiger is found mainly in Amurland in eastern Siberia and is usually hunted in winter by men on skis. In soft snow, the men can move faster than the tigers. Generally only cubs are taken, the adults being too large and fierce to be shipped.

To obtain Siberian tigers, arrangements would have to be made with the Russian government, by an exchange negotiated in Prague, for instance.

Lastly, I should consider the Komodo dragon as one of the world's rarest and most valuable animals—especially with the present $5,000 price tag put on them. Anyone who wants to charter a ship can stop at Komodo and get all he wants from the sultan at 1,000 rupias each. Then all he has to do is find a country that wants Komodo dragons badly enough to defy the government export rules.

I will go on working with animals until I die, in spite of increasing difficulties. It's my life. I know that people will always want to see animals. In Frankfort, Germany, the zoo was destroyed during the bombing but as soon as peace was declared, the population bought an elephant from a passing circus and started rebuilding the zoo before they'd rebuilt their own homes. In America, new zoos and wildlife exhibits are constantly being built, for hardheaded business men know that nothing so appeals to the general public. As the public learns more about animals, these zoos will become better and better, and large-scale breeding programs will be started to perpetuate rare species. Perhaps tracts of otherwise worthless land will be used as game parks where the animals can wander unconfined. When my collecting days are over, I hope to have a small part in these future projects. If so, I will not regret that the days of Lothar Behrend and the $100,000 cargos are over. It will be a new era, far more inspiring than any Frank Buck picture ever made, and I hope that I live to see it.